BLACK INTELLECTUALS COME TO POWER

INTERNATIONAL STUDIES IN POLITICAL AND SOCIAL CHANGE

Series Editor: WENDELL BELL, Yale University

1. The Democratic Revolution in the West Indies: Studies in Nationalism, Leadership, and the Belief in Progress
   edited by Wendell Bell

2. The Sociology of Political Independence: A Study of Nationalist Attitudes Among West Indian Leaders
   by Charles C. Moskos, Jr.

3. Black Intellectuals Come to Power: The Rise of Creole Nationalism in Trinidad & Tobago
   by Ivar Oxaal

4. Social Change and Images of the Future: A Study of the Pursuit of Progress in Jamaica
   by James A. Mau

Black Intellectuals Come to Power

The Rise of Creole Nationalism in Trinidad & Tobago

by IVAR OXAAL

SCHENKMAN PUBLISHING COMPANY, Inc.
CAMBRIDGE, MASSACHUSETTS

SCHENKMAN PUBLISHING COMPANY, INC.
Cambridge, Massachusetts 02138

PRINTED IN THE UNITED STATES OF AMERICA

Library of Congress Catalog Card Number: 67-29328

*For
Wendy,
Who Said 'Go'*

The bourgeoisie has through its exploitation of the world market given a cosmopolitan character to production and consumption in every country . . . In place of the old wants, satisfied by the production of the country, we find new wants, requiring for their satisfaction products of distant lands and climes. In place of the old local and national seclusion and self-sufficiency we have intercourse in every direction, universal interdependence of nations. And as in material, so also in intellectual production. The intellectual creations of individual nations become common property. National onesidedness and narrowmindedness become more and more impossible, and from the numerous national and local literatures there arises a world literature.

– Marx & Engels, *The Communist Manifesto*, 1848

. . . the whole problem of the Negro in the United States – and everywhere else – cannot possibly be viewed except in the light of the whole creaking and groaning world economy. If that problem is solved, and an era of peace and prosperity opens up before mankind, that is, the common man, the Negro's progress will be rapid. But if the world continues to indulge in the conflicts which have marked the twentieth century, the chances are that, in the increasing antagonism and dislocations, the Negro's claims to equality will be contested more fiercely than ever. The current Civil Rights controversy in the United States brings this out quite clearly.

– Eric Williams, *British Historians and the West Indies*, 1964

Preface

This study is a mere sketch, a synoptic sociological account of an island community up to the time of its attainment of political independence in 1962. My hope is that it will provide some measure of enlightenment for both the general reader and the professional scholar. I have not attempted to supplant earlier histories and monographs on Trinidad and Tobago; rather, one of my principal aims has been to place some of these earlier studies in a broader social and historical context, and to add some findings and chapters of my own concerning the development of this fascinating new nation. This may be viewed by local scholars as a rather audacious enterprise, but I am quite prepared to stand corrected on questions of fact or interpretation. Indeed, if this book can serve as either irritant or stimulant, provoking further research and intellectual controversy, I will consider my labors well repaid.

But these essays obviously do not tell the whole story. Readers who wish to probe further into the intricacies of Trinidad should consult the numerous books and documents listed in the footnotes to this volume, most of which should be available in metropolitan libraries. Also, the rising generation of West Indian social scientists are beginning to produce a scattered but growing list of manuscripts and publications. Still unpublished is Selwyn D. Ryan's detailed and solid analysis of Trinidad's political development entitled *Decolonization in a Multiracial Society;* for the past several years social scientists at the University of the West Indies in Kingston have bravely issued *The New World Quarterly*. Articles by Lloyd Best, Roy Augier, Archie Singham, and others have provided insightful and critical commentary on post-independence developments in Trinidad and the West Indies as a whole. It is still difficult, however, for scholars who wish to write from a national or regional slant to get their works accepted by metropolitan publishers. Nor, in these small-island nations, are they free from the sometimes arbitrary authority of official society. Of the major West Indian territories only Guyana seems to me today to be relatively spared the McCarthy-like atmosphere which has descended on the region in the years since the break-up of the West Indies federation. Visiting foreign scholars, secure in the knowledge of jobs to be had elsewhere, may speak their minds more or less openly, but the local man who openly dissents from the prevailing status quo is in a more vulnerable position.

As I have tried to show for the Trinidad case, considerable responsibility for this state of affairs must be assigned to United States policy in the area. Once the new regime was in office, the intellectual's question, "Which models of the future are desirable?" became quickly transformed into the politician's question, "Which models of the future are possible?" It is true that the social composition of the nationalist leadership in Trinidad predisposed that country to an accommodative posture, but always working to condition West Indian policies is the reality of the Caribbean as an American lake. Whether we look at the Bay of Pigs invasion, the Dominican intervention, the activities of the C.I.A. in Guyana, or the protracted quarrel over Chaguaramas in Trinidad, we continually encounter this sense of an overwhelming outside pressure to conform, and over-conform, to Cold War definitions of the world. These pressures have variously subverted and even corrupted the West Indian nationalist movement and will, I fear, ultimately result in further deterioration. Can this straitjacket be removed short of a radical redefinition of America's role toward the world at large? Impossible to answer.

Two central problems have concerned me in this study. The first has been simply to try to retell the singular development of the Trinidad society and culture as these pertained to the emergence, and problems, of the nationalist movement. Second, I have tried to suggest the impact of a telescoped version of European – particularly British – ideas and institutions on Trinidad. Social scientists will readily detect the invisible rubrics, theoretical issues, and concepts which have guided this narrative, but in a brief work of a quasi-popular nature I have tried to keep the conceptual baggage to a minimum.

In looking back over this manuscript, which I began writing in 1961 and had completed – after seventeen months of intermittent residency in Trinidad – by the end of 1964, it strikes me that my own basic attitudes toward the island may not always be clear. For one thing, I should have pointed out that unlike Jamaica and some of the other islands, Trinidad is not overrun by tourists. The beaches are public and barely inhabited; the island still affords a sense of individual discovery and remains a rich lode of ethnological diversity. If I have often written in a critical vein it is not because my personal experiences there were unpleasant; quite the reverse, the best days of my life may have been spent there. But I have tried to deal seriously with Trinidad as an objective, but involved, observer – and I hope no local reader will begrudge me some occasional lapses into irony and *picong*.

Literally dozens of persons in Trinidad helped me in fundamental ways after I arrived there, as a total stranger, in 1961. Dr. Eric Williams agreed to let me scout the perimeters of P.N.M. decision-making; Andrew Carr, W. J. Alexander, Nicholas Simonette, and other party stalwarts were helpful and candid; for the opposition, Dr. Rudranath Capildeo explained, as only he could, the historical and personal reasons underlying the alienation of many East Indians from the government. Cliff Sealy, Randolph Rawlins, Lennox Pierre, each provided valuable insights and information; Edna Roxburgh and Esla Molineaux not only provided emotional support – and fed me when I was broke – but helped me to understand that delightful and devious creature: the Creole woman. This knowledge has stood me in good stead since acquiring, in 1963, a Guyanese wife. Eugene and Phelma Borde, and all the little Bordes, have given me a home away from home; Dr. Andrew Camacho has ever been ready to debate points of interpretation; the Rialto Roti Shop and the Crossfire Steel Orchestra were unfailing sources of physical and esthetic refreshment. The list goes on and on; the boundaries between "field work" and life dissolved, like other rational distinctions, while I was in Trinidad.

Finally, I am indebted to the West Indies Study Program at University of California at Los Angeles, under the direction of Wendell Bell, and funded by the Carnegie Corporation of New York, for enabling me to go to Trinidad in the first instance for over a year in 1961–62, and for supporting me during the first half of 1963. In 1964 I received a Summer Faculty Fellowship from the University of California at Davis which enabled me to make a return visit. Sociological colleagues, teachers and friends such as Melvin Seeman, Kurt H. Wolff, Raymond J. Murphy, John Horton, Charles Moskos, James Mau, Andrew Phillips, and Daniel Crowley have all had an influence in the formulation of this study even though the family resemblance may not always be easily distinguishable.

IVAR OXAAL

May 17, 1967
Georgetown, Guyana

Contents

CHAPTER 1 Trinidad and the West Indian Setting

The populations in the British West Indies have no native civilization at all. People dance Bongo and Shango and all this is very artistic and very good. But these have no serious effects upon their general attitude toward the world. These populations are essentially Westernised and they have been Westernised for centuries.

— C. L. R. James, 1962[1]

At midnight on August 30, 1962, one of the most familiar and significant political rituals of the present historical period was enacted within a flood-lighted area in front of Red House in Port of Spain, Trinidad & Tobago. Local notables and a representative of the British monarchy stood in readiness for a ceremony which had already been performed on numerous occasions throughout the Asian and African colonies. Just a few weeks before, an almost identical ritual had been staged for the first time in the Caribbean as Jamaica became an independent member of the Commonwealth. Now, for the eleventh time since World War II, the Union Jack was slowly lowered in another outpost of empire and then the red, white and black flag of Trinidad & Tobago was run up the flagstaff.

Up to that point in the proceedings, the enormous throng of black and brown people who had assembled in Woodford Square had stood quietly by, almost transfixed. But as the new national flag came into view and a band struck up the new national anthem the entire crowd hesitated a moment, and then — as if rehearsed to respond on cue — broke into an incredible, jubilant roar. The nearby Gulf of Paria reverberated with a droning and tooting chorus emanating from the ships docked in the harbor. Church bells throughout the city began to peal maniacally. For at least that stirring moment there was no doubt that the people of the islands had achieved a sense of national solidarity and destiny.

"Here every creed and race find an equal place, and may God bless our Nation," were among the sentiments contained in the national anthem. A few moments later this faith was incorporated into the ceremony as Roman Catholic, Hindu, Protestant and Islamic religious leaders stepped forward to give their benedictions. Trinidad & Tobago (usually abbreviated to "Trinidad") must at that moment have struck the many foreign observers present as a fantastic place, as deserving of being called "the United Nations in miniature" which its citizens have rightly called themselves.

Political independence had come to Trinidad and its small neighbor island, Tobago, nearly five hundred years after Columbus sighted the Trinity Hills in southeast Trinidad during his third voyage to the new world. And British rule, which had begun when the colony had easily been wrested from Spain in 1797, was coming to an end after 165 years. Among the major milestones of that rule had been the abolition of slavery in 1833; the introduction of indentured laborers from India beginning in 1845 and terminating in 1917; the inauguration of universal adult suffrage in 1946, and the formation of the People's National Movement in 1956. Another recent milestone in the colony's history was now fading from public memory. In 1958 Trinidad & Tobago had joined with Jamaica and the British Leeward and Windward Islands in the attempt to form a West Indies Federation. Until a few months earlier it had been hoped that some form of federation would have been the means by which all the islands would have achieved independence together. The provisional federal experiment, however, was dissolved after Jamaican voters had opted out through a referendum held in September, 1961. Thus Jamaica and Trinidad went on to independence separately while the smaller islands were left stranded under colonial rule. The strongly-federationist but controversial leader of the Trinidad nationalist movement since 1956 had been a short, partially deaf, irascible, chain-smoking, brilliant, Oxford-educated Negro historian named Dr. Eric Williams. Dr. Williams was the founder and Political Leader of the People's National Movement and since 1956 had dominated the political life of the colony. In a few hours, at a vigorous 51 years of age, he would officially be installed as the new nation's first Prime Minister.

While the celebrations of independence eve were taking place in front of Red House, another important center of last-minute preparation for nationhood could be found a few blocks away on Frederick Street, at the offices of the P.N.M. publishing company. During the weeks preceding independence Eric Williams had been driving himself and the staff of the party's newspaper, *The Nation*, almost around the clock in order to prepare his *History of the People of Trinidad and Tobago* for distribution by Independence Day. The copies which reached the book vendors the following morning were immediately sold out and in the following days sales mounted quickly into the thousands. The appearance of a book of such importance, and its preparation within such a short period of time, were typical of the virtuoso intellectual performances "the Doctor" had brought to his new vocation as a politician. Because of such feats he had attracted a circle of middle class admirers who respected his dynamism and intellectual endowments, and who had joined with him in forming the People's National Movement. Not only Williams himself, but some of his closest associates during the six years in power were, or had been, persons of some intellectual stature themselves. Two of them, Dr. Williams and his former Marxist tutor, Mr. C. L. R. James, were major productive intellectuals with an international reputation. Five were persons who had made local intellectual and artistic contributions in the areas of history, anthropology and the fine arts. Four others were active patrons of local art or had disseminated "culture" and political commentaries via press and radio. Eight other members of the top echelon of the party were, if not productive intellectuals in the narrow sense, members of "the learned professions" – law and medicine – with broad cultural interests. And in Sir Learie Constantine the P.N.M. possessed a Party Chairman, widely renowned in Britain and the West Indies for his contributions to cricket, who had written a book on the perennial "colour question."

Thus, in addition to Dr. Williams and Mr. James, persons who could claim at least some degree of intellectual accomplishment or serious interest had combined to set the tenor of nationalist politics during the final years of "tutelary democracy" under colonial rule in Trinidad & Tobago. Surely no other political party has labored so diligently or sincerely to project the public image of a party based on the appeal to intellect and reason, or has ever brought into the political arena so many of the lofty ideals, and even the paraphernalia, of academic life. Major speeches by Dr. Williams in Port of Spain were held in "the University of Woodford Square;" branch "Colleges" had been established in other parts of the islands. At one point the P.N.M. even issued mock diplomas to "graduates" of the University. The University was not only an inspired public relations gimmick but also the natural outgrowth of a genuine desire to elevate nationalist politics to the status of adult education. It therefore immediately achieved a mass enrollment from among the majority Negro section of Trinidad society.

But the pursuit of what a Trinidad seaman once called "knowledgism" did not end there. Several years after the founding of the University of Woodford Square the East Indian opposition replied in kind by summoning "Trinidad's Most Educated Man," Dr. Rudranath Capildeo, mathematician, scientist and barrister, who was then an instructor at the University of London. Dr. Capildeo would first cross swords with Dr. Williams in the 1961 elections. Finally, three years after independence, in 1965, C. L. R. James began the formation of his own political party. In the general elections held in November, 1966, the voter could thus select from among parties headed by a famous historian, a brilliant scientist and a venerable Marxist intellectual.

This remarkably high standard of political leadership was perhaps not too astonishing because Trinidadians, like many of the four million people in the British Caribbean, speak and comprehend the English language with extraordinary facility. Few West Indians attempt to imitate the formidable accents of the B.B.C. newscasts which are relayed several times a day throughout the area, but West Indian speech has its own richness of vocabulary, metaphor, vivacity and wit. In Trinidad, as we will see, English has been in general circulation for less than a hundred years and has absorbed the spirit of many tongues. West Indians place a high premium on linguistic skill; they are thoroughly versed in its ceremonial and oratorical variants and will listen with evident pleasure to any amount of long-winded speech-making so long as it is apt and witty, and they will endure it in silence even when it is not. Street-corner political meetings frequently take up an entire evening, but they differ in style between, for example, Jamaica and Trinidad. The Jamaican political meeting tends to be a mass rally, highly emotional and demonstrative, in which songs and symbolic noisemakers often play an important role; the typical Trinidad partisan gathering, especially since the advent of the P.N.M., tends to be highly restrained, almost solemn. Dr. Williams' speeches in the University of Woodford Square sometimes have an *ex cathedra* quality. Thousands of lower-class auditors stand almost motionless for hours in the warm tropical night while the Doctor speaks in a carefully modulated, but still rather monotonous voice into the microphone on the square's Victorian bandstand. This scene often makes an uncanny impression on the visitor familiar with the more flamboyant, spontaneous, political style found elsewhere in the islands.

Reverence for the spoken word is not matched by universal comprehension of the written word, but the rates of literacy are extremely high in comparison to the level attained by other colonial territories. In Trinidad and Guyana, the only territories that have large East Indian populations, illiteracy is concentrated among the poorer, rural, sugar-estate workers, but even there the rate of literacy is steadily rising. Newspapers are widely read and journalistic standards are in several instances equal, if not superior, to the average run of newspapers in Britain and the United States. Jamaica has its daily *Gleaner* and *Star*, Trinidad its *Guardian*, and Barbados its *Advocate*. Aside from the local news, which has traditionally been treated as secondary to the world news (and events in other parts of the West Indies often ignored), the West Indian newspaper reader is given the international reportage from the wire services, editorials extolling the virtues of free enterprise in the Free World, and features including comic strips like *Li'l Abner*, *Blondie*, *Peanuts*, *Andy Capp*, which he might read in the newspapers of the United States. Locally-inspired advertisements for such indigenous manufactured products as rum and cigarets are often faithful imitations of Madison Avenue's approach to the mass market.

Even if he does not read the newspapers, the West Indian can hardly escape the ubiquitous commercial radio, particularly since the advent of the transistor set. Although the West Indian wireless has not yet acquired the frenetic, hysterical quality of American broadcasting – a somewhat more mellow British tone being the norm – the content is much the same. American popular culture dominates West Indian programming, and the radio, like the West Indian juke-box, vibrates with the current rock-and-roll hits from morning until late in the evening. Even in Trinidad, "Land of the Calypso," American popular music tends to dominate the airways from the early morning "wake up" show to the four o'clock commuter's program, and on into the evening disc jockey's selections. And with independence came commercial television. By 1963 10,000 sets were in operation and receiving *The Beverly Hillbillies*. In musical jingle, dramatic vignette and straight hard-sell commercial message (spoken in British, American, and even West Indian accents), the West Indian is exhorted to buy automobiles, radios, paint, beer, refrigerators, cigarets, rum and Pepsi-Cola and a host of other major and minor consumer products. Whether the consumer lives in Kingston; Bridgetown, Barbados; Georgetown, Guyana; or Port of Spain, these products can be purchased in modern shops and supermarkets. The hire-purchase, "never-never" system is as firmly established a way of life in the West Indian middle class, and increasingly in the lower class, as might be found in countries of much higher per capita income. The average West Indian can afford very few of these products, but commercial civilization has disseminated the idea of, and desire for, an economy of high mass consumption to a much greater degree than might be expected from an examination of the bare statistics on average personal poverty. West Indians have acquired, as C. L. R. James has written, a £500 mentality on £50 per year, but the elasticity of that £50 is one of the impenetrable mysteries of West Indian life.

West Indians must be classified with the poorer nations of the world, but they are far from being the poorest, and their lack of affluence has been very unevenly distributed both within and among the various territories. In 1957, on the eve of the federal experiment, the national per capita income for all the islands was about $200 (U.S.). Trinidad & Tobago, however, enjoyed what by world standards must be viewed as an astronomical figure of $400, and Jamaica had a figure of $300 – half again as much as the overall average.[2] It can be seen, therefore, that poverty was most acute among the 600,000 residents of the Leeward and Windward Islands, many of whom were eagerly looking to improved prospects through emigration, or to the possibilities of greater financial aid and economic opportunity within the federation. Because of its higher economic level and its calypso and steelband cultural pre-eminence, Trinidad has long been regarded in the Eastern Caribbean as an island of opportunity. Unknown numbers of "small islanders" have clandestinely migrated there, much to the irritation of many local inhabitants who understandably feel that they would be in a better position without labor competition from their poorer neighbors.

Relatively few Trinidadians, unlike the "small islanders" and Jamaicans, were drawn to an even greater island of opportunity – Great Britain, the Mother Country – which, until the restrictive Commonwealth Immigration Act went into effect in 1962 and sharply curtailed the flow, was viewed by large numbers of West Indians as a way out of the limited prospects at home. Like those who left the Caribbean to make the Puerto Rican journey to the United States, West Indians, on the eve of achieving national independence, flocked to England in ever-swelling numbers. From the beginning of 1958 until the end of 1960, over 82,000 emigrants went by ship and airplane from the islands of the federation to the United Kingdom. Sixty-six percent of these left Jamaica; only five percent of the total was drawn from Trinidad & Tobago. While the percentage of the total from the smaller islands was not large, in terms of actual numbers it represented a major exodus from some parts of the Lesser Antilles.[3]

As this massive wave of emigration was taking place in other parts of the West Indies, and as independence descended on Trinidad, Mighty Sparrow composed a calypso in which he asserted that "pound for pound we'll beat New York City." That may seem like an outlandish boast, but Trinidad has much of the internal complexity and élan usually associated with a major metropolis.

CHAPTER 2 A Sociologist's Baedeker to Trinidad & Tobago

In fact there is a tendency for most groups to retain their individuality in Trinidad. But on Sunday evening, at the Bel Air cabaret and dance, couples of every race take the floor together. The delicate ankles and precise beauty of movement which Chinese blood gives to a woman make something altogether strange of the familiar European dance, while South American rhythms which agree with Venezuelans on holiday are perfect, too, for the tall, velvet-skinned, African girl and her Indian partner.

— From a tourist brochure

Trinidad is a city-state; a tropical ruropolis enclosed by the sea, containing a variety of social types and traditions, but closely bound by trade, modern communications and transportation to the Anglo-American world. The island's remote geographical location suggests an entirely misleading notion of its psychological and cultural location. The ease with which many of its leading citizens have followed careers which moved through a circuit from Trinidad to England and North America, and thence back to Trinidad, would seem inexplicable unless one understands that the island is virtually a satellite city of London and New York. This pervasive dependency on, and intensive interaction with, Britain and America accounts for much of the content of Trinidad life; but the Trinidad city also has its own authentic *genius loci*, its own customs and sense of intimate social and spatial relationships. A quick tour of the country is the best means of focusing these factors and will provide a greater sense of familiarity for the ensuing reconstruction of its nationalist movement.

Despite the existence of first-class roads throughout contemporary Trinidad, the island today, as always, turns its back on the Atlantic and is developing chiefly along the western coast facing the Gulf of Paria. The most important functional areas, and correspondingly, the areas of greatest population density, are located within a richly endowed north-south crescent which runs from the northwestern to the

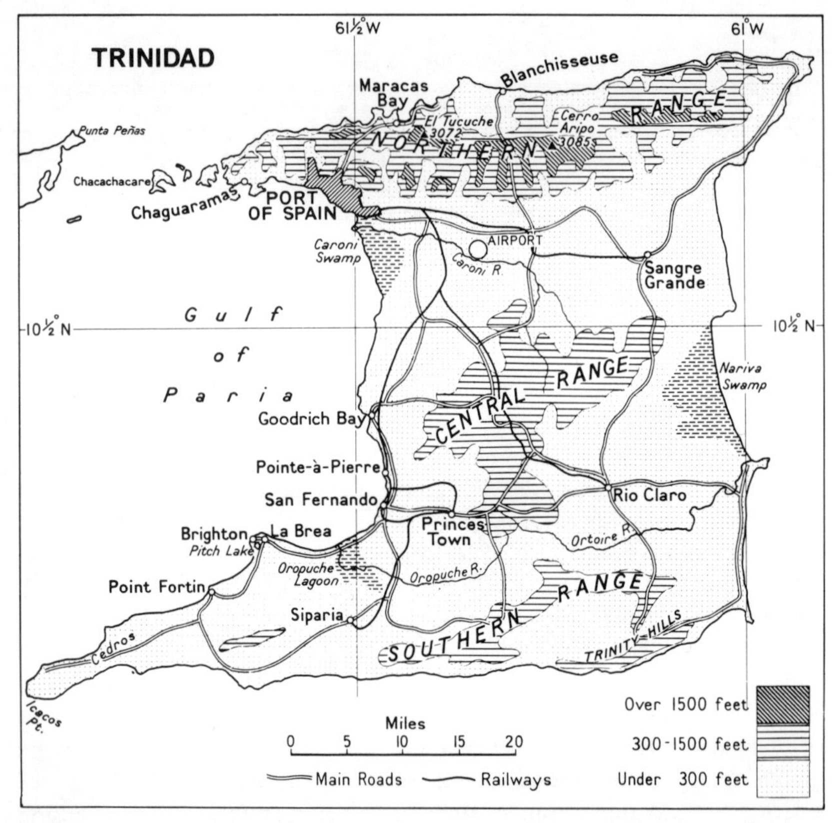

Trinidad (map), Courtesy John Macpherson, Longmans, Green and Co. Ltd.

southwestern tips of the island. These areas, from top to bottom, contain the former U.S. naval base at Chaguaramas Bay, with its excellent deep-water harbor; two major storage areas from which bauxite from Guyana and Surinam is trans-shipped; Port of Spain, the administrative and commercial capital; the sugar belt, which extends from just south of the capital's suburbs and on south past the town of San Fernando; the oil refineries and oil-producing region, which begins just to the north of San Fernando and extends down into the southwestern peninsula and out into the Gulf of Paria. Along this fertile, mineral-rich, industrial and heavily urbanized crescent has always lived the majority of Trinidad's residents. It is fairly compact, with the major urban clusters radiating out from Port of Spain and San Fernando. If one visits the North Post wireless station on the hilly northern shore above the suburbs of Port of Spain, one can easily discern the silver glitter of the Texaco storage tanks at Point-a-Pierre and the gray outline of the mesa-like Naparima Hill hovering over San Fernando some thirty miles to the south.

The South American mainland extends a long Venezuelan finger out toward Trinidad's northwest peninsula which, together with the rugged, sparsely-populated islands that in past geological ages helped to connect the island to the continent, today forms the boundary between the Eastern Caribbean and the Gulf of Paria. The calypsonian's "Matilda" who "took his money and run to Venezuela" must have been an exceptionally adventurous lass because, despite its easily visible and shadowy prominence, the South American mainland is culturally and socially remote from most Trinidadians. Latin American tempos in music and dance, the memories and family connections of a few Trinidadians who have roots on the mainland, and the Venezuelan students who board in Trinidad in order to learn English constitute the major cultural ties. On the whole, Trinidadians do not view Venezuela so much as a place that they might go *to*, but rather as a place where Venezuelans – political refugees, businessmen and smugglers – come *from*. The price differentials between the two countries have led to a fairly brisk, traditional illicit traffic across the Gulf in some consumer goods; for example, according to a Venezuelan of apparent experience, fancy edibles such as the canned ham (which Trinidad imports from Denmark) found on the east Venezuelan's dinner table originates mainly in the grocery stores of Trinidad. The grocers, he maintained, usually show a discreet lack of interest in the nationality of the stomachs for which this delicacy is destined.

The main channels through the islands separating Trinidad from the continent still bear the romantic name conferred on them by Columbus: the *Bocas del Dragon*, the mouths of the dragon. Far to the south, where the long southwestern peninsula of the island encloses the Gulf, the passage is named, with nice symmetry, the *Boca de la Serpiente.* The northwestern straits are usually referred to as "the Bocas," and this archipelago of small islands is called simply "out the islands." Few have occasion to visit this region except perhaps on a rare excursion, although some wealthy families maintain homes or vacation cottages here. The island of Chacachacare, which is host to a small leper colony, is regarded as some remote, Siberian outpost.

Setting off from Port of Spain for a trip by sea to Tobago on one of two daily government steamers, one passes through the Monos Boca out into the Caribbean. As the ship turns the corner from the placid Gulf into the choppy Caribbean and heads east, the mammoth radar screens of the U.S. missile-tracking station at Chaguaramas are visible on the high sea-cliffs looming nearby. The trip by ferry to Tobago is a long one (the ships do not operate at top speeds), taking about eight hours. For the holidaying Trinidad civil servant who, like the foreign visitor, will regard Tobago as a tropical paradise, the passage by ship has the advantage of permitting one to bring along an automobile at a nominal expense. The cruise along the north coast passes the popular public beaches at Maracas and Las Cuevas Bays, both accessible by excellent roads from the capital. Soon the entire north coast, which would appear to have considerable potential for the development of tourism, will be opened up as current road construction is completed across the region.

In a couple of hours the ship completes its transit across the north coast and passes far off-shore from the village of Toco near the remote northeastern tip of the island. In Toco the famous anthropologists Melville and Frances Herskovits conducted field work in 1939 in order to probe a *Trinidad Village* for the African cultural retentions which had been so marked in their pioneering study of the Bush Negroes in Dutch Guiana. Returning home in 1929 via sea from their field work down the Spanish Main, the Herskovitses passed through Port of Spain and their eye caught an intriguing item in the Trinidad *Guardian:* a letter from an "aroused citizen" expressing indignation at the worship of the African god, Shango, which he said was taking place near the city. The anthropologists returned to Trinidad ten years later. Selecting the locale for their investigation on the reasonable assumption that the further they were removed from the urban centers the greater the purity of the African retentions they would find, they settled down in far-off Toco. "Contrary to all our expectations," they later wrote, ". . . the remote community where we worked proved to be without Shango worship – without, indeed, any more Africanisms than would be found in almost any rural community in the southern United

States."[1] What they did claim to discover, however, was an outline of the ways in which the transition from African customs to a predominantly European way of life had taken place; notably, through the mixed worship of European and African deities practiced by the Shouter sect, and in the extra-legal, lower class marital arrangement called "keeping" which they saw as ". . . a reconciliation of European monogamic institutions and African relationship groupings based on a broader definition of kinship and plural marriage."[2]

I have, on various occasions, had the opportunity of discussing these, and other anthropological findings on Africanisms in Trinidad, with members of the relatively educated middle class. Their response was characterized by something less than scientific detachment, tending toward tolerant amusement; some, in an off-hand manner, condemned these cultural survivals as superstitious "stupidness" which education and better economic opportunities will eliminate. In a few instances, after apparently coming to the realization that such things are of great interest to the foreign social scientist, and therefore reflect credit on the island, some respondents were prepared to soberly consider the intricacies of cultural retention and mechanisms of readaptation. The chief attitude that one encounters however, (except among the educated few who are interested in local ethnography), in response to any marked interest in African retentions, is "why worry [bother] with that?" The African roots of part of Trinidad's lower class Negro culture are today generally viewed as colorful but vanishing anachronisms.

On arrival in Scarborough, Tobago, on a holiday weekend, the visitor will find the pier thronged with expectant relatives, tourist resort agents, and taxi drivers; indeed, apparently most of the town turns out just for the spectacle. Affluent foreign visitors may be setting off for the nearby Crown Point Hotel—new, small, very fashionable. But there are several other less expensive guest houses and hostelries in the vicinity of Scarborough. At the Bacolet Inn nearby, for example, rates are modest and meals will be served on a veranda with a view across the 30-mile channel to Trinidad, often dimly visible on the horizon. Although the claim is dubious, Tobago is taken to be the legendary island of Robinson Crusoe, and after surveying the island by auto, one quickly comes to appreciate how Crusoe and Friday, like the contemporary visitor from Trinidad or abroad, could develop a deep attachment for this lovely place. It is a favorite West Indies refuge of Princess Margaret, who honeymooned here; and Walt Disney made the castaway adventure *The Swiss Family Robinson* in Tobago. No visitor will miss the inexpensive and expertly-conducted boat tours to view the tropical fish at the coral Buccoo Reef, augmented by a dip in the shallow, white-sanded Nylon Pool in the

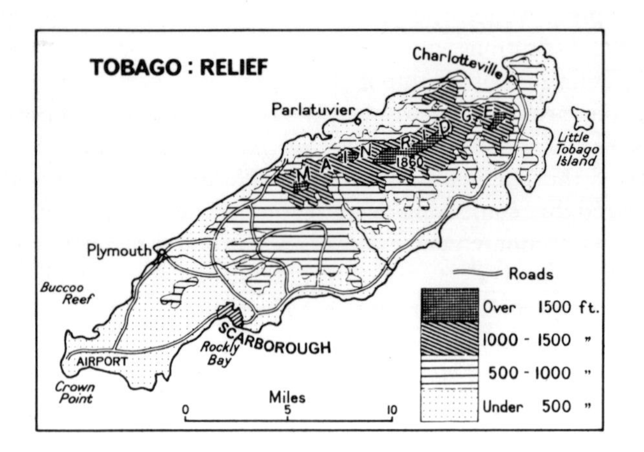

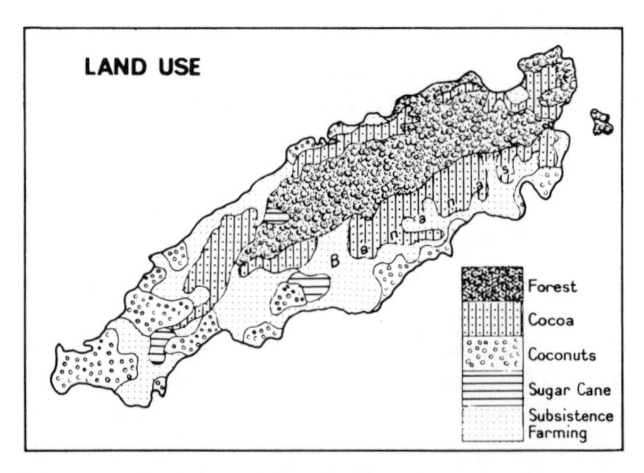

Tobago, Relief and Land Use (maps), Courtesy John Macpherson, Longmans, Green and Co. Ltd.

center of the bay on the return trip. Rewarding, too, is a drive the length of the island to the village of Charlottesville, during the course of which one can stop to bathe along seemingly endless miles of deserted tropical beaches. The really ambitious tourist will visit Bird of Paradise Island, an avian sanctuary for the beautiful birds transferred from New Guinea years ago. Secluded fishing villages, the preserved, romantic, remains of ancient Caribbean forts with cannon and balls in place – in short, a tourist brochure portrayal of a sunny, picturesque Caribbean island – all of this is epitomized in the external appearance of Tobago.

For the Tobagonians, however, Tobago falls somewhat short of paradise. Although not insensitive to the beauties that the foreign visitor continually extols, Tobagonians have long felt that they were residents of a neglected and backward district, remote from the colonial authorities in distant Port of Spain. To the credit of the P.N.M., when it attained office, was a concerted effort at improving air and sea communications with Tobago, and a substantial increase in public investment in the island took place in the attempt to bring it up to par with its larger partner. Before the P.N.M. undertook to upgrade the status of the island some Tobagonians were still talking, how seriously it is difficult to say, about secession – an example of that highly developed insularity which has persisted throughout the history of the West Indies, and which aggravated the separatist perspectives which plagued the foundation of the West Indies Federation. Today, however, Tobagonians have developed a much greater feeling of identity with Trinidad and many continue, as Herskovits discovered in Toco, to migrate to the larger island. The steelband movement flourishes, and with its overwhelmingly Negro population of around 40,000, Tobago is today a P.N.M. stronghold. The Minister of Finance in the P.N.M. cabinet as of 1966 was a young barrister and son of a Tobago schoolmaster, A. N. R. Robinson, who was regarded by some as a possible successor to Dr. Williams. Thus, the fishermen and small peasant proprietors in mountainous Tobago achieved greater benefits and attention in the hands of the P.N.M. Today it seems only slightly more remote from Port of Spain than some of the more isolated rural districts in the eastern section of Trinidad.

The return to Trinidad can be accomplished most quickly by air via one of the frequently scheduled, four-engined aircraft operated by British West Indian Airways. B.W.I.A., a former subsidiary of B.O.A.C., having been purchased by the Trinidad government in 1961, maintains an important service throughout the Caribbean islands and still acts as a feeder line for the parent British carrier. Some controversy surrounded the government's purchase of the airline. Critics pointed to the fact that it had been operating at a deficit, while proponents of the deal answered that it would guarantee the continuation of an indigenous air service for the British West Indies. Some skeptics saw in the acquisition of an airline by Trinidad a manifestation of the nationalist fever which has allegedly caused other small, newly-independent nations to embark on uneconomical purchases of national prestige items. Whatever the long-term merits of this particular transaction may prove to be, there is no denying that the flight between Tobago and Trinidad is swift, scenic, and inexpensive (about $15 round-trip).

Within a half-hour of leaving Tobago the passenger will be approaching Trinidad's modern new terminal at Piarco international airport, possibly when a giant Pan American jet is landing from Rio or New York. Flying over Trinidad one gains some aerial insight into the topography of the island. In contrast to Tobago, which consists almost entirely of low hills and mountains, Trinidad looks chiefly flat. The verdant Northern Range, which bears a striking resemblance to Tobago, extends southward only a few miles from the north coast and then tapers off in a series of slopes and valleys to join the central plain, which from the air looks as flat as a tabletop. The population of the Northern Range region, excluding several rich valleys, is sparse and similar in ethnicity and livelihood to that of Tobago. On the western expanse of the central plain, along the Gulf of Paria, the sugar belt can be seen beginning its winding 35-mile course from the Caroni swamp, located to the southeast of Port of Spain, down to the low-lying hills of the Central Range, which divides it briefly, then still further south, executing a deep, eastward flanking action around San Fernando and on down to the Oropuche Lagoon. The width of the sugar belt greatly varies, but soil and rainfall conditions favorable to sugar cultivation have extended it inland from the Gulf from five to ten miles on the average. By independence most sugar production, and all sugar processing, had been concentrated in the hands of Tate & Lyle, the British sugar trust. Moreover, like the sugar industry everywhere in the West Indies, Trinidad's major food export is dependent on the continuation of the preferential prices paid by Britain – a policy which might be terminated as the latter country attempts to re-orient its traditional economic links and seek entry into Europe.

The trip from Piarco airport to the capital by "drop" taxi – that is, individually hired cabs – is relatively expensive (about $5). The drive passes through the northern section of the cane fields on the Churchill-Roosevelt Highway (built by the American military during World War II), which can be a rather harrowing experience as the donkey-drawn carts of East Indian laborers, heavy diesel-driven trucks, and intrepid taxi drivers compete for the right-of-way. To the north, perched half-way up on the side of the Northern Range, is the Benedictine monastery, Mt. St. Benedict. If the taxi driver, eager to please the foreign visitor, is delivering one of his impromptu (and sometimes wildly inaccurate) travelogues, one may learn that Dr. Fidel Castro once visited the monastery during a brief stopover in Trinidad. This happens to be true, but in general the commentaries of the Trinidad taxi driver must be received with great caution. (Very little information about the Cuban revolution, for instance, penetrates the filters erected by language, the foreign-owned mass media and the anti-Communist stance of the government.) Between the highway and the mountains lies the government railway, the Eastern Main Road, and a series of almost continuous suburbs running along the base of the range from Port of Spain for some fifteen miles to the east. The ethnicity of this suburban region is mixed and has been an area of Negro-East Indian tension, engendered in part, perhaps, by the fact that despite its semi-urban character the classic division between Negro and Indian occupational pursuits to a large extent seems to be maintained here. Negroes commute by train and pirate-taxi into town, while many East Indians continue to work on the nearby sugar estates, or else cultivate vegetable gardens, or grow rice, near the Caroni swamp.

The road to "town" soon passes some of the experimental fields maintained by the nearby College of Tropical Agriculture, which has been made a division of the University of the West Indies and has been joined by engineering and liberal arts faculties. The institution has always been one of the highest ranking of its kind in the world. It conducts research on sugar and cocoa cultivation, and has recently conducted extensive research on forage grasses that might be used to expand local production of livestock. Along this section of the route can also be seen a few of the light industrial establishments which the government has been attempting to promote through tax concessions and the establishment of "industrial estates." After passing a drive-in movie theater and the Princess Margaret Highway, which branches off to the left through the Caroni swamp and the sugar estates toward San Fernando, the driver will take the visitor over the scenic Lady Young Road which climbs across the western end of the Northern Range to provide a spectacular vista overlooking Port of Spain and the Gulf of Paria. The Lady Young Road descends toward the city through a series of swooping hairpin curves and suddenly terminates at the edge of the Queen's Park Savannah. For accommodations in Trinidad the visitor can choose from a number of guest houses and hotels including Trinidad's independence-new Hilton, locally nicknamed "the upside down hotel" because the lobby entrance, reached by a driveway off the Lady Young Road, is located on the top floor, while the guest rooms are arranged in balconied tiers down toward the foot of the hill. The Trinidad Hilton represents an important government investment in the attempt to lure both trade and tourism to the island. The décor includes a swimming pool in the shape of Trinidad and a wading pool cast in the shape of Tobago, tastefully executed in a style that could perhaps be called "Hilton tropical." Local artists contributed murals, and in the "Carnival Bar" (coat and tie after six) a handsome metal frieze depicting Carnival characters complements a motif featuring lighting fixtures shaped like steelband instruments. The writer observed the opening of the Hilton with considerable interest because its initial social organization so closely paralleled that face of the West Indies social system which the islands' tourist industry usually likes to present to the world. At the top were the white, expatriate managerial personnel, some of whom, in accordance with Hilton policy, were to be replaced in the future by local staff; in one of the dining rooms were placed the predominantly fair, often French Creole "hostesses" who presided over a section of tables individually waited on by girls of more Negroid appearance; in the more important service capacities in the Carnival Bar and in the relatively plush La Boucan supper-club supervisors and waiters were predominantly East Indian, while the bus-boys, charwomen and other "behind the scenes" hotel employees were predominantly Negro. When the Hilton was opened, Mr. Hilton stressed that it was to be "a part of the community" rather than an isolated tourist enclave. For the Trinidad middle class and the upper social brackets this ideal was realized to a gratifying degree. But, as the local critics were quick to observe at the time, for the Trinidad masses the Hilton is almost as remote as the old colonial Queen's Park Hotel on the Savannah ever was.

Hotel managers and other impresarios have a great advantage in Trinidad: there is no shortage of local entertainers. The island boasts of not only the two popular musical traditions it invented – splendid steelbands and a large number of calypsonians ranging from superb to execrable – but abounds in dance orchestras, traditional folk choruses and dance troupes (not excluding the inevitable limbo dancers), and a small army of talented local performers who are veterans of Trinidad's flourishing night life. In a pinch, the management can always depend on the tens of thousands of seasoned troupers from the more elaborate Carnival bands. The gala opening of the Hilton saw a reenactment of a portion of the previous year's Carnival right on the premises. An entering guest that evening passed by an impressive row of (black) fur-bedecked and helmeted Visigoth warriors stationed along the corridor leading to the lobby, all solemnly performing their duties with spears at the ready. Later, portions of various bands, numbering several thousand, paraded and danced along the pool terrace with an invigorating zeal and earnestness and, despite an unfortunate cloudburst, put on a spectacular display requiring no rehearsal whatsoever!

Trinidadians certainly do not have to be taught about showmanship; so many are performers of one sort or another that the island has developed a kind of "show business" mentality. Every year Carnival impresarios strive to outdo the "hits" of previous years. Calypsonians are constantly attempting to compose a popular sensation for the local nightclub and records industry. In recent years, so it has been charged by students of the art, a growing number of calypsos have been composed in the hope of reaching the receptive ear of a foreign promoter. But this charge is exaggerated, for most calypsos are still satirical-topical commentaries on life in Trinidad and almost incomprehensible to the uninitiated.

The show business complex of Trinidad is most highly developed in the majority Negro-Creole community (although a protracted but less significant renaissance of classic and not-so-classic Indian culture has appeared as well), and it combines with the local enthusiasm for games of chance found in all groups to produce the ingratiating boom-bust attitude toward life that prevails. This is the core of the so-called "Creole way of life:" dance, drink, and be merry – play your mas' – have your fête and spree, that good, old-fashioned, Creole bacchanal. Toward all this, the more sober-minded of Trinidad's middle class leaders have held very mixed feelings. An old colonial notion that social stability can be enhanced if the government makes an effort to promote some increase in bread, while the Creole lower class provides itself with circuses, has not been entirely dispelled. The P.N.M. instigated a "Carnival Development Committee" as an indication of its solidarity with Creole culture, but a few P.N.M. leaders continued to feel uneasy about the stability of the support they enjoyed from the black lower class. As one rather nervous member of Dr. Williams' circle of advisors said, "Dr. Williams captured the imagination and the faith of the lower class. The steelband movement and the calypsonians have been important sources of support. But if something should happen, if we let them down or they lose their faith in the Doctor, they may turn on us overnight." During the independence period, when Dr. Williams introduced the sobering slogans of "Discipline, Production and Tolerance" and clamped down on plans to observe independence with the traditional spirit of Carnival, these measures were privately justified in some quarters on the grounds that unless they were taken there might be a repetition of the social chaos which

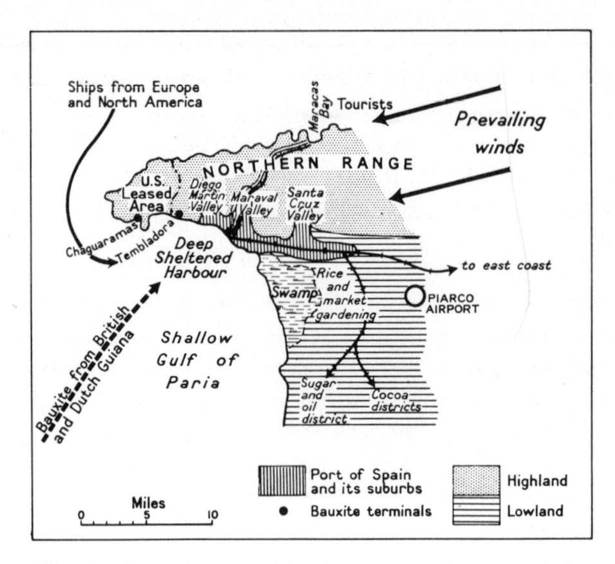

The Setting of Port of Spain (map), Courtesy John Macpherson, Longmans, Green and Co. Ltd.

allegedly accompanied the emancipation of the slaves. As a snackette, pirate-taxi, and steelband yard habitué, I could detect no trace of such attitudes toward the arrival of independence. But a belief in the volatility of the black masses is nevertheless widespread in Trinidad.

On the other hand, when Dr. Williams made a trip to Israel in connection with a European business tour after independence, he told a gathering that included Prime Minister Ben Gurion to come and visit Trinidad and they would be taught "how to live." And again, when during the final hours of the 1963 Carnival Dr. Williams and his party came upon a group of celebrants before the Port of Spain police headquarters who were *serenading the police*, he issued orders to the Planning Unit to consider how the resourcefulness and energy which Trinidadians put into Carnival might be harnessed in the interest of national development!

The city which supplies the central arena of Trinidad's Creole culture is located in a roughly semi-circular plain about two miles in diameter which is tilted slightly toward the waterfront. Rising above the irregular circumference of the city are the forested foothills of the Northern Range. The main road to the northwest and the Chaguaramas naval base passes along the sea far beneath the commanding heights of old Fort George, where only some overgrown breastworks, and antique cannon propped up among the weeds, are left as reminders of its former function. The main eastern traffic corridor follows the sea to skirt the Laventille Hills – their landmark a single, windmill-like ruin

Uriah Butler waves Trinidad flag on Independence Day, 1962.
Guardian photo.

Trinidad religious leaders say prayers for the new nation on Independence Eve.
Guardian photo.

Bringing in the sugar crop on a large estate. *Courtesy Paul Rupp Associates.*

Village women going to work. *Courtesy Noel P. Norton.*

Queen's Hall, designed by Trinidad architect Colin Laird, is a symbol of progress.
Courtesy Noel P. Norton.

Moslem youth puts the finishing touches on a *tadjah* float for Hosein festival. *Courtesy Paul Rupp Associates.*

Mighty Sparrow crowned as Calypso King. *Guardian* photo.

The final step in making a steel-band tenor pan, or "pingpong." Pans are usually played with wooden sticks around the top of which are wrapped strips of rubber. *Courtesy B.W.I.A.*

Combat troops, old and new, are popular Carnival roles. *Courtesy Government Public Relations Office.*

Kiddies' Carnival is held before adult event. *Guardian* photos.

of a military turret dating from Spanish times. These densely populated slums on the eastern hills of the city include the Laventille and John-John districts, both known by the generic name "on the hill." Below lie the sprawling wastelands of Shanty Town – now being demolished – and East Dry River, the latter called simply "behind the bridge" because of its location beyond the usually dry, deeply-culverted St. Ann's River. "Behind the bridge" can be loosely translated as "the wrong side of the tracks," and it is an area which has been frequently torn by open warfare between rival districts and cliques, usually organized around one of the area's many famous steelbands, *e.g.*, "Desperadoes" or "Renegades." These names give some indication of the fantasy life which the Creole lower class, inveterate movie fans, brings to its straitened circumstances, and there has been nothing restrained about their internal wars. Rocks, bolts, bottles, knives, pistols and even home-made bombs have been standard weapons in the arsenals of these descendants of "nigger-yard" culture and the original *jamettes*. Their periodic wars and assassinations – which have by far exceeded in violence and casualties the sporadic Negro-Indian feuds – have been regularly and predictably greeted by a chorus of shock and outrage from the respectable middle class. During the independence era two men were idolized behind the bridge: one was Francisco Slinger, a calypsonian immigrant from the nearby island of Grenada, better known as "Sparrow," and the other was "The Doc" – Dr. Eric Williams.

The major commercial district of the city lies along the waterfront, concentrated in an area of approximately six by ten blocks. The port area contains a single, connected line of berths running parallel to the water's edge which can accommodate at least six large vessels simultaneously. Nearby is the old St. Vincent Street jetty around which are berthed a myriad of small, often decrepit, island schooners. The scene here is one of unloading Barbados rum and loading Trinidad produce or biscuits. The traffic is small scale but brisk. Behind the customs sheds and warehouses of the central port area are located the main import-export houses, which run up to Independence Square where iron-balconied old business buildings are being steadily supplanted by a sterile mixture of stone, steel and glass facades favored by Trinidad's modernizing merchant princes and corporations. At one end of this long, rectangular, square stands a painted statue of Christopher Columbus. He looks upon the back of the old Roman Catholic Church, and this, in turn, faces toward a traffic circle in the center of which stands a black stone likeness of the father of Trinidad nationalism, Captain Andrew A. Cipriani. For some reason, possibly financial, Trinidadians have not had their culture heroes sculpted on an heroic scale. The statues of Columbus, Cipriani, and Gandhi (in San Fernando) seem barely life size. Cipriani's diminutive appearance is accentuated by his proximity to the new eight-story Salvatori Building from the top of which, as Sparrow once observed in a calypso commemorating this great, modern edifice, he looks like a boy. From its upper tier of penthouse residential suites, to its street-level offices of Barclay's Bank, D.C.O., the Salvatori Building arose as a monument to business self-confidence in a commercial community frequently wary about that nebulous, fickle, foreign spirit, "Investor Confidence." The building is a monument, also, to the memory of its builder, George A. Salvatori, popular businessman and sportsman from an old French family. He died in 1962 in a New York hospital whither he had been rushed by chartered plane from Trinidad for treatment of severe burns sustained while cleaning the engine of a yacht. Salvatori occupied one of the penthouse suites atop his building – a position of eminence roughly equivalent, by local standards, of owning and living on top of the Empire State Building.

Exploring the central business district on foot is as exciting and full of surprises as a tour of any of the world's great cities: the Central Market, reminiscent by virtue of its architecture, its bulk sales of meat and produce, and its bustle, noise and stench, of Les Halles; Henry and Charlotte Streets with their small bazaars run by Chinese, Syrian and Indian merchants. Here are Indian barber shops with photographs of turbanned pundits peering out from behind glass frames, rum shops, second-floor Chinese restaurants, sweepstake vendors, tailor shops – the sidewalks are thronged, and everywhere there is noise and commotion.

Bisecting the business district is Frederick Street, which runs from the old Spanish lighthouse on the waterfront for a mile back to the Queen's Park Savannah. A bigoted local white businessman once informed me that the Negro's lack of business acumen was nowhere better illustrated than in the fact that not a single foot of Frederick Street frontage was owned by a Negro. Along this thoroughfare are located the main department stores and tourist shops. Saturday morning is the major time set aside for shopping, and during those hours Frederick Street is filled with the island's cosmopolitan population and frequently with foreign merchant seamen, sailors, and tourists from cruise ships. Adjoining Frederick Street in the commercial district is the one-block wooded park named after a great nineteenth century British Governor, Woodford Square. It is bordered on three sides by buildings which were the embodiment of the doctrines of colonial trusteeship: the Anglican Cathedral, the Public Library, and the traditional center of administration, named after its color, Red House, in one second-story wing of which is located the legislative chamber. A parliament of an informal kind exists in Woodford Square itself. The square's central location and its lofty shade trees, which afford relief from the tropical sun, have made it for generations a refuge for town idlers and country visitors, and here has developed Trinidad's version of London's Hyde Park Corner. At almost any time of day one can find here an assortment of lay preachers, self-made political commentators, and a miscellany of local characters, holding forth vociferously before almost exclusively male audiences often numbering several dozen. Speakers on social or political issues often invite, or incur, pointed heckling from bystanders, and heated exchanges always produce appreciative guffaws and side discussions. These arguments are almost invariably carried on in the cleverly-insulting *picong* style of repartee, and speakers know that they must "come good" or they will be chastised by the sharp wits and tongues of their audience. Given its central location and its traditions of proselytizing and dissent, it was only natural that Woodford Square should have become the locale for formal political meetings. Many of the island's leading politicians have addressed audiences in the square, and its public traditions were officially entrenched when Dr. Eric Williams, speaking from the bandstand in 1955, dubbed his mass meetings there "the University of Woodford Square."

The city's old middle and working class residential districts, Belmont, New Town and Woodbrook, lie in an east-west zone between the commercial district and the more fashionable residential areas of St. Ann's, Cascade, and St. Clair. The latter has been the bailiwick, in the traditional social geography of the Negro community, of the local white, predominantly French Creole, elite. Here, with an unintended symbolic significance which will become evident to the reader later, Dr. Williams located his offices in a building ("Whitehall") flanked by the mansions of the Roman Catholic Archbishop and an old commercial dynasty.

St. James, which was the writer's base of operations, is an interesting quarter of the city because, unlike the eastern suburbs which have a heavy Negro-Indian mixture, the Negroes and East Indians in St. James live cheek-by-jowl in almost complete "inter-racial harmony." A part of the reason for this is that St. James, with its streets bearing names like "Hyderabad" and "Gandhi," was the old "Coolie Town" and contains Indians who have been urbanized and "creolized" to a considerable degree. Some evidence for this accommodation occurs during the annual Moslem Hosein festival when Negroes often serve as drummers and Negro children will be found taking part in the festivities. This event is mentioned simply to indicate that, although Negro-East Indian relations have often been strained, it is easy to overgeneralize about inter-group relations in even such a small place as Trinidad. In general, however, the more urbanized Moslem section of the East Indians—which in Trinidad, as shown in Table 1, constitutes a relatively small

TABLE 1. Races and Religions in Trinidad & Tobago at Independence

Race	*Number*	*Per Cent*	*Religion*	*Number*	*Per Cent*
Negro	358,588	43.3	Roman Catholic	299,649	36.2
East Indian*	301,946	36.5	Hindu	190,403	23.0
Mixed†	134,749	16.3	Anglican	175,042	21.1
White	15,718	1.9	Other Christian	108,520	13.1
Chinese	8,361	1.0	Moslem	49,736	6.0
Lebanese & Syrian	1,590	0.2	Other or none	4,607	0.6
Other, or not stated	7,005	0.8			
Total	827,957	100.0	Total	827,957	100.0

Source: *1960 Census of Trinidad and Tobago* (Bulletins Nos. 1 and 2).

* It will be noted that there are 61,807 more "East Indians" than the combined totals of Hindus and Moslems. This apparently reflects the fact that about one in five of those regarded as racially East Indian identify themselves with various branches of Christianity.

† "Mixed" is the official census category recognizing the racial "mix-up" of many Trinidadians. Alhough it contains many representatives from a number of racial permutations, most members of this category probably enjoy an appreciable degree of Negro ancestry.

proportion of the total Indian population—have gotten along more amicably with the Negroes than have the Hindus. There are a number of reasons for this, the ancient divisions between Hindu and Moslem being one, but an important additional factor seems to be the universalistic tenets of the Islamic creed. The Moslem religious hierarchy increasingly gravitated toward the P.N.M. politically, and one devout Moslem who served in the P.N.M. cabinet suggested to the writer an affinity between Islam and the African population based on the theory that many of the slaves had originally been Moslems because they had been drawn from the Mandingo kingdom! Few Negroes are aware of this historic bond; indeed, I even met a few who thought that the Moslems were simply another group within the attenuated Hindu caste system. Such egregious ignorance is exceptional, but it is symptomatic of the pervasive lack of mutual knowledge and communication between the various ethnic groups of Trinidad. This is a rather complicated phenomenon, but several major features of the situation must be mentioned. The first is that, owing to the diversity of cultural backgrounds of the various groups, and to the early tendency for certain types of occupations to take on a traditional character as being appropriate for certain groups and not for others; and owing, moreover, to the highly endogamous patterns of mating and marriage and the prevalence of stereotypy, Trinidadians have learned to *tolerate* the differing customs and peculiarities associated with various groups. But this toleration does not usually represent a positive acceptance of the intrinsic validity of the way of life and beliefs of another group. The usual response of the majority of Trinidad Negroes toward East Indian folkways and mores, and of East Indians toward Negro traits, is *negative indifference*, frequently accompanied by ridicule or sarcastic expressions of antipathy, mistrust and hostility. A "live and let live" outlook such as was implicit in the patriotic boast of the St. James snackette proprietor who assured me that "Trinidad going to show the *world* that cat and dog can live together" is constantly undermined by equally strong convictions that the customs of another group are morally reprehensible and "backward." Shading into this penchant toward a mutually jaundiced perception of many aspects of life, which is characteristic of inter-group relations, there has developed a sort of easy-going, picaresque relativism that frequently allows a considerable range of individual deviancy within each group. Although Trinidad is a small society, and therefore might be expected to impose rather strict sanctions on individual conduct in the classic modes of small societies, it is not so small, or, more importantly, so homogeneous in outlook as to impose successfully a unitary system of norms on its members.

Observing these anthropological oddities in the early 1950's, Daniel Crowley suggested that Trinidad is such a conglomeration of racial and cultural mixtures that each group has to some extent internalized, or learned to appreciate, the way of life of several other groups, and thus, through this process of "plural acculturation," a fluid yet stable system of inter-group relations is maintained.[3] There is considerable observational basis for this interpretation, and it is of great significance; but the existence of plural acculturation, while it provides one technique for the Trinidad *modus vivendi*, does not erase – indeed, probably works to preserve – the racial and cultural differences which are still relatively rigid categorical determinants of the basic social identities of persons belonging to the various groups. A belief in "plural acculturation" is, in effect, a major ingredient in middle class Creole ideology, an image of the society which emphasizes the cosmopolitan "mixture" and tends to regard the existing alienation of a large percentage of the East Indian population from the Creole majority as an aberration. It is, moreover, an ideology expressed in the tendency to regard Carnival as a "national" festival when in fact it is almost exclusively a Creole event, and which likewise was found in the pervasive tendency to equate the predominantly Creole P.N.M. with the nation. At least equally as important as plural acculturation in keeping

Trinidad society at a relatively low pitch of inter-group conflict is a pervasive state of mind which might be called *plural disassociation*, which is characterized by the attitude – a cardinal tenet in the philosophy of the Trinidadian – that each should attend to his own affairs and not go "interfering" in the business of other groups.

In reality, Trinidad's high rates of urbanization and sprawling quasi-suburbanization encompass the majority of the population and have produced, as suggested at the outset of this chapter, some of the major ecological and cultural ingredients of an *urban* way of life. The lack of ethnic-based residential segregation has placed Negro, East Indian, and the other minorities, side by side in many sections of Trinidad and thus has produced social conditions analogous to the early multi-cultural, immigrant-filled, American metropolis. Indeed, the proximity of conflicting or disparate ways of life is even more acute in Trinidad owing to the absence of urban ghettos. This, combined with the small size of the community, has produced that characteristic phenomenon of the folk community – intense gossiping based on high visibility of intimate behavior – which in Trinidad is practically devoid of any effectiveness as a means of social control. While Trinidadians are frequently rather sophisticated urban men in outlook, they live without the concealment of private lives which the anonymity of urban life typically affords. Moreover, because residential architecture tends to be so open and houses so close together, it is hardly metaphorical to say that in Trinidad one must become accustomed to living in a house of glass.

A quite different picture of Trinidad life is presented, however, if one takes a trip down into the sugar belt to one of the isolated and ethnically homogeneous East Indian villages. County Caroni in the northern section of the sugar belt has long been viewed by the Trinidad Negro as the most backward and isolated core of Indian culture. The social structure of one of these villages – the village of Felicity near the Caroni town of Chaguanas – was studied for a year by Morton Klass, who described his findings in *East Indians in Trinidad*. Reminiscent of the Herskovitses' quest for the retention of African culture in Toco, Klass's 1958 study, subtitled "A Study of Cultural Persistence," met with much greater success because there is no doubt that many East Indians have clung to ways of their ancestors. The degree and significance of these conscious retentions, however, is sometimes a matter of intellectual controversy in Trinidad. Klass concluded that his village (which he calls "Amity") was "in basic structure . . . an 'Indian' community and not a 'West Indian' community."[4] This conclusion provoked Eric Williams to include the following nationalist reprimand in his independence *History:* "A foreign student, with all the impetuosity of youth rushing in where angels fear to tread, may talk glibly of an Indian village in Trinidad not being West Indian, and predict that the Indians will never be assimilated. It is certain however, that he did not have to paint his face black or brown to ascertain this, as a compatriot of his had to do in respect of his native country."[5] The latter observation is true, for race prejudice on an interpersonal level in Trinidad is not acute, least of all between Indians and whites; but it hardly addressed the meticulous documentation on which Klass based his conclusion. Far from "talking glibly" about this finding, Klass took pains to qualify his generalization:

> The emphasis throughout this book has been on the persistence of Indian culture in Amity. This may have led to an under-emphasis of acculturation from the West Indian environment, but there is no desire here to deny that acculturation . . . There are radios and newspapers and even a telephone in Amity, and there are good roads leading to Port of Spain. Yet in some ways Amity is a closed world, and it is easy for an observer living there to forget that Amity is a part of 'Creole' Trinidad, which in turn is part of a greater West Indian complex. Amity is not really isolated from the world. Fluctuations in the price of sugar in London affect the personal income of every villager. Hindu and Muslim friendships in the village were strained during the early Indian-Pakistan conflicts . . .[6]

The issue at stake here, of no mean political as well as scientific interest, obviously hinges on the selection of the criteria by which one culture or community is judged to represent a different species from another. Although this problem, as it is manifested in Caribbean social research, has been intensively discussed by scholars,[7] the basic sociological distinction between "society" and "community" is useful in achieving some rudimentary clarity on the issue as presented in Klass's study. No one can deny, after spending a few hours, leave aside a full year, in Felicity or one of the other East Indian, rural, village ghettos in the heart of the sugar belt, that these people are different from the island's Negroes, and even from the Indians one has met in town. Klass describes a village which has an attenuated caste system, practices the religions of India and the public and private ceremonies and beliefs associated therewith, and thinks of itself as "Indian" as distinct from Creole. What he maintains, therefore, and he is obviously the authority on the question, is that the inhabitants of Felicity have a sense of *community* which includes a basic group identification as "East Indian" (or, a "we-feeling" distinct from that of the majority), and conventions and beliefs which constitute a distinct moral universe more akin to that of an Indian than a Negro-Caribbean village. At the same time, he goes out of his way to emphasize the inevitable interpenetration of Felicity's *society* – its functional interdependence with the economy and polity of which it is a small unit – with that of the majority culture. Klass neither states that Felicity is immutable and unchangeable, nor does he minimize the importance of outside societal influences.

The most likely explanation for Eric Williams' criticism of this study, which is recognized by many Trinidad intellectuals as the best study yet conducted of the Indian community, is that Klass discovered a community which some leading P.N.M. politicians felt *ought not* to exist. It so happened that Klass's study tended to confirm the "two nations" theory which, as will be shown, had been advanced as a justification for East Indian separatism in the early Twenties, and which was a spectre being raised again by a few militant East Indian nationalists in support of *partition* of Trinidad in the independence period. Dr. Williams rejected this radically pluralist conception of the society, as, indeed, did the majority of the population. But while Klass's study could be used to support the arguments of those who advanced a pluralist conception of Trinidad (and it was so used by one Indian leader in a conversation with the writer), Williams himself, in his independence *History*, seemed to subscribe to the idea that Trinidad still consisted of significantly divided and warring groups:

> . . . Two races have been freed, but a society has not been formed . . . The task facing the people of Trinidad and Tobago after their Independence is to create a nation out of the discordant elements and antagonistic principles and competing faiths and rival colors which have produced the amalgam that is today the approximately 875,000 people of Trinidad and Tobago.[8]

Nonetheless, one must raise the question of the degree to which Felicity is representative of the island-wide East Indian community, and on the basis of materials published by another team of anthropologists doing field work in the sugar belt almost simultaneously with Klass, a somewhat different perspective emerges. *East Indians in the West Indies* by Arthur and Juanita Niehoff is a study with less specific focus than Klass's, but it provides interesting comparative impressions obtained chiefly in the southern portion of the sugar belt, in the vicinity of the Oropuche Lagoon. The Niehoffs' study paid considerable attention to variations in the degree of retention of Indian culture in different areas. The Caroni swamp region where Felicity is located is viewed by them as a bailiwick of the more "conservative" East Indians. They do not attempt to say whether or not the communities they studied are predominately Indian in structure, but one gains the impression that they believe that, despite a high degree of retention of Indian culture, acculturation to European values and thus a closer approach to some aspects of the Creole value system had proceeded very far and at an accelerating rate.[9]

South Trinidad was brought most strongly under the influence of the Presbyterian missionaries from Canada in the nineteenth century, and this gave the East Indians of this region something of a lead in exposure to European values and educational opportunities. More important, perhaps, are the Niehoffs' findings which indicate a substantial breakdown in the traditional Trinidad division of labor. This division had established occupational myths about the suitability of the weak, scrawny East Indian for estate labor with cutlass and hoe, while the stronger, more durable and better-educated Negro was thought to be best equipped for industrial labor and white collar work. In compiling statistics on the ethnic distribution of employment in several major industrial undertakings in south Trinidad, the Niehoffs discovered that East Indians – much to the surprise of the manager of one sugar factory – had in recent years moved in substantial numbers into industrial and clerical occupations.[10]

The section of the sugar belt scrutinized by the Niehoffs overlaps with the economic zone known as "the oilfields," where Negroes number perhaps three-quarters of the total labor force. While Trinidad's chief agricultural product was developed from physical and historical conditions similar to those in most of the British Caribbean, its chief mineral asset exists by virtue of the island's proximity to Venezuela, which enables it to tap an extension of the Maturin basin. The oilfields of eastern Venezuela are not as prolific as those in the Lake Maracaibo region, but are nonetheless important to that country and indispensable to the economy of Trinidad, *accounting for 75 percent of the total value of its exports and paying at least 35 percent into the island's annual budget by direct royalties.* The town of San Fernando is situated at the hub of this southern industrial area. The giant refinery at Pointe-a-Pierre is a few miles away, and marine oil drilling platforms can be seen rising on the horizon to the south in the Gulf. With this overlapping of sugar estate and industrialization San Fernando has a strongly mixed Negro-Indian character. Here live a number of foreign technicians and key administrative personnel, in some instances residing in segregated compounds; and at the bottom of the social scale are the settlements of Negro immigrants from such smaller Caribbean islands as Grenada who, as at "Strikers' Village," gave violent support to their fellow Grenadian, Uriah Butler, in the oilfield demonstrations of the Thirties. From this period is dated a radical political tradition associated with "the South" which persisted up to, and even after, the formation of the P.N.M.

Finally, to complete this brief tour of Trinidad & Tobago, some mention must be made of the region east of the sugar belt, a land of large coconut estates, particularly on the east coast, and scattered small holdings of peasant farmers engaged in the production of cocoa. The beautiful, unbroken ten-mile sweep of ocean beach from Point Radix to Galeota Point is lined with coconut forests, but the population density in the "heel" of the Trinidad boot is very low. Climb the lighthouse tower at Point Galeota and the vista, including the nearby Trinity Hills, must look much the same as it did to Columbus when he first passed here. Along Mayaro Bay, however, devout Trinidad Hindus now flock to perform their traditional religious immersions.

Our tour has shown that while Trinidad & Tobago can be technically classified as one of the new, developing nations, it has the facilities, tempo and contrasts of a society already approaching European modernity, in comparison with most of the nations of Africa, Asia, and even neighboring Latin America. Table 2, showing the breakdown

TABLE 2. Working Population in Trinidad & Tobago by Industrial Group, 1960

	Number Employed	*Per Cent*
Total Working Population	262,570	100.0
Services	66,850	25.5
Agriculture, Forestry, Hunting & Fishing	55,407	21.1
Manufacturing	40,791	15.5
Commerce	34,932	13.3
Construction	30,016	11.4
Transport & Communications	16,250	6.2
Mining and Quarrying	12,826	4.9
Utilities	5,138	2.0
Not Stated	360	.1

Source: *1960 Census of Trinidad and Tobago* (Bulletin No. 6).

of the occupational structure in the islands, provides striking evidence for the economic factors supporting these impressions of the society.

In examining the relatively "developed" profile of this table, one important qualification should be noticed. The table is based on a distinction between the "working population" and the "labor force" of Trinidad & Tobago and therefore does not indicate the high levels of unemployment and underemployment prevalent in the islands. At the time this study was conducted official estimates of the number of unemployed in the labor force were not available, but inflated opposition estimates ranged as high as 60,000 and upwards to twenty-five percent. P.N.M. spokesmen, perhaps partially motivated by a partisan desire to obscure the magnitude of the problem, asserted that definitions of unemployment and underemployment utilized in richer industrialized societies were not applicable to the rural-squatting, casual, part-time labor still preferred by many citizens. This convenient stereotype of the Trinidad laborer was, however, incompatible with such incidents as the sudden appearance of hundreds of laborers who besieged the offices of the Minister of Public Works as he was preparing to undertake a major development scheme in 1961. (They were curtly dismissed by the Minister.)[11]

Of those Trinidadians who sought and found work in 1960, however, Table 2 shows how the urban-industrial sector of the economy swamped the rural-agricultural sector in terms of numbers formally employed. Barely one out of five members of the work force was engaged in distinctly rural occupations, with sugar cultivation both on the estates and by small canefarmers accounting for a major share of regular agricultural employment. Industrial, clerical and service occupations accounted for almost eight out of ten jobs available. Of the total working population, moreover, almost one in four – 68,963 – were females, of whom about one-half were employed in services, with commerce and agriculture employing about 11,000 each. Female estate laborers, domestic servants, retail clerks, secretaries – the latter including many representatives of that decidedly modern phenomenon, the middle class "working wife" – were a major force in the economic life of the country.

This economic superstructure rests chiefly – as everyone in Trinidad knows, and as Dr. Williams, like earlier politicians, has repeatedly emphasized – on the three letters "o-i-l." Moreover, by independence it was not simply the black gold within Trinidad's territory which accounted for its relative affluence, but the fact that the international oil corporations found Trinidad a lucrative spot for refining and trans-shipping imported crude. From nearby Venezuela, and strung out across the Atlantic and Mediterranean from Trinidad to the Near East, a fleet of gigantic tankers continually ferried a small portion of the incredible petroleum wealth of the Arabian Gulf to the refineries of south Trinidad. Had Britain entered the European Common Market on its first attempt, some Trinidadians feared, French petroleum from the Sahara might have dislocated the diminutive but established role of Trinidad in the world petroleum market. Thus, when Dr. Williams tells an audience of the unemployed poor that the government is doing its best to provide jobs, they tend to listen sympathetically to his recital of the gravity of the situation: the government can be viewed as a victim of the same uncontrollable, limited, economic circumstances which they

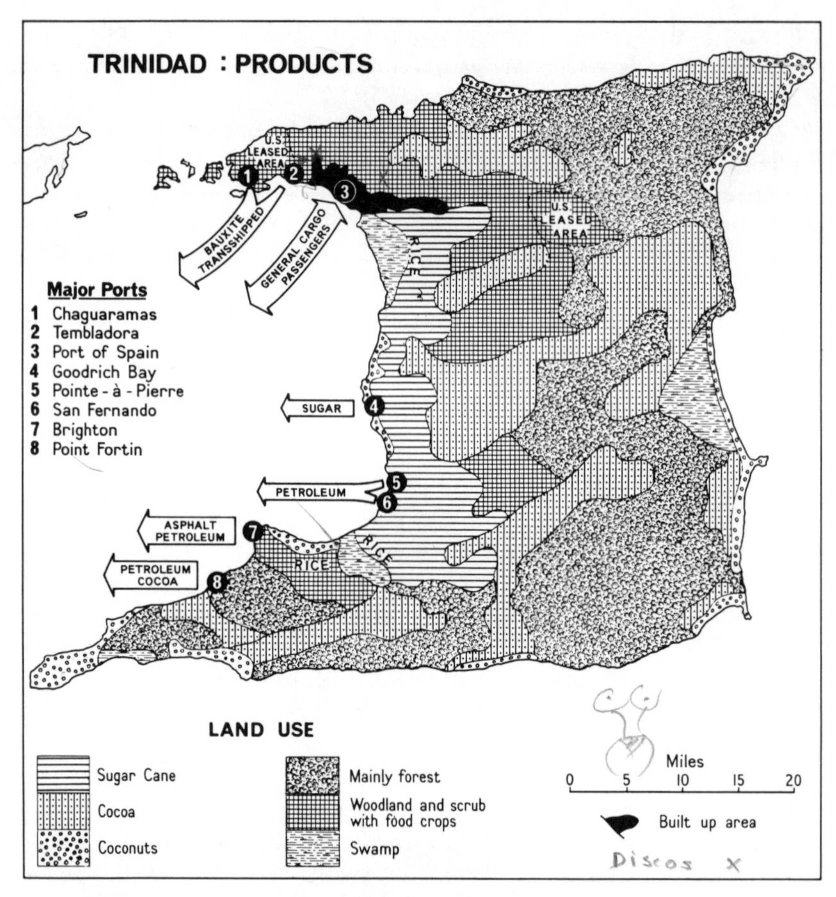

Trinidad Products (map). Courtesy John Macpherson, Longmans, Green and Co. Ltd.

themselves know. "The Doctor and them doing their best," was a widely held sentiment among a population sustained by an economic structure based largely on the processing and export of foreign-owned sugar and oil. The traditional British commercial slogan "Export or Die" is well understood by the common man in Trinidad, and a sense of powerlessness and insignificance in the face of massive, international economic currents has tended to dampen, if not stifle, post-independence public discussion of how Trinidad might attempt to transform the negative features of its colonial heritage from within.

Nonetheless, despite these limitations on Trinidad's economic security and affluence, its relative state of economic modernity in the West Indies combined with its generally stable racial relations led Sparrow to admonish foreign visitors during the independence celebrations that there had come into existence "a model nation at last." The self-image of Trinidad as a relatively prosperous and progressive area, although by no means universally shared, is one of the chief reasons underlying its low rate of emigration. But more: the widespread feeling that Trinidad is a good place to live is based not only on the relative economic prosperity of the country in the West Indies, but equally as much on the general quality of life. In spite of poverty, labor unrest, and occasional racial tension, there is an optimism which forms an important part of the world-view of many of its citizens. This sense of uniqueness and well-being is frequently encountered in the midst of conditions which in richer countries would be associated with acute despair or rebellion. As an unemployed, lower class youth, one of thousands whose *raison d'etre* was the steelband movement, said when asked if he would not prefer to go abroad to work: "No, man, I love this little Trinidad too bad." While the poor are by no means contented, and this is a major factor in the political stability of Trinidad & Tobago, the poor man's lot is eased not only by perpetual sunshine and the popular mass culture, but also by a number of ingenious popular institutions and practices which combine to give life in Trinidad its particular flavor.

Consider one of the hallmarks of the rich society: the availability of the automobile as a means of mass transportation. Relatively few individuals can afford to own an automobile in Trinidad (although ownership of a vehicle is widespread by West Indian standards and the key symbol of middle class status), but *everyone* rides in automobiles. This apparent paradox is resolved by a feature of Trinidad life which is as much a public institution as a system of transportation, namely, the pirate-taxi. The pirate-taxi system consists of several thousand automobiles which run on unscheduled routes throughout and between the major urban areas of Trinidad carrying up to five passengers at a time. The system began developing in the early years of this century and has been made possible partially by the relatively low prices of gasoline on the island. To a considerable extent, however, it is a consequence of the strong desire, particularly among East Indians, to own an automobile, and the possibility of maintaining one is enhanced by driving it on hire for at least part of the time. For an average trip of several miles within Port of Spain in 1963 the fare for each passenger in a pirate-taxi ranged in U.S. currency value from about five to ten cents; the forty-mile trip from the capital to San Fernando and the oilfields region was about 75 cents.

Not only is pirate-taxi transportation cheap, but it is abundant, flexible and entertaining as well. In Port of Spain there are literally hordes of pirate-taxis, and on some routes a wait on the curb of thirty seconds before successfully signalling a vehicle to a screeching stop is exceptionally long. Although the drivers follow traditional routes, they can sometimes be induced to deviate a few blocks to give the passenger a drop at his destination. The pirate-taxis are frequently the place where one hears the latest gossip, and often short-lived political debates develop.

The pirate-taxi system represents one important extension of the pluralist, yet intimate small-island ethos into an age of growing technological complexity. In Trinidad, industrialization and the spreading tide of urbanism have not produced to any significant degree the atomized, depersonalized social relationships which some sociologists have viewed as among the most salient features of technologically advanced "mass societies." With its less than one million citizens, most of whom occupy a well-defined position within an inter-twined network of groups based on familial, racial, religious, neighborhood, recreational, and occupational statuses and traditions, Trinidad life remains highly personal; one is continually running into acquaintances, even in downtown Port of Spain. This facilitates the perpetuation of the small-island agrarian code of interpersonal obligation and mutual aid, of a dependency on friends, relatives and superiors for assistance during personal difficulties. These strong survivals of the folk community that evolved out of slavery and indenture constitute some of the major social virtues of Trinidad. But they are not always regarded as virtues: this intense communal tradition is often viewed by the educated elite as underlying some of the major difficulties encountered in their attempts to modernize the country. These problems manifest themselves in various ways: in the ubiquitous tendency to read a personal motive into every political decision, in the assumption that personal "contacts" are necessary to get what one wants in dealings with official society, in the belief that conspiracy and wire-pulling are primary operational rules of ostensibly formal and impersonal transactions.

These are only a few of the ambiguities associated with the passing of the agrarian way of life in Trinidad. If the national legends and histories of older countries sometimes express a mood of nostalgia at the demise of the sturdy yeoman, the frontiersman or the independent craftsman, the Trinidad nationalist historian would be inclined to look back in anger at the slave, the indentured laborer and the prostitute. A negative image of the colonial past would play a major role in legitimizing the demand for independence, but it was, of course, only a part of the story. The post-slavery century in Trinidad produced local legends, traditions and social relationships which not only conditioned the form the nationalist movement itself would take, but provided an indispensable residue of collective memories and meanings without which a nationalist movement on this implausible island could not have emerged at all.

CHAPTER 3 Origins of a Sense of Nationhood

Much bless'd by Providence is Trinidad;
Flowers and fruits perpetual, trees evergreen,
Our scenery most rich and beautiful;
The people of all nations, countries, races,
French, English, Spanish, Scotch or Portuguese,
From Afric's or fair India's hotter shores;
Creoles, Coolies, Chinese, their language,
Manners, customs, everything so different.

— Trinidad Chronicle, 1876[1]

During most of the 300 years after Columbus thought he had distinguished a "Trinidad," a Trinity of hills in the verdant rolling landscape of southeastern Trinidad, and until the British captured the island in 1797, a handful of Spaniards, a few hundred free coloreds and slaves, and about 2,000 Amerindians were the sole human inhabitants of the place they called Iēre, the Land of the Humming Bird. That was the population in 1783, just before the ruling Spanish Cabildo opened the island to further settlement by colonists of the Roman Catholic faith. The beneficiaries of this new policy were chiefly settlers from the French Caribbean islands of Martinique, Guadeloupe, Haiti and the nearby island of Grenada, who, together with their slave retinues, established a French Creole culture in Trinidad, although the island would at no time pass under French control. By 1797, after just fourteen years on the island, the French settlers and their households had inundated the population of the Spanish era. In that year they numbered 16,000 and had transformed the economy of the island. They established nearly 500 plantations on over 85,000 acres of land, half of which they brought under the plow for the first time. Most of the land was put in sugar and 159 sugar mills were established; but there were undertakings in coffee, cotton and tobacco as well.[2]

After the British took possession of the island, a new, heterogeneous lot of settlers came in: there were freed American slaves who had fought with the British in Virginia during the War of 1812, discharged soldiers of African origin from the disbanded West India regiment, freed slaves taken from the vessels still plying a trade which had become illegal in the Empire in 1807, and even some admixture of peons who had come over to the island from the Spanish Main. By 1826, seven years before the beginning of the end of slavery was decreed in the Empire, the island had already acquired the characteristic ethnic complexity which would baffle colonial administrators for over a century. The census of 1826 revealed that the population of the island had almost doubled since 1797, rising from 18,000 to over 34,000. Three major social strata were defined in the census: first, there were the white inhabitants, numbering about 2,000; secondly, there were the approximately 8,500 free coloreds; and, third, about 23,000 slaves were enumerated. The aborigines who had been on the island to greet Columbus had become virtually extinct; barely 650 Amerindians survived by 1826. But if the major social strata could be easily defined on the basis of color and legal status, the cultural backgrounds within and cutting across each of the strata complicated matters a great deal, as shown in Table 3.

TABLE 3. The Population of Trinidad in the Pre-Emancipation Era (1826)[3]

Ethnic Origin	*Social Status*			
	White	*Free Coloreds*	*"Free" Totals*	*Slaves*
Spanish or Colonies	450	2,154	2,604	
French or Colonies	617	2,150	2,767	15,291 (Creole)
British or Colonies	938	1,594	2,532	
African		1,450	1,450	7,832 (African)
American		1,056	1,056	
Totals	2,005	8,404	10,409	23,123

As indicated, the whites were divided into three major nationalities; the free coloreds could be identified by these three background characteristics as well, plus two more, African and American; and the slaves were differentiated by whether they were "Creole," that is, born in the colonies, or "African," transported from Africa. In this potpourri of many nations it appears that it was the French, both white and free colored (a line which then, as today, cannot always be drawn with unambiguous precision), who set the pace socially during the first quarter of the nineteenth century. Port of Spain, Andrew Pearse has noted, seems to have developed a flourishing social and cultural life during the prosperous first decades of the century. One chronicler described this early golden age of the French settlers as ". . . a veritable aristocracy of colour no whit less urbane or distinguished than an aristocracy of blood."[4] Of the free coloreds among the French settlers, writes Pearse, the social scale ranged from the colored and black slave-owning planters and traders to artisans and petty cultivators. Some came from families of substantial property. Some built fine town houses, and during the early years of British rule they were given rights almost equal to those conferred on the whites. They were commissioned in the militia; their opportunities were such that they or their children could progress towards entry into the "*societé de couleur.*" And not the least of the elite social pastimes in which they engaged were the fêtes and merriment of the Carnival season which constituted the high point of the French Creole social season, running from Christmas to Ash Wednesday. Duels enlivened the course of this period, and it has been recorded as a time of "brilliant divertissiments," and ". . . a contagious gaiety, brilliant verbal sallies, and comic buffoonery which made the subject of morrow's conversation."[5]

From this early period of French Creole social ascendancy can be dated a controversy in the social history of Trinidad. It is maintained to the present day by descendants of the white French Creoles that they, and not the British, were the true progressive elite force in civilizing Trinidad; that, unlike the British planters and administrators, they mixed in an easy and familiar way with the lower class Negro population. Even Pearse, who seems wary of idealizing early French Creole society, maintains that they were

> . . . excelling in elegance, sophistication and ability in the arts, conversation, dress, music and hospitality, according to provincial French standards, rather than regarding the West Indian colonies as places to be tolerated for the sake of a quick fortune, the fruits of which might be enjoyed in the metropolitan country, as was often the outlook of the English planter or absentee owner.[6]

Whatever the merits of this particular interpretation, and it still lacks definitive historical documentation, its importance rests on the degree to which it was in fact believed. An important social distinction at the white peak of Trinidad's social structure was maintained as a consequence of this legend. Reinforcing this distinction was the difference in religion between the Protestant British and the Roman Catholic French and Spanish elite. The British Governors were compelled to maintain good relations with the leaders of a society two-thirds of which consisted of Roman Catholics. The first British Governor, writes Pearse, ". . . was at great pains to preserve cordial relations with the Roman Catholic authorities . . . and was a personal friend of the Roman Catholic Bishop."[7] From a government standpoint, the social power of the Church stood in continual potential opposition, as will be shown later, to such anglicizing and secularizing policies as the attempt to establish state control of education. This division between the old and new elites was complicated by the fact, as Miss Carmichael observed in her gleanings from the colonial documents, that following the influx of British planters after 1802, "the majority of the inhabitants were Roman Catholics, yet the owners of most of the property in the colony were British Protestants."[8] In the P.N.M. era the social power of the church was still regarded as a force that might be politically dangerous to have aligned against the government. In the end the P.N.M., after a period of church-state tension, was also at great pains to preserve cordial relations with the Roman Catholic authorities.

The social and cultural pluralism of Trinidad was destined to become even more complex in the years after emancipation. Because of a severe labor shortage caused by the reluctance of the newly freed slaves to continue to labor at low wages on the sugar estates, the planters and colonial government began to experiment with schemes that would bring in new laborers in place of the slaves. Trinidad in the nineteenth century, as Eric Williams frequently reminded his listeners and readers, was sugar, and major social policies were aimed at keeping the major British interest in the colony prosperous. After some efforts at encouraging immigration from other West Indian islands, and after the importation of a few Chinese and Portuguese laborers, most of whom soon went into trade, the British planters finally found the solution to their problem. In 1845 a shipment of indentured laborers from India arrived, the first boatload in a series which would continue until 1917. The East Indians, or the "Coolies," as they were called both officially and unofficially, soon came to dominate the labor force of the sugar estates. Thus began the formation of the major social cleavage at the base of the island's social pyramid (and, at the same time, of that of nearby British Guiana as well). The former Negro slave disdained estate field labor as work symbolic of an inferior status, a perception perhaps encouraged by the presence of numbers of free Negroes already ranking higher on the social scale. The Negro quickly acquired the tendency to look down on the "Coolie" as his inferior, while the East Indian, subjected to the virtual slave-like regime of the indentured laborer's barrack, hardly swept-out after the exodus of Africa, struggled to save money and return to India. In the early "indentured times," as this period is called among East Indians, many did in fact make the return voyage. Indeed, so many went back that the colonial governments in the Eastern Caribbean encouraged them to purchase or rent small plots of land at the end of their indenture. By this means an incentive was provided to retain them in the colony for the seasonal work of the estates, and thus the East Indian immigrant moved from the estate barrack to form the small Indian villages, like the "Amity" discussed in Chapter 2, which are still to be found today amidst the vast canefields. "This was not only pleasing to the laborer newly out of his indentures," Morton Klass observes, "but in making possible the formation of Indian villages it contributed in no small way to the circumstances under which Indian culture has persisted. The approach was also to the advantage of the Trinidad planter. Because of the long 'slack' season in Trinidad, many estates preferred to have a source of non-resident labor."[9] And the long-term social and political consequences of this policy for the development of the Trinidad social structure were summarized by Eric Williams in these terms:

> Thus, by a curious irony, the sugar planter who, in the seventeenth and eighteenth centuries, refused to grant land to the white indentured servant, who, after emancipation, tried to prevent the purchase of land by the former slaves, found himself obliged in the 19th Century to grant land to the indentured immigrant in order to reduce the expense of immigrant labour. Indian immigration, designed to compete with the Negro landowners, ended in the establishment of a class of Indian landowners.[10]

A *Guide to Trinidad*, written in the 1880's by an expatriate schoolmaster, J. H. Collens, gives the flavor of official thinking on the labor problem after several decades of substantial East Indian immigration:

> Fully one-third of the inhabitants of the colony at the present time are Coolies, immigrants brought hither from India by the Government, and indentured to the planters for a term of years. They are the chief labourers, having been found to work at a much cheaper rate than the natives, who are inclined to be lazy. Opinions are divided as to the wisdom of continuing to introduce this foreign element . . . but it must undoubtedly be acknowledged that at a time when the colony seemed to be in danger of imminent ruin, owing to the scarcity of labour, the immigration system stepped in and saved it. The remark above, alluding to the natural indolence of the natives, is intended to refer only to the lowest classes who, as in most countries, are not too fond of work.[11]

Note that Collens, writing *forty years* after the introduction of East Indian immigration, referred to them as a matter of course as a "foreign element" as distinguished from the "natives," meaning, of course, the Negroes, many of whom had arrived in Trinidad only a generation or two before the beginning of East Indian immigration and who, moreover, were still in the process of substantial immigration from other West Indian islands, particularly Barbados. Note also the apparently widespread official notion that the East Indians had "saved" the agricultural economy from ruin. Both of these notions, the identification of the East Indians in Trinidad as aliens, and the idea that they had saved the agricultural economy from ruin and were the rural "backbone" of the nation, would find a place in the political ideology of the East Indian community during the independence period.

In a chapter entitled "Habits and Peculiarities of the Lower Classes," by which he meant the lower class Negro, Collens presents an amusing analytical scheme for distinguishing different attitudes toward work on the sugar estates. They may, he states solemnly, be divided into three classes:

No. 1. Those who will not work.
No. 2. Those who do little or no work.
No. 3. Those who work regularly.

His description of the three classes is noteworthy in that it gives some conception, albeit stereotyped and impressionistic, of the way in which a part of the ex-slave work force, alienated from the chief economic institution of the colony, nonetheless managed to eke out a subsistence by squatting on Crown Land and through occasional estate labor.

> No. 1. Those who will not condescend to estate labour generally find some good soil, where water is handy, and build there a little shanty of timber with roseau partition laths, thatching it with palm leaves. Here, if the spirit moves them, they now and then dig an hour or two, planting maize, tanias, bananas – anything that gives no trouble. In the early morning, or on a bright, moonlight night, they go out with an old fowling piece, and a lean, mangy, half-starved cur, to pick up a stray deer, quenck [a small, wild pig], or lap, or it may be a 'wild-tame' [a neighbor's fowl]. If they are lucky enough to get more than they can eat, they smoke the remainder, and sell it to the nearest planter.
>
> No. 2 class also goes in for a 'squatting' life, but in the dry season they emerge from their obscurity to take part in some well-paid work which they like, such as driving cane-carts, etc.
>
> No. 3 are generally hard-working, but otherwise of primitive habits. Of the older men very few can read, and still fewer write. No man ever makes a mistake as to the amount of pay he should receive – rough notches on a stick, or an accumulation of pebbles in the corner of the one room he calls his house, being his perfectly infallible system of computation. . . . They are superstitious almost beyond conception, combining, in the country districts, a mixture of shrewdness and credulity that is as absurd as it is inconsistent. Smart and quick enough in business matters, they can drive a good bargain as well as any Yorkshireman or Scotchman, but if they once form the impression that occult influences are working insidiously against them, any argument you may adduce to the contrary will have about as much effect as the boring of an iron target with a wooden skewer.[12]

In contrast to this easy-going, marginal rural existence, is the bustle and efficiency of one of the new, centralized sugar-processing factories in which the schoolmaster is impressed not only by the technological modernity of the plant, complete with "Siemen's electric light," but by the work discipline imposed by an industrial enterprise:

> . . . the manager seems to have been attempting to reduce the system to something like working order. So far as the practical part of the work goes, every man, from A to Z, has his task to perform, and what is infinitely more to the point *he does it.* There is not a scrap perceptible of that listlessness and sleepiness one sometimes meets with in the cane-piece and mill. 'Sharp's the word and quick's the motion, or you'll be helped along,' is the prevailing motto. In the office are returns enumerating all the minutae relative to expenditure and results of the factory, and the expenditure and produce of each distinct estate from some years back, and posted up to date.[13]

What Collens was witnessing was the rationalization of production and concentration of ownership of Trinidad and West Indian sugar, a process which would continue apace and entirely eliminate the local class of British planters which, despite high rates of absentee ownership, were still very much in evidence during the schoolmaster's tour through the sugar belt.

British colonial society in Trinidad, partly by design and partly unintentionally, was responsible for considerable exposure to European modernity in the colony during the nineteenth century. When Collens wrote his guide, for example, the population of Trinidad stood at 180,000, fully one-fourth of whom were already town dwellers. Port of Spain boasted a population of 39,000 and San Fernando had 8,000 inhabitants. For a Victorian "underdeveloped area" this ratio was, of course, exceptionally high. The major metropolis might have been missing in Trinidad, but the cultural institutions, patterns of life and public services associated with the Age of Progress were much in evidence. Collens advised the British visitor to Trinidad that the ocean voyage consumed about two weeks (as compared to ten days by sea today); that he would find several good hotels ("with the telephone attached") as well as a number of respectable boarding houses; that he could expect to find well-stocked shops ("or stores, for we give them the American name"), two good "book depots," and a public library open to members at one pound per annum and featuring 21,000 books and periodicals. Moreover, no less than *five* weekly or bi-weekly newspapers are being published locally, and Collens remarks that ". . . we hear continually of fresh papers being started with a great flourish of trumpets, which, after a brief and sometimes rather inglorious existence, are buried with their ancestors."[14] A Philharmonic Union consisting of an orchestra and chorus is performing operas and oratorios ". . . creditably rendered in their entirety without the omission of a single bar."[15] A Scientific Association dealing with the natural history and products of the colony has been functioning since 1863 and is publishing a quarterly magazine. A post office is handling over a quarter of a million pieces of mail annually (and struggling to decipher the often indecipherable penmanship of a local population just beginning to become literate); there is a government railway with over a dozen engines and hundreds of pieces of rolling stock operating through the sugar belt to San Fernando and beyond at low rates provided by the government for the benefit of the planters. At the telegraph office in the bustling port area, the schoolmaster perceptively observed, "You will usually find a small crowd of men and boys congregated round the board, where are posted, as soon as they arrive, the latest telegrams from Europe."[16] As for the port itself, the statistics are revealing: in 1856 only 508 British ships and 133 foreign vessels, with a total tonnage of 106,000, called at Trinidad; by 1886, however, trade and commerce had grown to the point where 966 British ships and 1,247 foreign vessels with combined tonnage of 976,000 visited the island.[17] While it is impossible to ascertain the full impact represented by this ten-fold expansion in shipping on the social life of the colony, it is clear that at the very least it was responsible for increased employment in the port area. This increase included rum-shop proprietors and prostitutes, and at the upper levels it was associated with the establishment of foreign-owned business houses and consulates which, together with the other sections of the colonial superstructure concentrated in the capital city, employed thousands of lower class "natives" as laborers and domestics.

Prisons, orphanages, asylums, temperance societies — these and many other institutions associated with European civilization were to be found in Trinidad during the Victorian era. Over it all, from his splendid mansion in the St. Ann's district of Port of Spain overlooking the carefully tended and extensive botanical gardens, the vast Queen's Park Savannah with its cricket fields and race course, presided the British Governor, who was responsible only to the Secretary of State for the Colonies in London, and through him to Parliament and the Queen. British Governors in a Crown Colony system like that of Trinidad did not merely rule; they reigned. When Trinidadians of advanced years reminisce about past Governors they speak in the same terms as an old-fashioned history about the monarchs of Europe: Governor so-and-so was a "good and kindly man" and a real racing enthusiast; another Governor, it is recalled, was rumored to be quite a rake, but a jolly fellow . . . and so on. Local equivalents of court gossip developed as did an elite social stratum, a kind of provincial Establishment, in which deference to rank and protocol was maintained in the face of the pressures toward intimacy generated by the relatively small size of the white, ruling group, and a seldom-crossed color bar existed separating the leaders of official society from the majority of the population. The separation of the Governor and his official family from the colored middle class was not, however, absolute. At the bottom the colonial elite mixed with the local population in a number of ways in the line of official duty. There would be, for example, mixed participation in the professional societies and in some voluntary social and cultural organizations. In the twentieth century, with the expansion of the class of colored professionals this top stratum of colored society would increasingly be drawn into the system of official honors and awards. For the overwhelming majority of the population, however, the Governor and the upper strata of the colonial ruling class remained distant eminences: finely attired figures for whom the Police Band struck up *God Save the Queen* when they entered their official boxes at the Savannah race course.

Despite this Crown Colony stratification system in which the British held political sway, it does not appear that the social and political climate of nineteenth century Trinidad was oppressive in the extreme. Its chief characteristic seems to have been a *laissez faire*, benignly inefficient authoritarianism. What could go wrong? Britannia ruled the waves, life was pleasant and profitable. The lively newspapers which ingloriously came and went were, to be sure, censored; Governor Woodford, when annoyed by an article, would send a polite note to the editor requesting the loan of the handle of his printing press, thus enforcing suspension of the publication until his ire had passed.[18] But when James Anthony Froude visited Trinidad in 1887 he dined at Government House with English, French, Spanish and Corsican guests ("each speaking his or her own language") and sat beside the mayor of San Fernando who ". . . insisted much on the fine qualities of the leading persons in the island and the splendid things to be expected when responsible government should be conceded." Froude had arrived in the West Indies just after the Gladstone government had, in 1884, revived representative government in Jamaica, and this had given impetus to the middle class "reform movement" in Trinidad. Under the governorship of Sir William Robinson, whom Froude discovered was learning Spanish so that he could better communicate with that venerable minority, Port of Spain newspapers and reform spokesmen were openly denouncing the "degrading tyranny" of Crown Colony rule; placards announcing a political meeting on the Savannah were being circulated which contained language so violent that, according to Froude, the printer might have been indicted for high treason. During the meeting itself, which happened to coincide with a cricket match at the Savannah in which the Governor was participating, "The speakers did their best to imitate the fine phrases of the apostles of liberty in Europe, but they succeeded only in caricaturing their absurdities."[19] The "election virus" was clearly spreading to Crown Colony Trinidad, and through the newspapers and metropolitan orientation of the various minorities, awareness of events throughout the world was growing. Over a decade before Froude's visit, Charles Kingsley had arrived in Port of Spain and could immediately be struck by the presence of colored men "of all ranks" talking eagerly of business or politics.[20] Froude would report that the keener-minded Trinidad blacks were watching the development of the Irish problem. "They see the identity of the situation," he wrote. "They see that if the Radical view prevails, and in every country the majority are to rule, Trinidad will be theirs and the government of the English will be at an end."[21]

At the lower levels of white society among the missionaries, priests, schoolteachers and lesser civil servants, the colonial superstructure slowly achieved one lasting and significant penetration into the lives of their colonial wards. Collens noted that his pupils sometimes displayed an almost exaggerated enthusiasm in learning command of the English language. "In my capacity as Dominie," he wrote, "I continually had to check the disposition of my pupils in Trinidad to use long-winded words and high-flown phrases."

> Boys and young men spend hours poring over dictionaries, simply to try and master the meanings of words which for length might be measured by the yard . . . Only today, in the street, one man talking to another in the usual loud tone, said, while passing me, 'I estimate it to be my particular and elementary duty.' I should like to have discovered what duty combined those two essentials, but the speaker was out of hearing. I have heard, too, a woodcutter gravely tell his employer, 'It was with the utmost difficulty that I managed to disintegrate those logs, Sir.'[22]

Humorous? Yes – but the initial impulse to master the language for its own sake, or for the sake of the sometimes grotesque "school English" usages which became a standing joke in Trinidad, nonetheless laid the linguistic foundation for the communication of political ideas to mass audiences which reached such a high standard in the colony. Certainly since the days of Captain Cipriani, in the 1920's, popular political discourse could be conducted without fear of antagonizing lower class audiences through the use of "big words." On the contrary, receptivity to a high standard of political vocabulary seems to have been the established norm since the nineteenth century. The "gems of oratory" which had depressed Froude were an early sign of this tradition. Cipriani himself was a superb orator, as recordings of a few of his speeches bear evidence. He was gifted with a ringing, passionate tenor speaking voice which expressed with precision both fealty to the Crown and the justness of the cause of West Indian self-government. Uriah Butler's oratory was studded with the grandiose phrase and the involuted syntax which Collens probably had in mind when he commented irritably, "They positively do not believe in the sweet simplicity of the Saxon tongue."[23] Many other Trinidad orators were adept at the well-turned, if ponderous, phrase, but Dr. Eric Williams succeeded brilliantly, in a usually dry, unemotional style, in the presentation of complex issues before mass audiences; it was a style which at its best was almost indistinguishable from the lucid construction of his scholarly writings.

While the civil, religious and economic institutions of the colonial superstructure were exposing the local population to some knowledge of, and even some opportunity within, the life of contemporary modern nations, unofficial and undirected social changes were working out an accommodation between the diverse cultures at the wide base of the colonial social pyramid. Two major processes took place; one was "creolization" in which the diverse cultural strains of lower class Negroes tended to become mixed together to create a "native" folk culture; the other was the process of voluntary segregation which to a high degree marked the response of the East Indian immigrants to the local society.

Collens felt compelled, early in his *Guide*, to explain to the visitor the meaning of the word "Creole" as it was used in Trinidad. "It is generally applied," he wrote with a schoolmaster's care in definition, "to any person born, or article produced, in the island. Thus you hear of a French Creole, a Creole of Tobago, Creole cigars, Creole horses, etc."[24] Later, however, he refers to the Port of Spain Town Superintendent ("the wittiest man in the island") as a *creolized* European of Irish descent. Thus the schoolmaster recognized, at least implicitly, that "Creole" men were also being produced and that the term connoted a process of change not limited to the narrower French and Spanish colonial usage, which referred to persons or cultural traits originating in the colonial region of a usually "mixed" character, *e.g.*, racial mixtures or linguistic mixtures. Pearse has astutely analyzed the groups and cultural ingredients which were the basis of the Creole mixture in Trinidad. By the latter half of the nineteenth century the earlier colored settlers and former slaves, plus later Negro arrivals from both other West Indian islands and a few immigrants from Africa itself, had formed the nucleus of a Creole folk culture which was characterized by the tendency to adapt the French patois as their lingua franca while at the same time maintaining a multiplicity of customs. In the following passage Pearse neatly summarizes a) the basic character of Creole culture, b) its relationship to other groups, and c) the general impact of the colonial superstructure on it:

> . . . Beyond this nucleus were other folk groups, Indians, Chinese and Portuguese all less ready to merge. Whilst estate work was being taken over increasingly by the East Indians, the nuclear group . . . lived as occasional labourers, gardeners, semi-subsistence squatters, artisans in town and country, and fishermen. They were not under heavy economic pressure nor subject to tight control . . . but were subject nevertheless to the influence of the institutions of the superstructure, such as law, churches and schools, and also to the influence, manners and customs of the elite. Thus a type of rural life established itself in which law and custom, the African drum and the fiddle, the country doctor and the bush healer, the Catholic liturgy and the cults of Yorubaland and Dahomey, school English and Patois, lived side by side in easy accommodation, and a dual acculturative process took its course—creolisation, and accommodation to the institutions and standards of the superstructure.[25]

But if the cultural accommodation taking place within the Negro group could be called "easy," that group's relationship to both the growing East Indian minority and to the "institutions and standards" of the colonial superstructure was at times decidedly uneasy. The early antipathy between Negroes and the East Indian estate laborers has already been noted. Although there were many exceptions in villages and areas, particularly in south Trinidad, where Negroes and East Indians recall a bygone era of "racial harmony," and although the colony was at no time to experience the upheaval of a major race riot, the East Indians, prodded by feelings of fear and disdain toward Negroes, to a large extent apparently accommodated to Creole Trinidad by withdrawal and avoidance. A sign of the state of affairs prevailing in the sugar belt in the late nineteenth century is given in the 1890 government directive which prescribed separate latrine facilities for East Indian and Negro sugar estate workers.[26] And of the educational system, an Anglican clergyman and schoolmaster operating a school in Belmont, a district of Port of Spain, wrote in 1888 in opposition to an integrated Creole-Indian school, giving his reasons as follows:

> . . . a mixed school for Creoles and Indians will be a mistake. An Indian will not send his child to a Creole school. He is afraid of injustice being done to his child from the Creole teacher, and of ill usage from the

> Creole pupils. The Creole, as a rule, looks down on the Indian: he is a semi-civilized being, he speaks a barbarous language, and his manners are barbarous . . . He takes work cheaper than the Creole will do, hence he must be ill-treated where he can be ill-treated with impunity.[27]

The most likely interpretation of the government's attitude toward this mutual antipathy between Creole and East Indian is that it resigned itself to a phenomenon of mutual exclusiveness which, in fact, served as a not-so-very latent advantage for the British planters who had scoured the earth to find a pliant estate labor force after the end of slavery. If the East Indians came to emulate the Creoles in their general contempt for low-paying estate labor and were also drawn to the squatting life, or to employment opportunities in the towns which might be provided by increased education, then the labor problem would arise once again. Apprehension on this point was voiced as late as 1926 by a prominent representative of the planters before an official board inquiring into the educational prospects of the East Indian population:

> This is an agricultural country. Unless you put the children on to working in the fields when they are young, you will never get them to do so later. If you want to turn all these people into a lot of clerks, cane-weighers, and people of that sort, all you have to do is to prevent them working in the fields until they are 16 years old; then I guarantee you will have but very few labourers in the Colony . . . Give them some education in the way of reading and writing, but no more. Even then I would say educate only the bright ones; not the whole mass. If you do educate the whole mass of the agricultural population, you will be deliberately ruining the country.[28]

From this testimony Eric Williams (from whose independence *History* the above passage is excerpted), always keenly on the look-out for the determinants of history and social structure created by the self-interest of a powerful economic stratum, drew the obvious conclusion: "The Crown Colony system was based on sugar workers and needed only sugar workers. It did not need citizens."[29]

Although the antipathy between the Creole majority and the East Indian minority did not occasion the government any special difficulties in terms of keeping the peace, and although the Creole lower class may have generally shown the virtue of "politeness" toward the white elite, the Creoles nonetheless insisted on clinging to one custom which was a constant thorn in the side of British colonial administration, namely, Carnival. Unless one has experienced first-hand the degree to which personal economies and an annual Creole life cycle are oriented toward this one, massive spree which achieves a climax during the two days preceding Ash Wednesday, then the difficulties experienced by the British authorities on its account are not easily comprehensible. In 1881 a major armed clash, the so-called Canboulay riot, took place between colonial police and the local population in connection with the Carnival of that year. It was, writes Pearse, "a national issue" of the greatest importance.[30]

Before emancipation, as was indicated earlier, Carnival was observed chiefly by the French Creoles; however, after emancipation it came to be increasingly dominated by the Creole lower class, and featured duels between now legendary stick-fighters, torch-light parades, and open warfare between rival neighborhoods. There is a strong tendency in the literature on Carnival to interpret its social meaning and persistence in the face of official disapproval by reference to such notions as the need of the repressed colored middle class (and the irrepressible Negro lower class) for "a safety valve," a "period of license" and "role reversal."[31] However, considering that the Creole lower class had been participating in and developing Carnival for almost fifty years before the Canboulay riots of 1881, its traditional popularity would seem adequate to account for its resistance to official suppression. By the middle of the nineteenth century the Trinidad Carnival had already developed the prototypes of the mass, open-air theatrical extravaganzas of the contemporary Carnival. A visitor to the island in 1847 wrote:

> . . . The maskers parade the street in gangs of from ten to twenty, occasionally joining forces in procession. The primitives were Negroes, as nearly naked as might be, bedaubed with a black varnish. One of this gang had a long chain and padlock attached to his leg, which chain the others pulled . . . Parties of Negro ladies dance through the streets, each clique distinguished by bodices of the same color . . . For the men the predominating character was Pulichinello; every second Negro, at least, aiming at playing the continental Jack-pudding. Pirates too were very common . . . [characterized by] sneaking deportment . . . Turks also there were, and one Highlander . . . There were also two grand processions . . . one, judging from the royal arms in front . . . and a canopy of red glazed calico, trimmed with silver tinsel, shading a royal pair, who, in conscious majesty, sat within, representing the Sovereign pair of England. This brilliant cortege was marshalled forward by a huge Negro . . . who stalked along, spear in hand, as if intent on doing dire deeds.[32]

This early description has been quoted at length in order to emphasize the traditionally *disciplined and organized*, character of most Carnival masquerades. "Playing mas'," *i.e.*, "playing masque" – something of a misnomer since masks, except during the "old mas' " satirical bands, are seldom worn – was clearly as hard work in the nineteenth century as it is today. Writes one of the keenest observers of the modern Carnival: "The historical bands and sailors are the only masquers whose faces register pleasure, excitement or abandon. A much more common expression combines intensity, earnestness, exertion, fatigue, and a kind of fanatical zeal . . ."[33]

Carnival was, and is still, a great educational pageant which portrayed the diverse national characters, costumes and fads of the entire outside world, and which lampooned local customs, prominent personalities and events. All of this was developed by a largely illiterate population before the age of mass communications, and Carnival bands and characters underwent an unending series of changes of repertory. Each of the races and nationalities which constituted Trinidad society in real life contributed some characters to the passing parades. But many other characters, like the Pulichinello, Turks and Pirates mentioned above seeped into the colony from diverse sources. Local theatricals, vaudeville, newspaper stories, and later radio and the movies were major sources of role ideas. By the turn of the twentieth century, "Yankee Minstrels" and "Tennessee Cowboys" were popular. Crowley describes the former as a Negro imitating the Minstrel convention of blackface, wearing exaggerated white lips and an Uncle Sam costume. "He is thus," observes Crowley, "a Negro imitating a white imitating a Negro."[34] Here, certainly, was "role-reversal" with a vengeance! Congo and Shango bands turned inward and satirized the retention of African religious beliefs, reciting "African" prayers with fervor and selling charms. Combative Red Indians, with a series of songs and speeches in the language of the "Guarahoons" – a tribe of Amerindians who made regular trips from the mainland – were popular by the turn of the century also. Carnival served not merely as a safety valve for repression; it became an almost mystical celebration which sought to submerge the everyday pluralism of Trinidad in a wider vision of global diversity. Every year, in an instinctual gesture which they could scarcely explain, the masqueraders discarded their expensive costumes for new ones, thus signifying that the player, and not the play, is continuous and real. It is in this existential sense, and not simply because they display an enormous capacity for strenuous self-abandonment, that the Creoles are correct when they insist that only at Carnival can one grasp the essence of life in Trinidad.

Although after the Canboulay riots the colored middle class re-emerged to participate in Carnival, the lower class Creole group always dominated the festival in terms of numbers and boisterousness. Within the bowels of Port of Spain, in the lower class barrack-yard communities located within the perimeter of the city's respectable dwellings and shops, a colorful, indigenous, and unique lumpen-proletariat culture abounding in vivid social types had developed. The *diametres*, the "roughs and rowdies" who so irritated the civilized sensibilities of such bearers of European enlightenment as Collens, were the leading members of the urban, backyard underworld. *Diametre*, usually corrupted to *jamette*, referred to those beneath the 'diameter' of respectable local society. While the poverty-ridden and crowded "nigger-yard" was torn by inner dissension and violence, it was nonetheless the place where neighborhood loyalties developed and out of which would come a cultural tradition which produced both the modern calypso and the steelband. Writes Pearse of this colorful epoch:

> . . . in the pre-Carnival period, during rehearsals of the yard bands, the 'chantwell' or leading singer was expected to insult and provoke rival bands in his 'carisos' or Carnival songs, and when the yard stick-men went out into the streets, they sought out their rivals and single combats ensued. As a development from this, the bands of a region, led by the champions, would form up together. Canboulay itself was a fight between regional bands in which the rules of single combat were forgotten, and sticks, bottles and stones, etc., became the weapons of the bands and their followers, both male and female. And finally Canboulay in 1881 and a few other occasions, took on a class character, with the disappearance of band rivalries in united action against the police. It was the singers, drummers, dancers, stickmen, prostitutes, matadors, bad-johns, dunois, makos and corner-boys, that is to say, the *jamette* class, who dominated the Carnival of the day.[35]

The *jamette* class dominated Carnival, and the Carnival cycle came to dominate the *jamettes.* Despite their residential proximity to those who enjoyed, or were striving for, a place of respectability within the colonial working and middle class, the *jamettes* generally turned their backs on respectable society and within an economy of chronically high rates of underemployment and unemployment created an urban folk culture which was at the same time romantic, colorful, sordid, nihilistic and violent. This sub-culture had, as Pearse's account strongly suggests, a certain coherence and élan of its own which tended to distinguish the lower class Creole as a true "native" of the colony. After the Canboulay riot, when the government imposed stricter controls on Carnival, a calypsonian composed the following lament, which seems to have been one of the few local compositions to have expressed a positive preference for the emergent local ways of life looked down upon by the colonial authorities:

Can't beat we drum,
In my own, my native land

Can't have we Carnival,
In my own, my native land

Can't have we bacchanal
In my own, my native land

In my own, native land
In my own, my native land.[36]

The Crown Colony system may not have needed citizens, but under its loose supervision a society had taken shape in which middle class occupations, modern technology and civil life, limited opportunities for mobility through the educational system, local traditions and social types had developed. The dominant institutions and the leading classes, however, generally looked outward for a sense of belonging to a broader cultural entity. The East Indians would continue to cherish memories of Mother India, many French Creoles identified themselves as loyal descendants of Mother France, the expatriate British planters and administrators regarded themselves as temporary exiles from Mother England.

When the British Empire went to war in 1914 the West India Regiment, in which Trinidad's Captain Andrew Cipriani, a white French Creole of Corsican descent, occupied a high command position, was assigned to the Middle East where it performed well under Allenby. In the context of war, West Indians had a chance to match themselves against the performance of British and foreign troops, and, in Cipriani's opinion, they had not come off second best. The war period ushered in the beginnings of some major forces of social change within the Empire from which Trinidad would not be isolated. Mahatma Gandhi's agitation against imperialism in India had one important repercussion in Trinidad: in 1917 the Indian parliament put an end to the indentured labor system which had created the overseas Indian population, of which that of Trinidad and British Guiana was but one example. Equally significant for the development of the Trinidad economy was the decision taken by the First Lord of the Admiralty, Winston Churchill, who in 1912 inaugurated the conversion of the British Navy from coal to fuel oil. The existence of Trinidad petroleum had been known for many years and had been exploited on only a small scale, along with extraction of pitch from the celebrated Pitch Lake which had been used to Macadamise the streets of Baltimore; but the industry now began to grow under increased British investment and was to become the major source of non-agricultural industrial employment in the colony, "the goose that laid the golden eggs."

Local colonial government, too, underwent significant changes as a result of the more liberal social perspectives which had been accelerated by the democratic ideology of the Western war effort and its

A packet steamer negotiates the Monos Boca in the nineteenth century. From Charles Kingsley's *At Last: A Christmas in the West Indies*, London: Macmillan and Co., 1874.

Creoles, Indians, and Chinese waiting for the races to start at the Savannah in nineteenth-century Port of Spain. From *Kingsley's At Last*.

A nineteenth-century Indian couple in Trinidad. From J. H. Collens' *Guide to Trinidad*, London: Elliot Stock, 1888.

The Piano Warehouse.

H. STRONG'S

Celebrated Colonial Pianos,

Made expressly for the Climate.

UNSURPASSED FOR

TONE, DURABILITY, AND WORKMANSHIP,

CAN BE HAD FOR

CASH,

OR ON THE

NEW HIRE SYSTEM.

H. S. wishes to draw attention to the Repairing Branch of the Establishment, he having a very large stock of materials always on hand, suitable to the thorough repair of all kinds of instruments.

ORGANS AND HARMONIUMS ALWAYS IN STOCK.

Tunings in Town and Country on the shortest notice.

H. STRONG,

PIANO WAREHOUSE,

Port-of-Spain.

Tuner by appointment to His Excellency Sir W. Robinson, K.C.M.G.

Colonial merchants imported the implements of civilization for colonial elite. From Collens' *Guide to Trinidad.*

Captain A. A. Cipriani, founder of Trinidad's nationalist movement. *Guardian* photo.

C. L. R. James. Jacket illustration of *Mariner's Renegades and Castaways. Courtesy of Mrs. Selma James.*

Dr. Eric E. Williams. *Guardian* photo.

Port of Spain, Trinidad and Tobago. *Courtesy of Public Relations Division*, Office of the Premier, Trinidad.

settlement at Versailles. The principle of election to the Legislative Council of Trinidad was introduced for the first time. A British writer on the constitutional history of the colony has summarized the impetus to the political changes taking place in the West Indies during this period as follows:

> With the spread of education a coloured and black professional middle class was coming into being, and it was this class which now desired constitutional change, as much as, if not more than, the white community which in earlier years had been the chief source of such demands. Political activity among coloured West Indians had also been stimulated by the democratic sentiments and the ideas of self-determination engendered by the war, and these new elements in West Indian political life gave to the demand for constitutional change a potency which had been lacking before.[37]

The chief spokesmen for the extension of the principle of representative government to the Legislative Council (abbreviated 'LegCo') were a Legislative Reform Committee claiming to represent the middle classes and peasants. A member of this committee was Captain Cipriani, who had been persuaded to lead the budding working class political movement by reviving the Trinidad Workingmen's Association.

The British reader knows, but the American reader is probably only dimly aware that a feature of the British system of colonial administration was to send out to the colonies, from time to time, commissions of inquiry to gain an impression, independent of the routine reports flowing back to the Colonial Office from the Governor and the local administration, of what conditions were really like in the colony and what changes in economic, social or political policies might be warranted. These commissions were usually dispatched in connection with some particularly acute economic problem or civil disturbance which required looking into in order to assure the maintenance of "good government" and the general stability of the colony. Toward the end of 1921, the Parliamentary Under-Secretary of State for the Colonies, Major Wood, came out to the West Indies to investigate the potentials for constitutional change. In Trinidad he encountered at least three distinct points of view on the issue among the local population. One group, apparently consisting of propertied East Indians, the Chamber of Commerce and the Agricultural Society (the peak organization of the planters), opposed any departure from the prevailing system in which all of the legislators were appointed by the Governor. Another faction, the island's East Indian National Congress, advocated communal representation of East Indians. A third group headed by the Legislative Reform Committee was opposed to what it regarded as the divisive effect of the proposal for communal representation and advocated instead simply the establishment of an elected section in the LegCo.

Some comment is required at this point on these positions as presented to Major Wood. From what we know of these groups in later years, it seems plausible to attribute the resistance of both the propertied interests and the East Indian nationalists to an inclusivist form of political representation to a commitment regarding political progress which both of them shared, namely, the assumption that it was necessary or desirable to avoid making a coalition with the liberal reformers drawn chiefly from the colored middle class. To a large extent Trinidad political alignments would be determined, as in this first period of serious debate over constitutional reform, by the attitude one took toward the celebrated pluralism which was such a striking feature of the society. Those who saw emergent in the mosaic of Trinidad life an overall pattern, a Trinidad *suis generis*, were the leaders and participants in political movements which were at once broadly aggregative and most militantly nationalist. Such men could be nationalists because they subscribed to the necessary prior assumption – one that did not come automatically in Trinidad – that Trinidad, and perhaps even the West Indies as a whole, could be regarded as a primary unit of ethnic and territorial loyalty. The opponents of self-government, however, would stress the multi-national, plural aspects of the society in which the traditional bailiwicks and social privileges could only be safeguarded through the continuation of rule by the trusted arbiters in London. Between these two orientations were ranged the majority of the population, most of whom could be persuaded either way. That is, as the leaders proposed, so went the nation, or those sections of the nation that they represented. Actually, when the era of mass suffrage was introduced after World War II, white politicians, whatever private prejudices they might have held, could only hope to contest successfully in elections by stressing multi-racial, national principles; Negro politicians, depending on the location of their constituency, tended to stress the need for racial harmony; it was chiefly in the rural East Indian village ghettos that politicians were able to promote support by openly stressing minority solidarity.

In 1921 Major Wood considered these conflicting viewpoints and, on the basis of an interpretation of the desired direction of political development which the area should follow, formally initiated a policy aimed toward the development of ethnically-inclusivist politics. In Trinidad and British Guiana he rejected the proposals for communal representation. Though taking cognizance of the idea that ". . . the East Indians – the backbone of the agricultural industry in both colonies – are the 'underdogs' politically, when compared to the Negroes, owing to the superior educational advantages of the latter . . . ,"[38] he nonetheless advocated a policy which it was believed would promote social unity, while at the same time maintaining the colonies on a very short democratic leash.

Hewan Craig summarized Wood's reasoning in this way:

> Mr. Wood was . . . opposed to communal representation as, apart from the difficulty of deciding what the constituencies should be, he considered that such a system 'would accentuate and perpetuate differences which it should be the object of statesmanship to remove . . . By retaining the system of nomination by the Crown, it will always be possible to secure representation on the Council of races or important interests not otherwise represented by direct election.'[39]

The background of Wood's thinking, his sociological perspective of the West Indies, so to speak, was his belief that West Indian social conditions were such as to enable the promotion of developments which would create a society on the model of the Mother Country. Thus:

> Mr. Wood related the demand for representative government to the historical circumstances of the African population of the West Indies. Their whole history, he wrote, 'inevitably drives them towards representative institutions fashioned after the British model.' Having lost their indigenous social systems, their language and traditions of slavery, 'they look for political growth to the only source and pattern that they know, and aspire to share in what has been the peculiarly British gift of representative institutions.'[40]

The assumptions of colonial trusteeship in the West Indies have probably at no other time been expressed with greater clarity than in the passages just quoted. And, it is significant to note, they exactly coincide with the views expressed on the Legislative Reform Committee in Trinidad, of which Captain Cipriani was a prominent member. Moreover, this perspective represented an officially-certified image of the future for the West Indian democrats to aspire to; it would eventually be the text upon which Dr. Williams based his lectures on constitutional reform in the University of Woodford Square, and upon which the P.N.M.'s modernizing platform was based.

Early in 1925 Trinidad held its first elections to the Legislative Council. The franchise was highly limited by property and income qualifications, the number of registered voters being less than 22,000 out of a population of around 365,000. Only seven elected seats were contested and of the winners of these, only Cipriani would become a consistent, dynamic spokesman for the working class. The calypso, which had previously been used (usually in the patois which the British were unable to understand) as a covert medium for the expression of social protest by the Creole lower class, came into its own in the 1925 elections: "Who you voting for? Cipriani!" was the popular hit of the day. Through his seat in the LegCo, and in his position as Mayor of Port of Spain (to which he was re-elected for four terms), and in the columns of his trade union publication, *The Socialist*, Cipriani became the tribune of the people in a government still effectively under the control of the Governor and his appointees.

Since later Trinidad politicians, including Dr. Williams, often asserted that they were following in the footsteps of Cipriani, it is necessary to consider briefly who Cipriani was and what his politics were. First, he seemed to have represented in practice what many other French Creoles merely preached, or held up as a romantic ideal which differentiated them from the British section of the white elite stratum: a deep attachment to the local society, and a highly accessible, fraternal mode of interaction with its least privileged members (including, alas, the ladies). His private life and public conduct showed him to be, despite the undoubtedly strong charismatic attraction which he generated, a man with a strong populist streak. The political party which he formed, the Trinidad Labour Party, set the multi-racial precedent of later nationalist movements. With him were associated a number of prominent East Indians – by no means all favored ethnic partition. The first issue of *The Socialist* contained an article written by an East Indian emphasizing the need for unity between Negroes and Indians. An East Indian, Rienzi, was chief organizer for Cipriani's trade union in south Trinidad.[41]

Cipriani, under the slogan "Agitate, Educate, Confederate," was associated with a number of other early West Indian nationalists in advocating the most rapid possible advancement toward self-government in the area, preferably under some form of unified administration. His orientation toward social progress has been described by Lloyd Braithwaite in these terms:

> Even among the radicals this [general] straining towards acceptance of British values existed. The Trinidad Labour Party was modelled on the British Labour Party, and its leader, Captain Cipriani, was fond of saying that what was good enough for the British Labour movement was good enough for him. The demands of the Trade Unionist and Labour movement were for social services 'as is done in England' . . .[42]

The demands of the Legislative Reform Committee did not press for immediate self-government, but rather that tangible steps should be made in that direction, and while Cipriani helped to inaugurate 'representative institutions fashioned after the British model,' such changes were not made during his lifetime on a scale which would confer on elected members to the legislature the power to draft and execute policies. Furthermore, the day of reckoning when internal social cleavages would determine the distribution of political power in the legislature was indefinitely delayed. The radicals had not advocated immediate self-government, and, in any event, Major Wood had stated that such a development could not be entertained "within measurable distance of time."[43]

CHAPTER 4 The Education of Young Colonials at Home and Abroad

The planters do too much or too little in this matter. If they will educate the slave, then they do too little for their own safety in persisting to debar him from those privileges to which he will soon feel that he has acquired an equitable right . . . It will be impossible to march the Negroes on the road to knowledge and compel them to stand at ease within the old entrenchments of ignorance.

– H. Coleridge, *Six Months in the West Indies in 1825*[1]

But why march the Negroes, and much later, the East Indian estate workers, on "the road to knowledge" at all? If Crown Colony Trinidad, as Eric Williams charged in his independence *History*, was based on sugar workers and needed only sugar workers, not citizens, what purposes gave rise to the limited but in some respects excellent institutions of learning developed in nineteenth century Trinidad? Why was the lid of the Pandora's box which contained European ideas on enlightenment and progress raised even slightly?

There were three fundamental reasons, none of which were in direct conflict with the major interests of the sugar industry: first, there was the sheer necessity of colonial administration to bring some order into the colorful but vexatious *anomie* of Trinidad society; second, there were the proselytizing endeavors of the missionaries and priests; third, there was the unavoidable seepage of British humanitarianism and the doctrine of trusteeship into the colony through some of those who administered it.[2] These purposes combined to establish and expand the system of formal education in Trinidad, but they were not entirely complementary. Secular and religious educational authority clashed from the outset in the colony and resulted in a system of divided jurisdiction. That system was still in effect when the P.N.M. was formed, and the apparent intention of Dr. Williams and some of his closest associates to modify it heightened the crisis of political legitimacy which confronted them in the years immediately preceding nationhood.

From its very inception to the time of independence, the educational system of Trinidad has been divided between the overlapping, and at times conflicting, jurisdiction of church and state. At stake have been the competing aspirations of those persons and groups who have seen in the education of the young a means whereby a unified earthly city might be forwarded, and the descendants of St. Augustine who have been equally ardent in advancing the claims of the heavenly city. In the early 1840's Governor MacLeod, pressed by various religious groups for increased subsidies for the small denominational schools which had been established since emancipation a few years earlier, decided that the time had come to attempt to institute some unified, state-supervised system of education. In letters to the Secretary of State for the Colonies, MacLeod, as one historian has paraphrased the documents, pointed out:

> . . . Trinidad's unique position among British colonies owing to its very mixed population. The immigration of peoples from so many scattered nations as well as the differences of religion made it imperative that there should be some system in the colony. Education, he stressed, should be under Government control and should be accessible to all nationalities and religious groups. This would ensure that in future generations the English language would be understood by all the inhabitants, two-thirds of whom were still speaking French or Spanish.[3]

These circumstances could hardly be tolerated, the Governor stated; it was only proper that ". . . peoples living under British rule and claiming the benefits of British citizenship should at least be able to read the laws by which they were governed."[4] Aside from this compelling administrative necessity, he noted that the churches, each of which was using the schools to advance its own doctrinal points of view, would continue to claim government subsidies; the colonial government was already undertaking to pay half of their teachers' salaries.

Governor MacLeod's tentative inquiries addressed to the Secretary of State in the early 1840's did not result in any changes in the denominational school system as it was then constituted. In 1851, however, after East Indian immigration had begun, Governor Harris took steps to organize a system along strikingly secular lines, a move which met strenuous opposition not only from the Roman Catholic authorities, but from some of the other denominational leaders as well. The Harris educational reforms stipulated that primary school education was to be free, open to all children, conducted in English, maintained entirely from the rates of local districts, and devoid of any religious instruction whatsoever. The reforms further made the entire management and control of the schools, the hiring of teachers, the selection of textbooks and courses of instruction the responsibility of a Board of Education consisting of the Governor, members of the wholly-appointed Legislative Council, and such other laymen as the Governor might select.[5]

The Harris system was the high-water mark of secular education in Trinidad, but it neither flourished nor survived. As a result of denominational opposition the Secretary of State in 1869 sent one Patrick J. Keenan out to the colony to recommend changes. Keenan had been Inspector of Schools under the Commissioners of National Education in Ireland, and because of the nature of his suggestions, a later writer suspected that he ". . . was obviously not a liberal choice for the job . . ."[6] The Educational Ordinance of 1870, which embodied many of the recommendations of the Keenan Commission, saw the substantial beginning of the reassertion of denominational control of education. The dual system, as it was called, involved the maintenance of both government and denominational schools, with the latter enjoying considerable autonomy, and with the passing of years, ever greater subsidization by the government. Power to appoint and dismiss teachers in the grant-aided church schools was given to the religious managers of the institutions. By 1890 the government was paying three-quarters of their salaries and operating expenses. In 1878 there had been 47 government primary schools in operation as against only 35 denominational schools; by 1898 the number of government schools had increased only by ten, to 57, while the number of denominational schools, assisted by increasingly generous subsidies, had leaped to 147. During the same twenty-year period at the end of the century, enrollment in primary schools of all types swelled from barely 7,000 in 1878 to almost 25,000 in 1898. More Trinidadians were receiving a rudimentary formal education, but it was increasingly being taken over by the humanitarian and missionary program of the Christian churches.[7]

One of the most remarkable of these missionary endeavors was that conducted by the Presbyterians of the Canadian Mission led by Reverend John Morton. The program of the Canadian Mission, which addressed itself to the neglected education of the rural East Indians, illustrated how the Government, in effect, abdicated the responsibility for education to the priest and missionary. In 1869 Morton proposed to the Governor that his administration should undertake to fully underwrite the Mission's expenses. The Governor admitted to the Legislative Council the need for a greater effort at educating the East Indians, pointing out that ". . . hardly an Indian child has attended a ward school, whilst the small number of these immigrants who are receiving any education are almost exclusively to be found in private schools of the strictest denominational character and uninspected by the State."[8] Very little financial assistance for Morton's mission to the East Indians was provided by the government, however. By 1874 Morton had opened twelve primary schools in southern Trinidad, only one of which was government supported, one supported from the funds of the Mission itself, while the remaining nine were paid for by the (presumably British Protestant) planters of the area who had been receptive to the Mission's appeals. Many later prominent East Indians were educated in the Canadian Presbyterian primary schools and many, too, received their secondary education at Naparima College in San Fernando, one of the first three secondary-level institutions in the colony.

Secondary education was not intended for the masses in Victorian Trinidad. It was an educational system geared chiefly to teaching both spoken and written English and the verities of the British Empire and the Christian religion. In addition to Naparima College, secondary school education in the last quarter of the century was available at only two other institutions. One was the government-operated Queen's Royal College which provided a secondary education free of charge to the sons of civil servants; the other was the Roman Catholic St. Mary's College. Both were located in Port of Spain. From its foundation in 1870, however, Queen's Royal College offered a limited number of scholarships and exhibition prizes by which a few exceptionally-promising primary school graduates could continue their education. This introduction of scholarships at the secondary level was of great importance in that it opened up the possibility of higher education to at least a few of the most gifted sons of poor local parents. A secondary school certificate eventually became the ticket of admission to junior positions in the civil service, and it was likewise the necessary formal prerequisite for those few who sought a university education and a berth in the private professions. With the addition of the so-called Island Scholarships as another link in this embryo meritocracy, a few of the most talented of the secondary school graduates could, on the basis of performance in gruelling, competitive examinations, obtain a university education in Great Britain and then possibly enter into studies in medicine or law. The "scholarship boys," as they came to be called in Trinidad, were exemplary figures in a society which otherwise provided very limited opportunities for the vast majority of its citizens; they were the exceptional ones who rose in the social scale by virtue of brains and hard work. There would be three Island Scholarship winners in the first P.N.M. Cabinet: Dr. Williams himself; the P.N.M.'s Deputy Political Leader, Dr. Patrick Solomon (M.D.); and Dr. Winston Mahabir, an East Indian physician. Ellis Clark, a brilliant constitutional lawyer, pillar of the Roman Catholic Church, who was appointed as

Trinidad & Tobago's first Ambassador to the United Nations, also began his career as an Island Scholar from Queen's Royal College, or, as it is nicknamed, "Q.R.C."

There thus appeared during the Victorian era an avenue of social mobility based on the educational system which led to a growing degree of correlation, within the Negro community, of social status and education. From this ladder of opportunity the East Indians, owing to their rural location, neglect, and an official bias against drawing them off the land through education, were relatively excluded until much later. These rewards for exemplary academic performance were the limited expression of the official colonial policy which aimed at providing some avenues of advancement into the professions and civil service for talented local persons. Collens, the experienced British schoolmaster living in Trinidad in the nineteenth century, eulogized that policy in these terms:

> In consequence of the liberal exhibitions and scholarships open every year to deserving pupils of elementary schools no matter of what nationality or creed, 'the humblest peasant,' to quote . . . from a report of the Inspector of Schools, 'may aspire to a college course at Cambridge or elsewhere free of expense, and enter as a candidate for the Civil Service of India. The advantages offered to boys by our educational system are hardly surpassed in the world . . . It may indeed be said that the highest positions in the British Empire to which mental acquirements are a passport are opened to the poorest boy in Trinidad by the educational advantages at his command.'[9]

Not only the exceptional scholar, however, benefited from the establishment of the education system: that system had to be staffed and, although a great many of the primary grade teaching positions and virtually all the secondary level posts were filled by expatriate teachers, the growing school system provided expanding opportunities for local citizens to achieve at least the status of a minor professional. Naturally, there were other criteria which became the basis of social ranking within the Negro community in Trinidad, color being perhaps the most important of these; but with the growth of the professions and the civil service, education and the opportunities which education provided began to assume ever greater significance in the twentieth century. At the top of this status hierarchy would be the university educated professionals, below them the more educated of the civil servants, and, still lower, the primary school teachers who had been trained by the "student teacher" method, perhaps supplemented with a course in the local teachers' training college. But the exportation of education from the "advanced" nations of the Victorian era to Trinidad was not without difficulties, aside from the government's periodic differences with the denominational authorities. The attempt to maintain the same standards "as at home" is unrealistic, the schoolmaster quoted above laments, because of the heterogeneous nature of the population. "Speaking from experience," he wrote, "I can truly say a teacher's life 'is not a happy one.' "[10]

Just after the turn of the century, two members of the new stratum of Negro primary school teachers in the Arima district of Trinidad, east of Port of Spain along the base of the Northern Range, acquired sons who would make their mark on the world in a rather exotic profession. One of the boys was named Cyril Lionel Robinson James, the other, Malcolm Nurse; both would achieve distinction as professional revolutionary organizers and intellectuals. The fathers of the pair were good friends. The James family was descended from the class of free colored artisans; James's grandfather had been a respected mechanic and first Negro engineer on the government railroad.[11] Later James's young brother, Eric, would continue in the family occupational tradition and become an important railway official himself. The father of the young Nurse was also an exceptionally successful colored man by the standards of the colonial society of the period, for he served as an Agricultural Advisor to the government Department of Education.[12]

The young James and Nurse seemed to have been casual friends in their boyhood days. Writing many years later, James nostalgically recalled that they had together explored their rural and forested environment, tramping along the base of the Northern Range and bathing in the Arima River.[13] Both boys eventually attended secondary school. James was a precocious scholar and won an exhibition at nine years of age to Queen's Royal College; Nurse attended St. Mary's College. Not that opportunities for secondary education had increased very much by 1911, the year in which a Negro clerk in the Port of Spain post office acquired the distinction of becoming the father of the future Dr. Eric Williams, and which was approximately the year in which James and Nurse were preparing to embark on their secondary school education. Secondary education was expensive, straining the limited resources of the colored middle class and practically out of the question for the sons of parents living in regions so remote from the urban centers as to make necessary the boarding of their sons in town. The official scholarship bridge between primary and secondary school, and from the latter to a university education abroad, was in reality a razor's edge of competitive scholarship. The government itself provided only four free places in the secondary schools, and the university scholarships for the United Kingdom numbered but three annually.[14]

However, the quality of the secondary school instruction was, in comparison to the ordinary level in the primary schools, deemed to be extraordinarily high. On this point there is the testimony of a leading West Indian educator, Dr. Eric Williams himself. As an alumnus of the system, he later wrote that both Q.R.C. and St. Mary's had a (chiefly expatriate) staff and curriculum the equal of the British public schools after which both were modelled. Classical literature, languages, geography, mathematics, history – even a course in West Indian history – were all taught and taught well. Also of the greatest importance in accounting for the high level of competitive scholarship in Trinidad was the fact that the colony's secondary schools were the first colonial institutions to participate in the external examinations of Oxford and Cambridge.[15] Thus identical criteria for performance were established for the local scholars, whose work was thereby ranked and locally acclaimed in an inter-Empire educational system. The Trinidad scholars did very well; as Eric Williams, "old boy" from Q.R.C., wrote later in a newspaper article dealing with the social anatomy on the island in the year of his birth:

> . . . One of the island scholars of 1911 was placed first among 57 candidates in the British Empire in Agricultural Science . . . He gained distinction in five subjects; so did four other students in the Empire, one in Ceylon, three in England. Of 83 candidates who gained distinction in history, four were from Trinidad . . . At the 1910 examinations one island scholar from Queen's Royal College was placed first in the Senior Cambridge examinations throughout the Empire, whilst another from St. Mary's College topped the candidates in the entrance examination to St. Bartholomew's Hospital in London. W. J. Locke, island scholar for 1879, became a successful novelist; another, scholar for 1884, became Sir Robert Falconer, President of the University of Toronto.[16]

Another avenue of advancement for the secondary school graduate who had been unable to obtain a university scholarship was to go to the United States and attempt to work his way through a university. Malcolm Nurse would take this route in the 1920's. However, the only profession in Trinidad which could be entered on the basis of an American degree was that of dentistry. In 1911, twenty of the twenty-four dentists practicing in the island had been trained at American schools, indicating that this avenue of advancement which thousands of West Indian students would later take was already well trodden.[17]

And then there was cricket. The stem of one palm tree branch provided a bat, and three more propped up against each other supplied a wicket for the plebeians who had observed the British gentlemen engaged in their favorite sport. Inter-colonial cricket had been inaugurated in Trinidad in 1893, the year in which the elite Queen's Park Oval Club was organized. In 1895 a team from England had been beaten by an all-Trinidad side; two years later, during the centennial celebrations of British rule, cricket was prominent on the agenda, and in 1900 the first West Indian team visited England. Cricket clubs, and the inevitable village cricket pitch, could be found all over Trinidad. Everyone knew the game; young C. L. R. James was a cricket fanatic, and so was Learie Constantine, whose father had himself been an outstanding exponent of the game. In the 1920's Learie Constantine went to England to play in the County leagues for Nelson in Lancashire. He soon established a reputation as being one of the best "all-rounders" that the game had ever seen, a sportsman of legendary prowess and one of the early heralds of the phenomenal ability that West Indians were to bring to the game.

Someday, perhaps, a Trinidad writer will attempt a full-scale social history of the complex little island civilization that was Trinidad in the early years of the century. In his cricket memoirs, *Beyond a Boundary,* James provides glimpses into such facets of the period as the Puritannical code impressed on the Q.R.C. schoolboy, the metropolitan sophistication of a group of local intellectuals and literateurs, and the manner in which membership in the various local cricket clubs was determined by very fine class and color distinctions. The excellence of the cricket played was a product of the sublimated class conflict which found an outlet in the keen rivalries between the clubs; also of importance was the ready, informal, availability of top players for matches at every level. Under the veneer of class and caste there had taken shape a self-confident, robust, uninhibited national character for which cricket — like Carnival? — provided a disciplined, formalized, means of expression. West Indian social conditions of the period, particularly in Trinidad, James seems to be saying, were analogous to the vigorous, pre-Victorian ethos which had produced W. G. Grace and the modern game of cricket: an England still unconquered by the Industrial Revolution, not finicky in morals, committed to enjoying life with gusto.[18] The parallel, if tenuous, is nonetheless fascinating. In Trinidad the lively, competitive, innovative neighborhood organizations of the urban *jamettes* had counterparts in many areas of the countryside. Tunapuna, the native district of James, Constantine and Nurse, has been described by Dom Basil Matthews as a frontier town, intensely clannish, and united as a semi-secret organization against outsiders. The cultural background, and the perhaps subconscious origins, of the intense populist faith which James developed into a unique method of revolutionary organization during his years as a sectarian radical, are suggested in this portrayal, by Reverend Matthews, of the Trinidad from which he emerged:

> Beneath the geographico-economic conditions of the village neighborhood, a human factor was active and creative. The flight of runaway slaves and the forging or assimilation of novel kinship links (godparent relationships) in the social pattern, to say nothing of the development of folk literature, are evidence of creative activity. Nevertheless, the neighborhood, that is, the village, frequently cast or drawn into the shadow of the plantation, largely conditioned and also determined the structure, form and expression of the traditional Trinidad family and society. Just as before Emancipation the slave plantation was the center of all life; and, as in recent times all life and activity, even in the remotest village, point, like the roads, to the commercial towns and industrial centres; so, in the intervening hundred years, the shut-in village neighborhood was the hub and matrix of society . . .
>
> Membership in a territorial group used to be a test of manhood. Initiation involved the spilling of blood of the petitioner in a war-like ceremony which has been witnessed by many people who are today [circa 1953] not above twenty-five years of age. The secret society aspect of the territorial group is nowhere as remarkable as in Tunapuna where . . . the original Tunapunians hold their community secrets to this day against all comers, whether they be the law or private citizens.[19]

During this period Cipriani seems to have made a deep impression on many youths in Trinidad, an impression which was more than political; it was emotional as well. While many members of the colored middle class, directly dependent on remaining in good grace with the British authorities to maintain their standing within a tight little social structure, were leery of supporting Cipriani openly, they sympathized with his cause and gave him covert support and encouragement. When speaking at Woodford Square Cipriani would often point rhetorically toward St. Vincent Street (the "lawyers row" of Port of Spain) and, apparently without great success, exhort its timid denizens to join in the struggle for democracy. James has written a reminiscence of Cipriani in which several incidents are suggestive. At one time he and a friend were listening to Cipriani speak: "As Cipriani came to a pause at the end of his opening words I felt thrills running up and down my back and I looked at John: his eyes were filled with tears." On another occasion, when in his capacity as English tutor to the French Consul in Trinidad, the latter official asked James, "If the Governor arrested Captain Cipriani, what do you think would happen?" James immediately answered, "The people will burn down the town."[20]

This, then, was the curious mixture of the rustic and urban, the provincial, yet cosmopolitan environment to which schoolboys and young men born after the turn of the century would be exposed in the Trinidad of the Twenties. During that decade Malcolm Nurse tried his hand at local journalism but then set off for Fisk University in Nashville, Tennessee, and then moved on to Howard University in Washington, D.C. James taught at Q.R.C., at the Government Teacher's College, and was also on the verge of leaving the colony by the end of the decade. Eric Williams had a series of successful scholarship competitions behind him and was about to climax his graduation from Q.R.C. by winning an Island Scholarship.

On a day in 1931 James ran into Eric Williams on a street near Q.R.C. They knew each other well, for James had been a tutor to Williams while the latter was a pupil at the secondary institution. Both had made plans to leave the colony. James had been working on a biography of Captain Cipriani and was determined to go to England and become a writer. Williams, having just won his university scholarship, had decided that the conventional career pattern of the scholarship winner — law or medicine — was not for him; he was going to Oxford University and do History.[21] His father, who had favored a regular professional career for his son, protested, but to no avail, for after all, as the Trinidad scholar-statesman dryly observed during a B.B.C. interview in 1962, "It was I who had won the scholarship — not he."

Thus the two Trinidad intellectuals set off, like many other bright, adventurous and ambitious young men from the provinces of the Empire, in search of an education, and possibly even a career, in the metropolitan country. Many had, of course, preceded them, and even more would follow. Not all, however, went to the Mother Country; some, like Kwame Nkrumah who left the Gold Coast about three years later, or the son of a poor East Indian estate overseer, Cheddi Jagan, who left British Guiana in 1936, would go to the United States. All, however, shared the status of "foreign student" in an advanced country. In both the university and by exposure to the intellectual milieux of these countries, they found individuals and groups which instilled and encouraged nationalist aspirations which gave the impetus to the incipient colonial revolution.

"The colleges and universities," writes Edward Shils, "attended by the students of underdeveloped countries became academies of national revolution."[22] In London, the Fabian-founded London School of Economics which had Harold Laski as its leading political theorist upheld a universal democratic ideal for the young colonials; the *New Statesman*, under the editorial guidance of Kingsley Martin and with

J. M. Keynes and the Guild Socialist, G. D. H. Cole, as the dominant influence in the paper's approach to economic affairs, made the cause of independence for India its own during the Thirties. Notes Shils:

> . . . It was not only the universities of London and Paris but the cafes and cheap restaurants and dingy hotels and boarding houses where they spent most of their days and the offices of their nationalist organizations which educated the students in nationalism, gave them first some degree of national consciousness, made them see how retrograde their own countries were and what they could become if only they became their own masters and modernized themselves. Personalities like Mr. Krishna Menon, Dr. Nkrumah, Dr. Banda, *et al*, were themselves formed in these milieux and in turn formed many of those who were to play an active part in the movement in their own countries.[23]

The intellectual and political *Zeitgeist* which greeted James and Williams in the England of the Thirties was perhaps more strongly to the left than it had ever been before, or would become thereafter. The Western democracies were entering a period of intense political ferment and crisis associated with the Great Depression and the skirmishes, both ideological and military, between fascism, Communism, and capitalist democracy. In this highly-charged political period the education of colonial students tended to acquire great ideological intensity and significance. But not all of the young colonials were exposed to, or gravitated toward, identical left milieux. Their status and experiences had much in common, but the theoretical and practical social knowledge which they acquired bore the differing stamps of the conflicting schools of thought within the European Left of the day. Between Keynes and Lenin, between Laski and Trotsky, there were important differences in the strategy of attaining a better future society. These were distinctions which the seriously political colonial student would at least be aware of, and toward which he might often acquire at least tentative leanings and ideological preferences. Political education in the metropolitan country was not uniform, although there was a broad common exposure to everyday British life. Cricket was everywhere cricket, but Oxford was not Bloomsbury.

In the diverging careers of James and Williams in the England of the Thirties these differences in milieux stand in sharp contrast, partially because James was not a university student, but perhaps more because his was a more radical and romantic temperament, and he lived chiefly in London. Another colonial intellectual who was a university student in London (studying anthropology under Professor Malinowski), Jomo Kenyatta, was a member of the same radical circle that attracted James.

James arrived in England in 1932, apparently a few months ahead of Eric Williams. He spent three months in London and then went to live for some months with Norma and Learie Constantine in Lancashire, where he found employment for his literary skills in helping Learie write his first cricket book. Returning to London he made his living by reporting county cricket for the *Manchester Guardian* while, as he later wrote, "I educated myself." There was to be, however, a curious similarity in the careers of these Trinidadians in the Mother Country, and that was that though they came to learn, *they stayed to teach.* Constantine was an acknowledged master at cricket, James would teach them politics, Williams would teach them history; and, some years later, Dr. Rudranath Capildeo would undertake to teach them physics.

As Williams began his career at Oxford, James, then just over thirty years of age, almost immediately embarked on the education of the British. He plunged into the radical haunts of London. More than a spectator, and fresh from completing his *Life of Cipriani,* he began to participate by lecturing on *The Case for West Indian Self-Government* which Leonard and Virginia Woolf's Hogarth Press published in 1933. At the same time, he later wrote, "I was reading hard and I was already a long way towards becoming a Trotskyist."[24] In the midst of this formative period in London he was invited one day to attend a speech by "a great Negro Communist" named George Padmore in Gray's Inn Road. He was going to every meeting in those days, and the Negro aspect of the invitation was an added attraction. He went and found about 50 people in a small auditorium, most of them Negroes. They waited for some time and then ". . . in stepped Malcolm Nurse." His old chum, James learned during a reunion which ran far into the night, had pursued an exciting career since he had left Trinidad and gone to the United States. At Howard University Nurse had shown signs of a militantly revolutionary temperament when he had (so the story went) thrown a sheaf of anti-imperialist pamphlets in the face of a visiting British Ambassador. He then entered into organizational work for the U.S. Communist Party in Harlem and took the party name of George Padmore.[25]

Well-educated, cultivated young Negro radicals like Padmore and James were at a premium in these early days of the stirrings of Negro radicalism in the United States, the West Indies, and Africa. First Padmore, and later James, rose very rapidly in the hierarchy of leadership and notoriety of the various contending branches of the international Left. Compared to Negroes in the United States and Africa, the West Indian colored colonials had had educational and social advantages far superior to those attained by the Negroes suffering under the American caste system or under the cruder, less "enlightened" British trusteeship in Black Africa. In 1928 the Sixth International Conference of the Communist International established a new world-wide trade union organization, the Profintern, and in charge of its Negro department, with offices in Moscow, was placed George Padmore. Despite his outward air of a respectable, cultivated colored Englishman, Padmore appears to have been an ingenious and indefatigable organizer. One of his early achievements had been the organization of the first international conference of Negro workers staged in Hamburg in 1930, which had involved him in considerable world travel, often of a dangerous, clandestine variety.[26]

Padmore invited James to assist him in his work for the Communist International, which had then brought him to England, but James was already too far committed ideologically to take up the offer. "Between Communism and Trotskyism," he wrote almost thirty years later, "there was a line of antagonism and conflict, stained with blood, incredible cruelties, murders and death." Nonetheless, both James and Padmore were Trinidadians, "sons of the soil," and as old friends in an alien land they never quarrelled: ". . . the simple stream of home kept us together."[27] They would see each other intermittently during the next several years, and soon it would be Padmore who changed ideological ranks and became for many years a central figure in the early efforts to organize African students into nationalist movements in London. During the 1940's when James was living in New York as leader of a Trotskyist sect named the Johnsonites (James had also, as was the fashion, taken a revolutionary alias, J. R. Johnson), he wrote as a matter of routine a letter of introduction to George Padmore for an African foreign student named Kwame Nkrumah who was then enroute to London.[28] In his autobiography Nkrumah states that he learned the techniques of underground organization from James, and in London his association with the other revolutionary from Trinidad would result in the latter becoming political advisor, until his death in 1959, to the founder of the newly-independent state of Ghana.[29]

In examining the ideological exposure of the young colonials in Britain, and in assessing the world orientation of nationalist politicians in the British colonies, it is important to remember that the dominant British leftist orientation of the Thirties on the question of global alignment was, if not actively pro-Communist, at least pro-Russian. The Bolshevik Revolution and its aftermath had been examined by the Fabian leaders, Beatrice and Sidney Webb, for example, who thought that in Soviet Communism a new civilization was being created. Aside from the general admiration of the Soviet Union which was widespread in the Labour Party and among the intelligentsia, there was a strong, clinching *Realpolitik* argument, strenuously advanced by such periodicals as the *New Statesman*,[30] that the only practical defense strategy available to the Western democracies against the rising militarism of fascism lay in alliance with the Soviet Union. As history is re-written from year to year in modern times, and even from week to week, these basically rational and persuasive political assumptions of the decade, created by the domestic and international crises of the times, tend to be forgotten, or are at best viewed as temporary, youthful aberrations which new times and new problems have made obsolete. But exist they did, and it is important to recall how pervasive and unexceptional such views were at the time. Many years later, Eric Williams would twit an opposing Trinidad politician for having paid tribute, during World War II, to the Soviet system and the Red Army, though these were hardly exceptional views at the time, particularly among labor politicians. Thus one finds, too, in Learie Constantine's book, *Colour Bar*, that despite vigorous disclaimers of any advocacy of the Soviet system, he is nonetheless convinced that Soviet racial policies could serve as a model for other nations.[31]

When C. L. R. James became a Trotskyist in the Thirties, therefore, he went against the prevailing currents of the British Left. Instead, he joined forces with a group of Marxist, anti-Stalinist radicals within the Independent Labour Party which was presided over by a fiery M.P. from Glasgow, James Maxton. The I.L.P. had been a ginger group within the Labour Party for many years before it withdrew to form a small, separate organization which published an influential weekly newspaper, *The New Leader*. Among the best known of the British members during these years were Fenner Brockway and Aneurin Bevan's wife, Jennie Lee, and author George Orwell. Among the colonials there were James, Kenyatta and Padmore. Fenner Brockway performed valuable services for the young colonials, providing them with entrée into the left-wing politics of the period and assisting them in various ways. In the first installment of Brockway's autobiography, *Inside the Left*, there is a glimpse of James in the thick of I.L.P. internal politics moving a resolution "in a typically torrential speech." During the speech he "appealed as a black worker for help for the black population of Abyssinia" on an issue which would nearly split the organization within which "the Marxist Group" was continually prodding its labor officials and parliamentary members from the left.[32]

For political activists and writers interested in reaching a wide audience, the climate of receptivity to radical authors in British publishing circles was obviously important and requires brief mention here. In publisher Frederic Warburg's autobiography the political climate of the time and the place of anti-Stalinist writers like James and Orwell within it is vividly portrayed at first hand. Left-wing publishing during the period was dominated by Victor Gollancz, a leader in the pro-Soviet United Front against fascism and founder of the highly popular and influential Left Book Club. From 1933 until 1939 Gollancz, wrote Warburg, held a virtual monopoly on this section of the book trades.

But in the mid-Thirties Warburg, who had just established the house of Secker and Warburg on a shoestring, challenged the prevailing pro-Soviet tendency represented in Gollancz's venturies in political publications. The circumstances are interesting: Fenner Brockway had approached Warburg and suggested that some of the I.L.P. writers would be interested in bringing their works to him. The publisher realized that he would be running a considerable risk in view of the unfashionable anti-Soviet bias of the group. "If Brockway's proposal was tempting, it was also double-edged. Despite my association with him over a book on the Routledge list a year before, he would never, I felt, have approached me, had he been able to place the work of his members and friends with a stronger and better established house."[33] However, Warburg decided to make the plunge, not so much out of ideological affinity with the I.L.P. writers, whose libertarian doctrines he viewed with tolerant skepticism, but because "my little firm needed authors as an army needs banners," and because his wife — their conversation on the subject consumes four pages of the autobiography! — strongly and wittily reinforced his uneasiness over what he viewed as the currently uncritical and unprincipled support in British intellectual circles of the Soviet Union.

Warburg decided to gamble on Brockway's proposition, and the returns formed an important chapter in British publishing history. He picked up Orwell on the road back from his Gollancz-sponsored trip to *Wigan Pier* and sent him to Spain, out of which came the classic study of the Spanish Civil War, *Homage to Catalonia.* Moreover, once embarked on an anti-Stalinist policy, Warburg published Andre Gide's account of his observations of the U.S.S.R. (whither he had been invited on the assumption that this apparently pro-Soviet dean of French letters would pen another one of those paeans of praise to socialist construction which became almost a literary *genre* in itself during the Thirties). Gide, however, wrote a brief, spare account of his observations in which he related his surprise and dismay at the social pretentiousness and privileged status which he perceived to be so prominent among the Stalinist leadership and bureaucracy, and he opined that "I doubt whether in any other country in the world, even Hitler's Germany, thought be less free." This statement, wrote Warburg, "spread consternation and rage through the Communist ranks. Members of the Left Book Club, carefully shielded by their committee from the truth, must have rubbed their eyes in astonishment if they happened to light on these lines of Gide. Blasphemous, treacherous, reptilian . . . the futile outpourings of a decaying homosexual, such were the anathemata launched against Gide's pamphlet."[34]

Into this bitterly controversial climate of political opinion the biographer of an obscure West Indian politician entered during the early Thirties. "One of the first authors introduced to me by Brockway," Warburg recalled, "was C. L. R. James, and his book, *World Revolution,* became a kind of Bible of Trotskyism. We published it in 1937. It was dedicated to the Marxist Group. How many members composed this group at the time I don't know, probably less than fifty, for it was a quality of Trotskyist groups to break in two, like an amoeba when reproducing itself, and to continue doing so until the fission process had reduced the group to a mere handful . . ."[35] The Trotskyists, and James foremost amongst them, Warburg stated, believed in the wickedness of capitalism and regarded Nazism as simply capitalism gone rotten. They loved the U.S.S.R. like children love their mother, but they regarded Stalin as a wicked father who had debauched her and produced a miscarriage. They therefore felt free to criticize the U.S.S.R. for Stalin's crimes, while loving it for the beautiful thing it might have become — providing Lenin and Trotsky had survived in power to create the Utopia that was just around the corner:

> Despite the atmosphere of hate and arid dispute in his writings, James himself was one of the most delightful and easy-going personalities I have known, colourful in more senses than one. A dark-skinned West Indian Negro from Trinidad, he stood six feet three inches in his socks and was noticeably good-looking. His memory was extraordinary . . . Immensely amiable, he loved the fleshpots of capitalism, fine cooking, fine clothes, fine furniture and beautiful women without a trace of the guilty remorse to be expected from a seasoned warrior of the class war . . . Night after night he would address meetings in London and the provinces, denouncing the crimes of the blood-thirsty Stalin until he was hoarse and his wonderful voice a mere croaking in the throat. The Communists who heckled him would have torn him limb from limb, had it not been for the ubiquity of the police . . .
>
> If politics was his religion and Marx his god, if literature was his passion and Shakespeare his prince among writers, cricket was his beloved activity. He wrote splendid articles on county matches for the *Manchester Guardian* during the summer. Indeed, it was only between April and October that he was in funds. Sometimes he came for the week-end to our cottage near West Hoathly in Sussex and turned out for the local team. He was a demon bowler, and a powerful if erratic batsman. The village loved him, referring to him affectionately as 'the black bastard.' In Sussex politics were forgotten. Instead, I can hear

> today the opening words of Twelfth Night delivered beautifully from his full sensitive lips: 'If music be the food of love, play on; give me excess of it.' Excess, perhaps was James' crime, an excess of words whose relevance to the contemporary tragedy was less than he supposed.[36]

James did not, however, limit his productivity to Trotskyist polemics. He wrote a perceptive short novel on Trinidad, *Minty Alley*, and in 1938 Warburg published his classic study of the San Domingo slave revolt led by Toussaint Louverture, *The Black Jacobins*. Research for this brilliant work had taken James to the archives at Bordeaux where he discovered that another Trinidad scholar, Eric Williams, had been before him during the course of examining documents in preparation for the doctoral thesis he was writing at Oxford.

For the Trinidad Island Scholarship winner, the England of the Thirties did not afford such strong inducements to political engagement as had characterized the careers of Padmore and James. His niche was not in the urban, radical milieux of the metropolitan country, but rather in the more serene traditional atmosphere of the British university. At Oxford he was motivated chiefly by the determination to continue in the prodigious feats of scholarship which had marked his educational career from the beginning. From a published fragment of his yet unpublished autobiography, Williams has described the environment and dominant concerns of "A Colonial at Oxford." It is a dramatic account of scholarly discovery and of the widening of intellectual horizons.

Williams arrived in Oxford in October, 1932, just after his twenty-first birthday (celebrated at sea) and fresh from "a few days' bewilderment in the vast metropolis of London." He described the institution around which his life centered for over seven years in these terms:

> Awed but exhilarated I was, for seven years, to be a part, however small, of noble and inspiring traditions which have no equal anywhere in the world. Carfax, the tower of Christ Church and Magdalen, the Bodleian and the Radcliffe Camera, the several colleges, the Parks, the meadows of Christ Church, the towpath along the river – buildings and gardens, architecture and nature, all enthralled. But it was the human interest, the literary, religious and political traditions, Man, in short which fascinated me most. It was not the Oxford of the tourist or the antiquarian which most attracted me but the Oxford of scholarship, the Oxford of the Reformation, the Civil War and the British Empire.[37]

The history and literature he had studied in Trinidad came to life at Oxford as he trod through the same corridors which Gladstone, Peel, Fox, Canning, Cecil Rhodes and a mighty host of other historic giants had walked. In a Welsh clergyman named Trevor Davies he acquired not only a tutor, but a guide, philosopher, and friend, who counselled him during his three undergraduate years. In discussions with his tutor, Williams wrote, he took a "very independent line" – arguing that Aristotle was a "dyed-in-the-wool reactionary," and that Hobbes had a "fascist mentality." Although at Oxford he was not insulated from the ideological fervor of the time, his actual participation seems to have been very limited. James later recalled having attended a meeting with Williams in which the latter, during question period, had challenged the speaker, G. D. H. Cole, on some point or other.[38] After Williams and James fell out in 1960, however, James wrote of Williams' political activities in the Thirties that his former pupil had associated with him and Padmore, had criticised and taken positions, but that he had never joined any organizations.[39] This appears to have been roughly the case, with one near exception. When Williams, on the verge of entering nationalist politics in Trinidad many years later, felt compelled to give himself an ideologically clean bill of health, he stated: "I had never had any connection whatsoever with any political organization at all, except that at Oxford I had attended regularly meetings of the Indian nationalist students in their club, the Majliss."[40]

Williams was, it seems fair to say, only incidentally involved in the political struggles of the period; the primary objective to which he directed most of his energies was to graduate from Oxford with a top degree. In aiming for a First, he later wrote, he had the advantage of "the necessary personal discipline, for which the ordeal of the Island Scholarship was admirable preparation."

> . . . I worked steadily throughout the entire period . . . and in the excessively long vacations . . . I made it my practice to spend three weeks at Christmas, three at Easter, six in the summer in Oxford, which was at those times almost like a dead city, reading steadily in my rooms and in the college and university libraries . . .[41]

The image of the young West Indian scholar, working diligently through major portions of vacations in the deserted university, is strikingly similar to the reputation for superhuman effort which became a legend in the early years of the P.N.M. government in Trinidad. "You could drive by his office late, late at night," the writer was often told, "and see the lights still burning." Given his diligence and native ability, Williams cleared his final exams at Oxford easily and was awarded the coveted First Class degree, placing first, with two other students, in that class. His *viva voce* examination was a mere formality, but in his recollection of the brief exchange with his examiners Williams indicated that despite his love of cloistered Oxford he had developed a pragmatic attitude toward knowledge and had retained his colonial roots:

> . . . The chairman of the board of examiners . . . asked me where I came from, and then what subject had interested me most in my course. I replied it was my special subject in colonial history. He stated that this was borne out in my marks and asked me why; I answered, in some surprise, 'Well, I am a colonial . . . and I replied that I could not see the value of study unless there was that connection with the environment.' His reply was: 'That is one of the most interesting answers I have ever heard.'[42]

He then embarked on research for his doctoral dissertation which, after some further research, would be published in 1944 as *Capitalism and Slavery* – his *magnum opus*, and the work on which his reputation as an historian chiefly rests. In this study Williams attacked, and sought to disprove, a currently received theory in British historical circles concerning the reasons underlying the abolition of slavery in the British Empire in 1833. The theory which he attacked was the notion that abolition of slavery had been due to the humanitarian agitation and propaganda of the British abolitionists. The thesis which he advanced was, briefly, that although the West Indies plantation economy and its slave labor force had been responsible for the development of mercantilist capital in the metropolitan country, the rise of the industrial bourgeoisie in the early nineteenth century brought into being new forces whose interests were at variance with those of the older capitalist group. The support given to anti-slavery measures by this rising class was but a part of their general economic self-interest and was the decisive factor in the emancipation of the slaves. Where did Williams obtain this thesis? In a bibliographical footnote he cites James's *The Black Jacobins* and states that "on pages 38–41 the thesis advanced in this book is stated clearly and concisely and, as far as I know, for the first time in English."[43] In examining *The Black Jacobins*, James is indeed found discussing precisely the process which Williams so thoroughly documented. But a full reading of *The Black Jacobins* reveals the rather startling fact that *this was not James's thesis;* rather, it was only one-half of the Trotskyist writer's theory as to the causes of the abolition of slavery in the Caribbean colonies.

Both Williams and James agreed that the end of slavery represented the ascendancy of the industrial middle class interests without which, as James put it, abolitionists like Wilberforce and Clarkson would have preached themselves as black in the face as any Negro. For Williams, in *Capitalism and Slavery*, this was the key point: slavery was abolished because it happened to have been in the interest of the most powerful economic faction in the British ruling class; moreover, he argued in his conclusion, the process had been substantially the same in the French colonies, hence the justification of a general title like the one that he had given to the study. For James, however, the ascendancy of the industrial interests were only a necessary *precondition* for the abolition of slavery, the root cause of which was not to be found in the interests of the strong, but in the revolt of the weak. "The Haitian revolution," he concluded, ". . . killed the West Indian slave-trade and slavery."

> It is true that abolition was but one stage in the successive victories of the industrial bourgeoisie over the landed aristocracy . . . Those who see in abolition the gradually awakening conscience of mankind should spend a few minutes asking themselves why it is that man's conscience, which had slept peacefully for so many centuries, should awake just at the time that men began to see the unprofitableness of slavery as a method of production in the West Indian colonies.
>
> But the process worked itself out blindly . . . Had the British held San Domingo and started to exploit that colony, the slave-trade and slavery in the West Indies might have lasted another half-century. As it was, driven out of the West Indies, the English were so disgusted with their own half-bankrupt colonies that they stopped the slave trade in 1807 to prevent cultivation of new lands.[44]

Moreover, wrote James, even the European working class had played a significant role in the final liquidation of slavery: "One of the first things that the revolution of 1848 achieved was the abolition of slavery, the workers completing the good work of their ancestors; and so weak were the slave-holding interests that when the revolution was crushed emancipation was not reversed."[45] And on the positive side, James insisted, the Haitian revolution gave the impulse to, and subsidized, the first national revolutions in Spanish America; Simon Bolivar came twice to Haiti for respite, encouragement and supplies. Thus, for James, considerable moral credit had to be given to the active struggle of the oppressed in significantly accelerating and maintaining the changes *made possible by* the shifting distribution of power in the European ruling class, and thereby effecting historical progress. In Williams' study, however, there were no historical bouquets for anyone; while conceding that some of the abolitionists were sincere in espousing the cause of emancipation and that the slave revolts had by 1833 produced an acute crisis in the maintenance of the slave system, he implied that the slave revolts had not triggered the emancipation: they might have, but the British industrial elite beat them to the punch.

Which interpretation was correct? Or were they complementary? Both studies stressed the decisive role of class conflict in history. Williams attacked the moral complacency associated with Britain's understanding of its slave-owning past; James sought to demolish the historical lie of Negro passivity under slavery. Both were radical works of scholarship written from the perspective of a marginal, black intellectual whose personal experiences had made him aware of the hypocrisy behind the metropolitan country's pious self-congratulation over its dealings with the colonies. From the beginning of his career Williams takes the role of a tough-minded prosecutor calling a white elite to the bar of historical justice — a habit of mind toward the uses of knowledge which led naturally to the founding of the University of Woodford Square.

But there is this intriguing difference between the two: as in *Capitalism and Slavery*, Williams would continue to interpret West Indian social and political change through an *historicist* lens; that is, his political philosophy would, when the chips were down, be conditioned by the assumption that the economic self-interests of the strong tend to be the final arbiters of history; and the West Indian territories were not to be numbered among the strong.[46] James, on the other hand, will always look to the weak, the exploited, for the motive power to break historical continuity and establish qualitatively new societies. This theoretical difference, clearly evident in the contrasting theses of *Black Jacobins* and *Capitalism and Slavery*, was probably maintained and reinforced by the diverging careers of the two men: Williams would become a respectable and expert social science technician, an administrator close to the center of West Indian decision-making. The intellectual role James pursued — one equally institutionalized in healthy Western societies — would remain that of the outsider, the nay-sayer inspired by a millenarian vision of human potentialities.

As World War II descended on England, both James and Williams left for the United States. Williams had accepted a post at Howard University; James, it is said, came to deliver a set of lectures but was overtaken by illness and then the war. Padmore and Constantine stayed on in London, the latter being awarded an M.B.E. for his services as a social welfare officer in the Ministry of Labour. During the war years and immediately thereafter Williams and James kept in touch, although Williams was a rising academic (Associate Professor at age 35 in 1946) while James stuck out the life of the independent radical writer and philosopher in a political atmosphere which, as the Cold War began, was becoming increasingly intolerant of radical ideas. By 1942 Williams had published *The Negro in the Caribbean* in which he praised the rise of working class leaders in the West Indies and issued a Cipriani-like exhortation to the middle class to join in the struggle for independence. James's intellectual interests, however, had taken him far afield from the Caribbean. The Trotskyist movement was an international movement and James had no difficulty in gaining admittance into the circle of Trotsky's followers in New York. Indeed, according to one version, he travelled to the U.S. via Mexico where he spent some time with Trotsky. He then entered the politics of the American Left as a fervent apostle of revolution. Within a couple of years, however, he broke with the orthodox followers of Trotsky and in April, 1941, led his small band of adherents, known as the Johnson-Forest 'Tendency,' out of the Socialist Workers Party. The 'Tendency' joined with another small group, the Workers Party, during the war, then left to enjoy an independent existence until July, 1951, when it went back into the S.W.P. Its membership later quit the S.W.P. again, and then splintered.[47] It is easy to lampoon these amoebic tendencies of the radical left, and Dwight MacDonald has hilariously done so in his *Memoirs of a Revolutionist*,[48] except that the protagonists in these microdramas rightly felt themselves to be the inheritors of a great tradition which could count among its martyrs the German *Spartakists* and Trotsky himself.

As a Trotskyist James, or J. R. Johnson, was of course also a Leninist. He therefore shared in the Leninist belief that a small, tightly-disciplined group of revolutionary conspirators could, when the historical situation was ripe, be the critical force in propelling society into a new era. In this assumption – had it not been validated by the Bolshevik revolution? – lies the basic explanation for the perpetual tendency of sectarian splits to develop. The group did not have to be large, but it was essential, as Lenin had repeatedly insisted, that it have a correct theoretical grasp of historical conditions and revolutionary tactics. Since these were open to a variety of interpretations, each of which was potentially of world-shaping importance in the eyes of its adherents, the splits often took on an acrimonious, fanatical tone. In his book *World Revolution*, James had sharply criticized even the murdered *Spartakists* for having failed to act with Leninist resoluteness.

We do not know the details of James-Johnson's life as the charismatic leader of a small radical sect; we do know, however, that following an intensive restudy of the historical dialectic as first formulated by Hegel, the Johnson-Forest Tendency repudiated not only Trotsky, but Lenin and the very idea of a vanguard party as a necessary or valid agent of social revolution! By 1950 James could write that "The great organizations of the masses of the people and of workers in the past were not worked out by any theoretical elite or vanguard . . . the new organizations will come as Lilburne's Leveller Party came, as the sections and popular societies of Paris in 1793, as the Commune in 1871 and the Soviets in 1905, with not a single soul having any concrete ideas about them until they appeared in all their power and glory."[49] But if this were so, what was the point of continuing, for example, the Johnson-Forest Tendency – or any other radical group? Apparently it required, as the nineteenth century Russian Populists had urged, going "back to the people."

> Jimmy developed the theory [the writer was told by an ex-disciple] that all proletarian parties had suffered from one fatal defect: namely, the intellectuals were always telling the workers what was going on in the world. This, he argued, was completely cockeyed because it was obviously the workers who, being closest to the system of production, were first exposed to the imminent changes resulting from changing patterns of production. Therefore he maintained that the intellectuals should shut up and listen to the workers for a change. He firmly believed that was the only way we could find out what was going on. So the group was divided into what we called 'layers.' The real proletarians were put in the first layer; people of mixed status, like housewives, in the second; and the intellectuals were put in the third layer. Our meetings consisted of the now highly-prestigeful first layer spouting off, usually in a random, inarticulate way about what they thought about everything under the sun. The rest of us, especially we intellectuals in the third layer, were told to listen.

The workers not only had the floor at cell meetings, but in Detroit the group also founded a periodical of worker opinion entirely produced by workers themselves. It was a remarkable experiment. (Had a reading of Heidegger's insistence on truth as accessible through everyday *dasein* influenced James? It is possible.) In any event, he had travelled the road from revolutionary elitism to proletarian populism. The latter, surely, was most consistent with his Trinidad background and temperament.

Somewhere in the course of his American sojourn, J. R. Johnson discovered Herman Melville, and he lectured widely on the social meaning of the great American novelist's works. Perhaps James's fervent and poetic view of the world is best summarized in a passage from the introduction to his Melville study, *Mariners, Renegades and Castaways:*

> The totalitarian madness which swept the world first as Nazism and now as Soviet Communism; the great mass labor movements and the colonial revolts; intellectuals drowning in the incestuous dreams of psychoanalysis – this is the world the masses of men strive to make sense of. This is what Melville coordinates – but not as industry, science, politics, economics, or psychology, but as a world of human personalities, living as the vast majority of human beings live, not by ideas, but by their emotions, seeking to avoid pain and misery and struggling for happiness.[50]

In 1952 James was caught in the very totalitarian madness which he thought Captain Ahab had foreshadowed and was sent to Ellis Island for deportation back to England. Williams, in the meantime, had left the United States in 1948 under more auspicious circumstances. From his position as consultant on Caribbean affairs while he was at Howard, he was drawn into full-time work for the Anglo-American Caribbean Commission, and thus, he later wrote, was given an opportunity to be of practical service to the area and community of his origin. He soon became Deputy Chairman of the Commission, in charge of the research division in Port of Spain. There, in 1952, Lloyd Braithwaite was completing his field study of the class system of his native island and noted that the traditional attraction of the Trinidad middle class to a charismatic leader was well exemplified in the way that Dr. Eric Williams was being lionized.[51]

CHAPTER 5 Trinidad in Transition —1935–1955

Rum and Coca-Cola; go down Point Cumana,
Both mother and daughter working for the Yankee Dollar.
— Lord Invader, 1941

During the third week of June, 1955, two Oxford University graduates who would play key roles in altering the political structure of Trinidad & Tobago reached, almost simultaneously, a climactic point in their respective careers. One was a black intellectual who had just lost his job. Eric Williams, Ph.D., announced before a mass audience in Woodford Square on the evening of the twenty-first, just four hours after he had ceased to be Deputy Chairman of the Caribbean Commission, that he would "let down his bucket" in Trinidad despite the possibility of attractive employment outside the colony. The other Oxford graduate was Sir Edward Betham Beetham, K.C.M.G., C.V.O., O.B.E., newly appointed "Governor and Commander-in-Chief in and over the colony of Trinidad & Tobago" who was capping his many years of service to the administration of the British colonies. On June twenty-third he arrived in Port of Spain aboard the *S.S. Cottica,* and after brief welcoming ceremonies at the quay he and Lady Beetham were escorted to the Legislative Council chamber in Red House where the notables of the colony, in accordance with long-established ritual, had assembled to greet and address him on the state of his domain.[1]

Governor Beetham, who would be the last British Governor of the colony, was no stranger to the West Indies. He had just completed three years of service as Governor of the Windward Islands, and thus, while he may have been, as the West Indians say, "a bird of passage" through this his final post before retirement, he was already versed in some of the complexities of the area's politics. None of the territories of the British Caribbean, however, had a more complex social and political structure than had Trinidad & Tobago, and it had undergone rapid changes during the preceding twenty years.

First there had been the mass demonstrations begun in the oilfields in 1937 by a Grenadian immigrant lamed in an oilfield accident, Uriah

Butler – demonstrations which ushered in a period of labor uprisings throughout the West Indies and led to the establishment of a royal commission to investigate the social conditions of the islands. This commission, headed by Lord Moyne (assassinated a few years later in Egypt by Zionist terrorists), produced findings which were withheld from publication during the war because of the conditions of extreme deprivation which they depicted. After the war, however, the Moyne commission report was a key document in triggering the decision implemented in Montego Bay in 1947: that the West Indies should be set on the road toward Dominion status under a federal form of government. In the meantime, in 1940, a celebrated real estate transaction had been concluded between Prime Minister Churchill and President Roosevelt in which the latter obtained a number of military bases in the West Indies in exchange for several dozen antiquated warships. The Yankees then descended on Trinidad in force, building airstrips and a major naval installation at the excellent deep-water harbor at Chaguaramas Bay. "The American Occupation," as this period is called in Trinidad, brought about a tremendous acceleration in the exposure of Trinidadians to the outside world. Tens of thousands of local people were employed in the construction and maintenance of the wartime facilities. The white American and Canadian military personnel, while criticized for their Jim Crow racial attitudes and for the military expropriation of some of the best recreational areas near Port of Spain, created something of a boom times atmosphere in the island. They drank great quantities of rum and Coca-Cola with local ladies of easy virtue at Point Cumana, not far from the entrance to Chaguaramas, where an observant calypsonian noted that both mother and daughter were working for the Yankee dollar. Prostitution and organized vice flourished under the entrepreneurial skill of Boysie Singh, zoot-suiter and later mass murderer, who considerably enhanced Trinidad's reputation as a Caribbean fleshpot, a vastly inflated stereotype of the island nonetheless cherished and perpetuated by some as part of the national self-image.

On the positive side, however, the American occupation provided considerable employment and income for the local population. The writer encountered many Trinidadians who looked back on the war years as times of relative prosperity; moreover, as Braithwaite has observed, the spectacle of foreign white men engaged *en masse* in manual labor in connection with military construction tended to break down the aura of superiority and automatic deference previously accorded persons with a white skin.[2] The U.S. Navy Seabees, with the assistance of local laborers, undertook major public works projects, chiefly in road construction; a North Coast road to Maracas Bay was built to offset the recreational facilities lost at Chaguaramas. American efficiency and know-how, easy money and exposure to the attitudes of wartime affluence, North American racial attitudes – these were the mixed influences to which Trinidad was subjected during the war years which led to the formation of ambivalent, somewhat condescending, but generally favorable attitudes toward the Yankees on the part of the local population.

And in 1945 occurred an event of the utmost significance in the social life of the colony: the steelband movement was born. Like the origins of calypso, the precise origins of the steelband are not known. Some local authorities date its evolution from the immediate pre-war years; others maintain that it emerged after the war when the wartime suspension of Carnival was lifted. What is certain, however, is that the modern multi-octave, finely tuned "pans" which are the pride of Trinidad were not developed until the post-war period, using as raw material the 50-gallon oil barrel. Every district, almost every neighborhood, would acquire its own steelband. The rippling finesse of the tenor pans, the deep pulsation of the bass pans – a sound impossible to capture even with the best recording equipment – in a matter of a few years took their place alongside the calypso as an integral, Creole musical tradition. District Carnival bands would now be organized behind such famous early steelbands as the Woodbrook Invaders, whose leader, Ellie Manette, is generally credited with some of the major breakthroughs in the development of the instrument. The majority of the early steelbands were from lower class districts, and the old neighborhood rivalries of the *jamettes* and stickfighters were resurrected in the steelband wars which began to rage, particularly at Carnival. This gave the steelbands a bad name among the middle classes and in official society, and several years passed before their true artistic worth was recognized.

By 1946 the war was over and most of the American troops of occupation were withdrawn, although the bases, in accordance with the negotiated 99-year lease, were retained in deactivated or semi-activated status. Now came the era of universal suffrage with its radical but confusing array of splinter parties and politicians. Butler, who had been tricked, captured, and then imprisoned by the British early in the war, emerged as a popular hero and the leader of the most successful campaign in the elections of 1946, but his radical minority party with its demands for "home rule" and nationalization of major industries was not invited by the Governor to participate in the formation of the Executive Council. Nonetheless, the proletarian movement led by Butler and the apparent leftward movement of European politics in the immediate post-war period provided a setting for the emergence of a few middle class radicals who attempted to link up their more sophisticated socialism with the mass movement. The attempt proved abortive.

Writes Morley Ayearst of this period of groping middle-class radicalism:

> Even the more serious attempts to base a permanent party upon a political philosophy were not successful. The West Indies National Party, for example, was founded at San Fernando in south Trinidad in November, 1943, by Dr. David Pitt who had been elected previously to the San Fernando Borough Council as a socialist. The W.I.N.P. was organized as a socialist party and in its early history grew rapidly in importance and attracted the allegiance of a number of Trinidad's active politicians. Some of its candidates were elected to municipal councils but it never managed to organize a corps of voters whose first loyalty would be to the party. Successful W.I.N.P. candidates owed election to personal qualities rather than to party designation. Lacking an island-wide following, the W.I.N.P. tried to ally itself with organized labour under the name of United Front. Some union leaders came in but the best-known of all, T. U. Butler, refused to do so. Only three U.F. candidates were successful in the elections of 1946. These included two W.I.N.P. members, Dr. Patrick Solomon, a coloured physician, and Roy Joseph, a Syrian with a large personal following in San Fernando. The other was Albert Gomes, an ex-socialist and trade unionist of Portuguese descent who had been expelled from the W.I.N.P. but who joined the U.F. and gained celebrity by defeating the famous Butler. The euphemeral nature of parties at this time is indicated by the fact that in 1950 all three U.F. candidates again sought election but under different designations. Gomes was now sponsored by the Party of Political Progress Groups, a rather conservative, middle-class organization. Dr. Solomon was now president of the Caribbean Socialist Party, successor to W.I.N.P., and Roy Joseph ran as an independent.[3]

The mainspring of the United Front was Jack Kelshall, a local white barrister of distinguished ancestry (his father, as a nominated member of the LegCo, had frequently crossed swords with Cipriani), who had just returned from service as a member of the R.C.A.F. The West Indies National Party had opened a branch in British Guiana during the war and Kelshall, when political developments under the P.N.M. a decade later proved disappointing, moved to the nearby mainland colony where he became private secretary to his friend and political confrere, Dr. Cheddi Jagan. Dr. Pitt, on the other hand, had left Trinidad and gone to England where he became an (unsuccessful) Labour Party candidate to the House of Commons! Some of those who had been associated with the West Indian National Party viewed it as a possible Trinidad nucleus of a Marxist movement to be associated with the Jagans in British Guiana and with the Hart faction in the left wing of Manley's Jamaican P.N.P. Nothing very tangible in an organizational sense ever developed from this perspective; communications between the various Marxist groups seems to have been infrequent, and the suspension of British Guiana's constitution in 1953 was a blow to the development of an area-wide Marxist leadership from that quarter.[4]

Captain Cipriani had died in 1945 and so did not live to see the advent of the era of universal suffrage. During the late Thirties the aging nationalist warrior had indicated his disapproval of the tactics of mass demonstration initiated by Butler, demonstrations which were not, and could not, be free of violence, including one notorious incident in which a despised police official in south Trinidad had been doused with gasoline and burned alive. A major difference between Cipriani and Butler was that the former had begun by defending a semi-industrial "barefooted man" while Butler came out of the highly industrialized oilfield regions during the trough of economic depression fifteen years later and led men who were not only barefooted, but hungry as well. The immediate post-war political climate, therefore, was very much to the left; but it was a divided and disorganized left. Trade unionists competed with middle class radicals for the same ballot. When in the 1946 elections the leaders of two of the islands' major unions were defeated at the polls, it could be interpreted as only a technical defeat for labor because their victorious opponents were equally pro-labor.[5] The 1950 elections, moreover, did not see any consolidation of the forces of individual politicians and splinter parties. If anything, the state of affairs became even more fragmented. Butler was obviously the logical popular hero around whom the radical forces might unite, and he did attract to his ranks several young East Indian professional men; but he lacked finesse, organizational ability and the education which might have attracted a wider middle class following. "Buzz" Butler was a showman-politician; a hymn-singing, charismatic rabble-rouser of whom practically everyone was fond, but the Chief Servant himself seemed to many too quixotic to form the basis for building a unified left party. These, at any rate, are the impressions formed from interviews with persons who had collaborated with Butler, and some who might have but did not.

Another divisive tendency in the politics which developed after the beginning of the universal suffrage, and which inhibited the development of actual labor politics, was the increasing tendency of the Hindu voters to cast their ballots on the basis of ethnicity. This development was enhanced by a swelling sense of ethnic pride which accompanied the achievement of national independence by India after the war and precipitated a renaissance of enthusiasm for Indian culture. By the early 1950's this regeneration of Indian culture received a forceful, organized character with the emergence of Bhadase Sagan Maraj, who had accumulated a fortune in the disposal of surplus war goods from the American bases, as a strong leader of the Hindu community. As president of the chief Hindu cultural organization, the Sanatan Dharma Mahasabha, through acts of direct personal philanthropy, and by initiating the construction of Hindu schools, Bhadase Maraj acquired a wide following among a people who still placed high value on the *praja* relationship, on the traditional Hindu bond of mutual obligation between the powerful and the weak. Maraj and his successors to political leadership of the Hindu population thus transformed major sections of the sugar belt into an ethnic vote bloc.

The arrival of Bhadase Maraj as political boss of the Hindu community was symptomatic of the chief structural factor inhibiting the development of political parties with a broad mass base. Despite the official multi-racial nationalist outlook inaugurated by Cipriani, the social structure and basic group loyalties which characterized Trinidad society were made to order for the development of splinter parties. Crowley, for example, in his analysis of the Trinidad social structure, concluded that there were no less than *13 largely endogamous ethnic enclaves* in the early 1950's. Braithwaite's study of social stratification in the colony during the same period, although it excluded the East Indians, also provides a highly differentiated portrait of the dominant Negro-European class system. As adapted from Crowley and Braithwaite, a composite model of the Trinidad social structure during the decade preceding independence might be drawn as in Figure 1 on the following pages.

No diagram can do justice to the degree of plural acculturation and racial permutations which Trinidad had acquired by this time. Nonetheless, the basically pluralist dichotomy between two major social orders can be safely posited. The Negro social pyramid, as discussed earlier, arose first. The chief means of mobility were through the professions and the civil service. At this time Dr. Eric Williams, while he was at the Carribbean Commission, would have ranked in the upper strata of the Negro pyramid. However, since the time he had left Trinidad to spend fifteen years abroad, significant changes in the lowly position of the East Indians had begun to take place. They had begun to move out of exclusively agricultural occupations into industrial and clerical work; capital initially acquired through land ownership was beginning to be converted into mercantile and industrial channels. The traditional Creole view of East Indians as third-class citizens was about to receive a sharp jolt.

FIGURE 1. Trinidad Social Structure in the Early 1950's

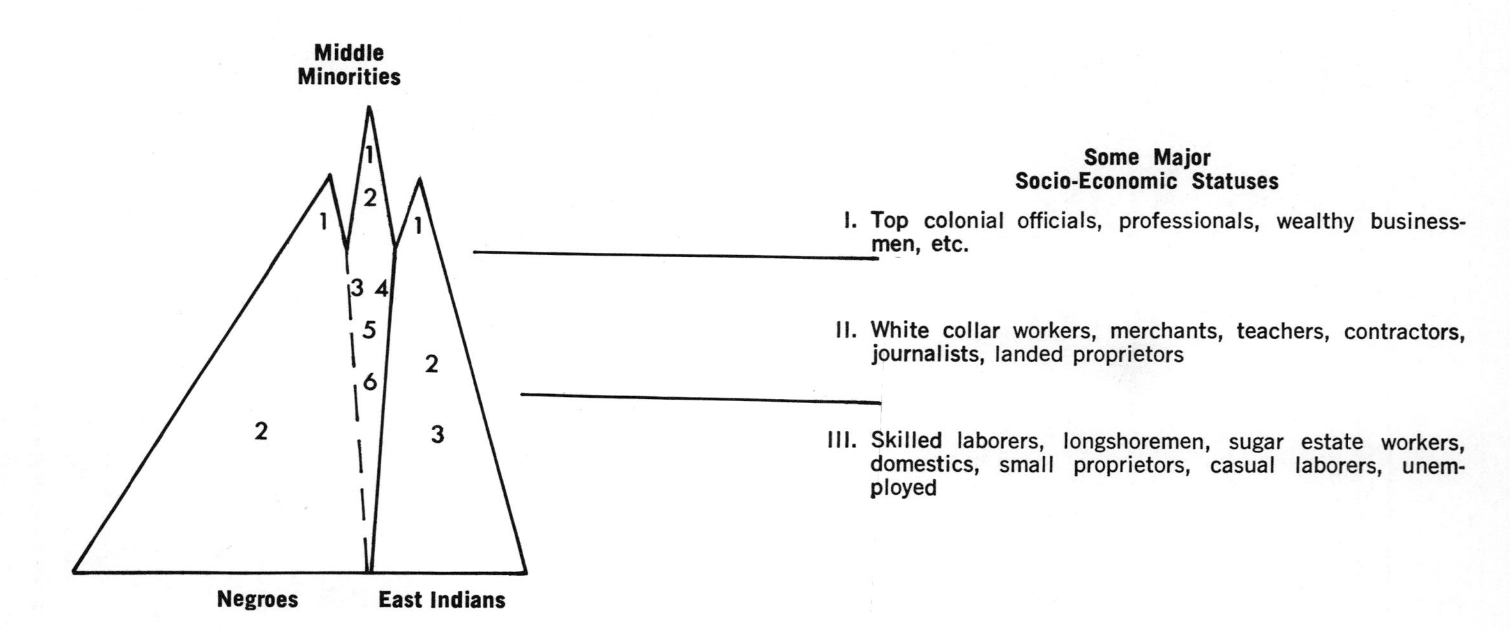

Major Ethnic Distinctions[6]

Negroes

1. "COLOREDS" of both French and English origin; former Roman Catholic, latter chiefly Anglican and Methodist. Traditional colored middle class, some drawn from smaller islands, especially Barbados. Range from Supreme Court justice through planters, civil servants, professional men, shop clerks. Members of this group may or may not feel a sense of identity with "Creole" folk culture.
2. NEGROES or CREOLES, black lower and lower-middle class. Predominantly Roman Catholic, Anglican and other revivalist sects.

Middle Minorities

1. FOREIGN WHITES, including Governor and top aides, U.S. Naval officers, Canadian oilfield employees, Irish and Flemish priests, Scottish Canefield Overseers.
2. LOCAL WHITES, mainly "French Creoles" representing Roman Catholic elite, and ranging occupationally from planters and landowners through businessmen and bank clerks.
3. CHINESE AND CHINESE-CREOLES, Anglican and Roman Catholic, some major business families, but chiefly small shopkeepers.
4. PORTUGUESE, often of Maderian origin; Presbyterian, ranging from a wealthy rum distiller through businessmen, politicians, small shopkeepers.
5. a) VENEZUELANS and other "Spanishy" locally born people, b) SYRIANS, LEBANESE and a few EUROPEAN JEWS, chiefly shopkeepers, drygoods merchants, street peddlers.
6. "DOOGLAS" (Hindi word meaning "bastard"), Indian-Negro mixed bloods; not a distinct endogamous group as those listed above tend to be.

East Indians

1. CHRISTIAN converts have had greatest opportunity for mobility; include politicians, clergymen, civil servants, a few still engaged in traditional estate labor — rice cultivation livelihoods.
2. MOSLEMS, sometimes distinguished by lighter skin color and Armenoid features. Cluster in cities and towns as shopkeepers, includes a few professional men, many small farmers and some cane laborers.
3. HINDUS, largest group in Indian community, second in size only to lower class Negroes. Chiefly poor rural laborers. Caste lines, both real and assumed, still carry weight; high caste include leading businessmen, politicians, small shopkeepers. Also, taxi drivers and lower caste laborers.

Note: Position of numbers within the diagram should not be taken to mean that all members of a particular ethnic group occupy the indicated socioeconomic level. There are obviously many lower class Christianized Indians, numerous upper class Hindus and Negroes and lower class Chinese and Portuguese. "Dooglas" may appear at any level, and often do. The diagram represents a very gross approximation of the overall structure in the 1950's, and continuous mobility in ensuing years has blurred many of these distinctions.

The acquisition of wealth by poor East Indians has long been a favorite topic of speculation in Trinidad. Some have argued that the East Indians came from a civilization which understood the social value of money; others have suggested that Indian family organization has been much more tightly knit than the looser Creole system of matrimony and thus has provided a social base for investment and accumulation. From early indentured times Trinidad commentators noted the Indian passion for thrift, a laudable trait which was held up for the spendthrift Creoles to emulate. A few years ago an American anthropologist, Walter Mischel, conducted a psychological field experiment testing the difference between Indians and Creoles in their capacity to defer gratification. Mischel argued that the greater security in father-child relations inherent in the more stable Indian family would make Indian children more prone to accept an experimental promise of a greater future gift in place of a smaller immediate gift; conversely, he anticipated that the instability of father-child relations in the Creole community, and the relative absence of a male authority figure, produced a greater tendency among Negro youths to take the immediate gift rather than to chance the wait for the promised larger one. This ingenious experiment, carried out with Negro and Indian school children, generally confirmed the hypothesis that children from fatherless homes, particularly Creole homes, were much more inclined to take the proffered immediate gift.[7] These findings, supporting the cultural stereotypes which inspired the study, are interesting and lend credence to the popular interpretation stressing the role of the Indian family in fostering the motivational structure conducive to the accumulation of wealth.

And while Indians had advanced into business, they were also making rapid strides in achieving professional status. A few statistics are suggestive. In 1952 there were 131 barristers and solicitors bearing European names residing in Trinidad, who had been admitted to practice since 1920 (and therefore could be assumed to be still relatively active). It is difficult to estimate how many in this group were Negroes, but certainly the majority of them were. Of these, 54 had been admitted to practice before 1941; 77 had begun practice in the eleven years following. Now, what about the East Indians? The figures for practitioners in the legal profession with Indian names were these: 13 had been admitted to practice between 1920 and 1940, and 22 had been admitted thereafter. Considering that the East Indians numbered only slightly over one-third of the population, and particularly considering their disadvantageous educational opportunities, the rate of their entry into the legal profession from 1941 to 1952 was certainly on a par with that of the Creole community. The statistics on the emergence of East Indian physicians are even more striking: of those in practice in the colony in 1954, only 6 had been licensed before 1941, but in the following thirteen years no fewer than 26 entered practice. To be sure, during the same period, 102 practitioners with European names were licensed, but here again the ratio of emerging Indian professionals is almost holding its own in relation to the size of the East Indian population.[8] Though they retained exclusivist loyalties, and though they could most certainly be viewed as an ethnic group which tended to be largely endogamous, the traditional country "Coolie" had clearly produced sons who had reached educational heights attained by the Creoles, and who had excelled them by far in business enterprises. By 1955, then, the Indian middle class included not only professionals, but members of the commercial classes who took their place in the councils of the Chamber of Commerce, thus establishing a bond of mutual interest with the local white commercial elite. This bond, vaguely foreshadowed during Major Wood's visit in the 1920's, would soon take the form of a tentative political coalition against what both groups professed to perceive as the rising tide of black totalitarianism.

As shown in Figure 1, wedged between the Indian and Negro middle class were several ethnic minorities which might be termed "middle minorities" by virtue of the fact that they were mainly middle class and belonged to neither of the two major racial groups. These groups, particularly below the level of the local whites, occupied a strategic position in the social structure because, although many of them had been strongly creolized, as indicated by the broken line dividing them from the Negroes in Figure 1, they were viewed as neither Negro nor Indian, nor as occupying the same exalted plane as the white elite. Moreover, they were not primarily identified with either the mainly Negro professions or the civil service, and they could move fairly easily between a number of milieux while retaining their separate identity. Because of their marginal social position and knowledge of the workings of commerce, they were potentially ideal brokers and emissaries between the two major and sharply-split social factions, and could use their perceived independence in dealings with the white elite.

The most notable instance in which one of this group played the broker's role to the hilt was the case of Albert Gomes, a Portuguese of intelligence, oratorical power, and legendary girth. He was *the* leading politician in Trinidad from 1950 to 1956, holding several major portfolios simultaneously, and he was generally regarded as Chief Minister in all but name. Gomes knew the business world well, and since he had begun his career as a trade unionist, and had initially been elected to the Legislative Council as a candidate of the socialist United Front, he was able to attempt to mediate in the troubled relations between business and labor. During the course of the early 1950's, however, it was becoming evident to many of his former associates among the colony's trade unionists and socialists that Gomes was using his Ministerial prerogatives on the side of the employers. In 1952, when the president of the Oil Workers' Trade Union, John Rojas, had indicated his union's preference for affiliation with the international Communist trade union organization, the Gomes government summoned a British trade unionist, F. W. Dalley, C.B.E., to make an investigation of the situation. Dalley, among his other activities, found time to deliver a lecture to the West Indian Methodist Synod on "Methodism and Trade Unionism" and concluded his report with an appendix on "Communism as a Religion" in which the evils of Marxist class struggle were exposed.[9] Another one-time admirer of Gomes, Ulric Lee, the youthful chief organizer of the clerical workers, became disillusioned when Gomes apparently sided with powerful commercial interests during an attempt to organize a local insurance company. Lee later joined the P.N.M. and became Dr. Williams' chief personal assistant and go-between after having personally unseated Gomes in the election of 1956.

Lee would play an intermediary role perhaps partially because he, like Gomes, was a member of one of the middle minorities, the Chinese Creoles. And it was hardly a coincidence that Governor Beetham's successor, the first West Indian to be Governor of a British colony, would be Solomon Hochoy, a career civil servant of Chinese extraction. Thus, these men in the middle of the major divisions of Trinidad society, while small in number, nonetheless played in a few key instances a role in facilitating social communication, and to some extent, social integration. On the whole, however, the political involvement of members of these small ethnic enclaves remained slight; for the most part they remained aloof from political struggles and tended to their business affairs.

The formal system of rule which greeted Governor Beetham was that of "tutelary democracy," a mixture of ultimate metropolitan supremacy, status and interest representation, and mass democracy. The symbol and embodiment of metropolitan supremacy was the person of the Governor himself, whose ultimate recourse to ruling by naked force, if by some mischance the peace of the colony was threatened, was to summon, as had been done during the Butler demonstrations of the Thirties, troops and warships loyal to the Crown. The chief formal policy body of the government was the Executive Council, over which the Governor presided. The Executive Council was in theory, and by 1955 to some extent in practice, a proto-Cabinet in which were mixed three principles of representation. First of all, there were three official members drawn from the upper echelons of the government establishment; secondly, a prominent member of the local community nominated by the Governor; thirdly, five elected politicians who had been selected to act as Ministers in charge of various branches of government. Who the official members should be was prescribed in the constitution of 1950, and the Ministries which should be represented were also prescribed, but the Governor was legally free to select for Ministerial posts either his own appointees or the elected members to the Legislative Council.

This is not the place for a lengthy analysis of the different types of colonial administration which were employed by the British during their long tenure in the West Indies, but it is necessary to describe the main outlines of the formal process by which power was being slowly transferred to the local inhabitants of Trinidad & Tobago in order to obtain a general appreciation of the point in that evolution which had been reached by 1955. The introduction of the principle of election to the central Legislature, albeit on a severely limited franchise occurred, as discussed earlier, after World War I. But this concession to the radical middle class opinion of the time in no way altered the essential hegemony of the expatriate administrators who, in league with upper class, local white civil servants and business interests, constituted a white, hereditary ruling caste. Although an occasional man, or even woman, of color might be nominated to the LegCo, and although a few talented local colored professionals established reputations for sound views and were called upon to serve the public interest in some major official capacity, the local aristocrats of color and position were not dedicated to the proposition of the self-liquidation of imperial control with any noticeable enthusiasm. And while Cipriani had influenced legislative deliberations on a few issues in an apparently important way, he tended to be regarded by his social peers among the colonial expatriates as at least a black sheep, if not actually a traitor to his class and race.

The great divide in Trinidad and West Indian history came in the Thirties when it became clear that the old system of elite control was no longer workable and could no longer assure social stability. The British, it seems fair to say, were not inflexibly committed to the principle of Crown Colony rule *per se;* what they became most concerned with was a *modus vivendi* by which their paramount economic interests – in Trinidad, petroleum, sugar and finance – could be best safeguarded. They were, moreover, committed to the notion that the responsibilities of trusteeship required the maintenance of "good government," and this required at least the passive acquiescence of the local population to the established laws of the colony. Uriah Butler's role in accelerating a change in Trinidad's political status was literally to demonstrate, as Cipriani had never done, that the old system of laws and the process by which they were determined were no longer adequate to insure social stability and a relatively peaceful, on-going social order. The major battle for the extension of parliamentary institutions to the colony was fought and won in the late Thirties, and what came after were essentially protracted rear-guard actions by which the local ruling class, motivated by a defense of their traditional privileges and fearful of the radical proclamations of the rising politicians – for a time abetted by a fearful Indian minority – sought to delay the inevitable transfer of political power which the granting of universal suffrage in 1946 heralded. During this period the major task of British administration was to gradually phase-in the power of elected politicians and to construct a parliamentary system along the British model, by means of which the conflicting values and interests of the society could be peacefully negotiated – all the while keeping a sharp eye on the investments of the metropolitan country in the area.

Thus the period under review here was a time in which British colonial administrators, in collaboration with local parliamentarians who were chiefly British-educated barristers, introduced a gradual series of constitutional reforms during the course of which the legal forms of government were brought successively closer to the British model. The *sine qua non* of the model was a cabinet system of government responsible to a fully-elected lower house which ideally would be composed of a majority party cohesive and disciplined enough to assure the enactment of legislation, and a strong opposition party to serve as a watchdog of the national interest and prepared to offer the nation an alternative government on short notice. All of this was, of course, elementary and self-evident to the colonial administrators and their local colleagues who attempted to re-draft a traditionally authoritarian constitution in order to increasingly fulfill the ideal criteria of British parliamentary democracy. By 1955 Trinidad had experienced two transitional colonial constitutions under mass suffrage and was preparing to embark on a third. The constitution of 1950 had established the principle of Ministerial responsibility in the hands of elected politicians, and the juggling of the ratio of appointees of the Governor to the number of elected politicians holding executive responsibility was being increasingly weighted in favor of the latter.

But while voters and Ministers could be created by constitutional reform, political parties could not. The difficulty was not that Trinidadians had shown no enthusiasm for politics. Rather, as we have seen, individual politicians and special interest groups, particularly in the divided trade union movement, had been unable to unite for the purpose of creating an organized, disciplined political party capable of winning a majority of seats in the legislature. Such a party would not fully emerge until 1961 when the P.N.M. contested in general elections for the second time. The P.N.M.'s showing in the elections of 1956 – 39% of the total vote – was impressive, but, as will be seen, in order to obtain a secure majority to the legislature the party required the collaboration of Governor Beetham and the Colonial Office in the appointment of nominated members of the legislature who were loyal to the P.N.M. The achievement of Dr. Eric Williams, therefore, was not in persuading the colonial authorities to institute parliamentary democracy, although he would certainly agitate for a complete transfer of power as quickly as feasible, but rather in forging a majority party for the first time.

Recognizing the need for at least the appearance, if not the actuality, of a Government-versus-Opposition legislature, the LegCo elected in 1950 had dutifully divided itself in order to simulate a two party system, with Butler leading the major faction in the opposition. The artificial nature of this working arrangement was exposed in 1954 when the principle of "collective responsibility" of the elected members of the Executive Council broke down on an important vote concerning adoption of the first constitution drafted in London for a West Indies Federation. An East Indian member of the Executive Council, accompanied by the elected East Indian members of the LegCo, opposed the plan because federation with the overwhelmingly Negro populations of the other West Indian islands had traditionally been a *bête noire* of the Indian community, whose reportedly higher birth rates had established the notion that they would eventually become the majority ethnic group in Trinidad.

British colonial policy in Trinidad therefore faced a number of difficulties and dilemmas in the transition to self-government. First, there was the question of whom to sponsor in the transitional period for political leadership. Albert Gomes had proved himself efficient and responsible, and a strong federationist, but he was drawn from a tiny marginal ethnic group and was rapidly losing his rapport with his former radical and trade unionist supporters. His appointment as *de facto* Chief Minister had the advantage of side-stepping the difficulties which might arise from the selection of either a Negro or East Indian for this position of eminence, but this situation was only made possible, if not necessary, by the fragmentation of the legislature into individual politicians and splinter parties. The East Indians – especially after Bhadase Maraj, with his reputation for shady deals and strong-arm methods entered the legislature, and after they had demonstrated definite opposition to the master plan of federation for the area – were not likely heirs for the slipping mantle of official responsibility. Finally, there was the radical lower class threat, represented in the form of Uriah Butler and his endless, often almost incomprehensible harangues in the legislature. What had failed to materialize in Trinidad, as had emerged in predominantly Negro islands like Barbados and Jamaica in the aftermath of the turmoil of the Thirties, were cohesive, middle-class-led parties enjoying substantial trade union and lower class support.

Until such a time the individual broker-politician would be in his heyday in Trinidad, maneuvering and negotiating between the established but waning political power of the old colonialists and the groups of elected politicians and special interests who were dividedly contending for a place in the sun. It was, the new P.N.M. politicians would charge, the era of the "Deal" – not the old, ordered, authoritarian deal meted out under Crown Colony rule, and not the democratic, honest, New Deal for the masses (the announced mission of the P.N.M.) – but rather the manipulative, back-room, and sometimes corrupt deal of opportunist politicians ready and able to seize personal advantage in the confused transition from one system of political authority to the next. The old order was dying – that much was certain. Indeed, in the West Indies it became increasingly impatient with the protracted death agonies it suffered while attempting to arrange for the disposition of its historic political estate and to place in reliable hands the protection of its economic investments in the region.

New political rumblings of uncertain portent could be heard during Governor Beetham's first week in spacious Government House. Eric Williams had made a tour through the slum of "John-John" and had pronounced it the worst he had ever seen, a national scandal. But, across town, life in the colonial establishment went on as usual. The Colonial Secretary, Mr. Maurice Dorman, held a small cocktail party in honor of the new Governor. The Roman Catholic Archbishop was there, as was the Church of England Bishop and his wife; the Chief Justice was on hand, and business was represented in the imposing figure of George de Nobriga (who would later be characterized as a leading "die-hard" defender of the old order by the P.N.M.). Also in attendance were the members of the Executive Council and the Governor's appointees to the LegCo. If any of the ordinary elected members of the legislature were honored with an invitation, which is unlikely, their presence was not mentioned by the *Guardian's* society page chronicler. Who knows? Perhaps they had been excluded from this polite society on the grounds that they were thought to comport themselves too much along the lines of the vulgar, gauche, lower class politicians later portrayed by Vidia Naipaul in *The Mystic Masseur*.[10] The next day the Governor attended the summer race meeting at the Savannah, and on Sunday he rounded out his first week of official duties by following Mr. Dorman in reading the second lesson at Matins in the Anglican Holy Trinity Cathedral.

CHAPTER 6 Founding the University of Woodford Square

Thy gift o'vrflows and nourishes our land,
Great genius, scholar, teacher — of this age.
The world's your audience, our nation your stage,
Vessel of rare clay moulded by God's hand.
Cease not to share with us thy wealth — oh man
Whose knowledge is from God a heritage.
Master builder . . . historian — noble sage,
Daunt not thy pow'r to lead and understand.
Resplendent star, that shines above the rest
Of thy contemporaries; great and small.
Pour out, "dark Moses" — louder still thy best
That no more into bondage may we fall.
And never let thy labours seek vain rest.
But in thy wisdom live, and lead us all.

— "Sonnet to Dr. Eric Williams"[1]

No real grasp of Trinidad politics in the last years of the colonial period can be achieved without understanding the bases of the charismatic authority wielded by Dr. Eric Williams. It was the *deus ex machina* which propelled the independence movement forward, revolutionized the political life of the colony almost overnight, and shattered the complacency of the sputtering transition to self-government. The central institution, the symbol and embodiment of this process, was the University of Woodford Square, the direct charismatic bond established between Dr. Williams and the Negro masses of Trinidad & Tobago. Much of his power as an elected politician and his position of continuing supremacy within the political party that he organized resulted from the fact that he alone was the focal point of the aspirations and faith of the major ethnic group in the colony.

However, to paraphrase Marx, although historians may make history, even they cannot make it exactly as they please. Dr. Williams, it was widely believed, was the indispensable hero without whom the People's National Movement would disintegrate into rival factions based on the competing ambitions and interests of his lieutenants; but the limitations on his control over internal developments in the colony were decidedly formidable. The locus of charismatic authority is in the heart of the follower, and the Trinidad public was far from unanimous in its adoration of Dr. Eric Williams. The society was too highly differentiated culturally, and had lived too long under the traditional social divisions, to respond as one nation to the nationalist appeals of the aggressive Negro intellectual who burst onto the political scene in 1956. Nonetheless, for many Williams approached the status of philosopher-king, and here we will explore how and why Dr. Williams initially triggered the mass adulation which became the major weapon in his arsenal of power as a practical politician.

It began, appropriately enough, with a debate over the doctrines of a philosopher whom a Trinidad undergraduate at Oxford had once attacked as a dyed-in-the-wool reactionary: Aristotle.

Before Dr. Williams denounced some of Aristotle's political views at the Public Library in November of 1954 he had been a well-known and highly respected intellectual leader, particularly in some sections of the educated and "cultured" middle class, but he was by no means the public figure, the household word, that he became thereafter. In attacking Aristotle, Dr. Williams was in fact challenging the moral authority of the Roman Catholic Church, particularly on the question of church versus state control of education, which was, as we have seen, of ancient vintage in Trinidad. It was not surprising, therefore, that he would gain the allegiance of a number of local teachers who were acutely dissatisfied with the existing system of dual control; but what did come as a surprise to everyone was the unprecedented mass interest which developed in connection with his debate over Aristotle with a noted Catholic educator and sociologist, Dom Basil Matthews.

Dr. Williams had returned to Trinidad to live in 1948, two years after the first elections held under universal suffrage. In 1950, as was described in the last chapter, elections to a Legislative Council incorporating a ministerial system had been held. A fact of great significance which emerged from these elections was that although some members of the colored middle class were ready to join forces with the labor leaders who had come to the fore during the Thirties – as Williams had urged eight years before in *The Negro in the Caribbean* – newly-enfranchised labor, especially lower class Negro voters, did not leap at the opportunity of elevating their traditionally aloof middle class friends to the seats of power. The defeat of Dr. Patrick Solomon, leader of the Caribbean Socialist Party (which was allied with one of the most politically-conscious and advanced trade unions in the colony,

The Seaman and Waterfront Workers), and champion of popular causes in the Legislative Council since 1946, was taken by many as symptomatic of the precarious political popularity of the educated professional man. Braithwaite, who was on the ground at the time, interpreted the 1950 elections as indicating, in part, that the mass of lower class voters preferred candidates who gave the most convincing demonstrations of being *of* the people in addition to being *for* the people. Braithwaite wrote that Dr. Solomon's successful opponent ". . . cultivated the steelband movement and showed himself personally prepared to mix with the lower class by attending its functions."[2]

After the 1950 elections there appears to have developed a general mood of pessimism among many members of more educated, professionally-employed colored middle class. The prospects seemed poor for creating in Trinidad a responsible, educated political leadership such as Norman Manley symbolized in Jamaica and Grantley Adams in Barbados. The Trinidad Creole community lacked a middle class hero – a man who, like Manley and Adams, had emerged in times of social crisis to declare their common cause with the lower class at considerable personal risk and sacrifice. The chief political task of the aspiring middle class politician was, therefore, to build widespread mass support in a period which, compared to the trauma of the Thirties, provided very limited opportunities for decisive political gestures, or for dramatic and convincing demonstratons of solidarity with the common man. Dr. Eric Williams achieved this by founding a University, and he maintained his reputation by dramatizing the wickedness of the colonial system as symbolized by that doddering arch-foe of progress, Massa; by holding a ceremonial burning of The Seven Deadly Sins of Colonialism, followed by a March in the Rain to the American Consulate to demand the return of Chaguaramas; and, not least in importance, by giving the colony good government and by addressing mass audiences as if they were mature, educated citizens.

When he returned to Trinidad, Williams soon became involved in various public appearances in which he spoke on West Indian historical topics. As a son of the soil, now holding a high position in the prestigious Caribbean Commission, he was naturally in demand for forums and public lectures sponsored by culturally-conscious middle class organizations. From his vast knowledge of the West Indian past Williams lectured on the area's history and even attempted to explain the origins of some peculiar West Indian folkways. "He told us," said an early Williams supporter with devastating simplicity, "how we had become what we were." For many in these early lectures, Eric Williams opened a window on the West Indian past; later, when he was freed from the vows of apoliticism imposed by his affiliation with the Caribbean Commission, he would open a window on the future.

Eric Williams opened the window on the West Indian past and what he saw there mightily displeased him. A sorry political heritage of Crown Colony rule, economic stagnation under the reign of King Sugar, the social evils of race and color prejudice – all of these he indicted from his scholarly platform. One theme on which Williams repeatedly touched, which offended some, was what they viewed as Williams' retrogressive obsession with the Original Sin of West Indian history, namely, slavery. As a Negro (they argued and argue still), Williams harbored deep racial resentments; his status as an "ambitious black boy" in a career at home and abroad in which white men dominated had given him a warped historical perspective. Slavery had become his *idée fixe* and European supremacy some sort of obsession. Had not the real burden of *Capitalism and Slavery* been an elaborate effort aimed at undermining faith in the sincerity and moral scruples of the white Mother Country? As for slavery, they observed, it had been laid to rest over a hundred years ago; peace unto its ashes.

Such was a common early reaction to Williams' ventilation of the West Indian past among both colored and white who identified themselves with the leading institutions of the colonial society, and who had faith in the good will and sincere intentions of the colonial authorities to insure orderly political and social progress. For some, perhaps, the window on the past was also a closet door which opened on the family skeletons of a small local society, one of which was the historical memory of slave ownership. Another skeleton in the family closet which Williams disinterred during his historical discourse was the servitude of the East Indian indentured laborer, of which he spoke in stinging moral terms as having been tantamount to slavery. This theme of national solidarity, that Negroes and East Indians should be united because of a common heritage of suppression on the sugar estates, was repeated many times in Williams' nationalist speeches over the years; but it was a notion that some East Indian leaders found distasteful because, in their view, the voluntary indenture of the East Indian "pioneers" who had "rescued" the agricultural economy represented quite a distinct social species from the slave who after emancipation had turned his back on the land and cultivated his Creole passion for irresponsibility.

While Williams spoke of the heritage of slavery, *inter alia*, the impact of these disclosures on his Negro auditors must often have been profound. To cite just one example of many which I encountered among P.N.M. followers of slight formal education: After a series of excellent weekend lectures on emerging African nations given by Dr. Williams and other P.N.M. leaders at a Port of Spain constituency headquarters shortly before independence, a number of party members rose to express their appreciation to the speakers for their comprehensive and thorough treatment of the subject. Trinidadians are firmly addicted to prolonged ceremonies in voting thanks to speakers at formal meetings, but these particular terminal ceremonies conveyed the degree to which ignorance and a vague sense of shame about Africa and the slave background of the Trinidad Creole were still a barrier to the achievement of a sense of personal dignity. One woman stepped to the front of the assembly and, in moving her vote of thanks to the speakers, noted in an emotional voice that before Dr. Williams had begun his lectures ten years earlier she and many others had actually believed that their African ancestors were subhuman animals living in the trees of the jungle. An official from the American consulate seated beside me quietly groaned, "Oh, gawd," at this exhibitionistic testimonial of how Dr. Williams had liberated the minds of his people; but from the murmurs of approval around the room it was clear that the woman expressed the sentiments of many in attendance. For many lower class Negroes, particularly Creole women, Dr. Williams was nothing less than a messiah come to lead the black children into the Promised Land. This messianic tradition had been firmly entrenched in the Butler movement and was an important basis of the P.N.M.'s mass support as well. As pro-P.N.M. placards announced during a political rally in San Fernando before the 1961 elections: "The Master Couldn't Come So He Sent Williams." The title, under a rough caricature of Williams, was "Moses II."

There can be little doubt that Williams' discussions of the historical origins of the slaves, the nature of the slave regime and economy, and the consequences of slavery, were important themes in stimulating the mass notoriety which projected him into politics. The degree to which this was a calculated political maneuver, rather than an unforeseen outcome of public lectures on a subject which had been the focus of his interests as a scholar, is impossible to say. My personal guess is that initial statements by Williams on this subject were not made with any particular political end in view, but once their political potency had been revealed he used them in a very shrewd manner as rallying symbols. On the one hand, he always denounced racial prejudice and affirmed the multi-racial convictions of the P.N.M., but on at least a few occasions at the University he insinuated racial undertones into his oratory. Perhaps the most notable instance of this technique was the speech, *Massa Day Done*, in which "Massa" meant not the white ruling class as such, but rather the colonial institutions over which they had traditionally maintained control. Nevertheless, for most of his auditors "Massa" had a very personal reference to the local whites. This interpretation of the latent racist appeals of Williams' oratory is not simply the independent judgment of one who has heard him speak on dozens of occasions over a three-year period, but is a view privately held by some in the top echelons of the P.N.M. leadership itself, and was certainly a criticism maintained by most P.N.M. opponents. The most charitable interpretation, perhaps, was given by a P.N.M. Cabinet member who said, "I think that very often it's not simply what Dr. Williams says, but rather what his followers *hear* that is the crucial point. Whatever he says, they believe, in their hearts, that he speaks principally for the Negroes." To which might be added one further point: the image of Williams as a racial messiah was not limited to the black lower class, although it was strongest there, but could be found in the Creole middle class as well. Among members of the latter, however, the belief in personal and collective salvation through Dr. Williams often shaded over into a more secular variant of the True Believer in which the *rationality* and *honesty* of the Doctor were so fervently espoused as to occasion the willing surrender of independent judgment and will, associated with an intense hostility to any form of criticism, direct or implied, of the Political Leader.

While in his early speeches Williams was acquiring something of a reputation in the Negro lower class, during this early period he also acquired the status of sage and seminar leader among some members of the colored middle class. At his home in the elite residential district on Lady Chancellor's Road he held evening adult education seminars which attracted a number of persons who would become his most active supporters when he prepared to enter politics. One such group in particular, calling itself *Bachacs* (a ferocious species of ant), contained several men who would later become P.N.M. Ministers. As one member of this group, Gerard Montano, later to become a P.N.M. Minister, recalled these meetings:

> We met to present papers on various social and economic problems and then tore each other's arguments apart. This was a stimulating exercise which probably got us nowhere except that we learned to appreciate the enormity of such issues as the population explosion, the need for industrialization, and so on. As an historian and as the man in charge of economic research at the Caribbean Commission, Dr. Williams had the answers to many of the questions we raised, and which were being asked by many thinking people since independence was clearly just a matter of time. But at one point I told him, 'Bill, you're a goddam fraud. You have made us aware of all these problems, but you don't put forward the solutions.' He replied that so long as he was with the Commission

he couldn't put forward any ideas publicly counter to those of Gomes and the other politicians of the time.

Another later-prominent P.N.M. member who never participated in one of these discussion groups, Ulric Lee, recalls having been taken to one by a visiting Canadian trade unionist. Afterwards he remarked to his companion, "When that man decides to enter politics I will support him." Thus, both formally and casually the research director at the Caribbean Commission, occupying a social status near the top of the Creole system of prestige, developed a diffuse popular reputation, a wide circle of middle class admirers, and a coterie of associates and disciples who participated in his study groups.

During these years, in 1950, he published *Education in the British West Indies*, which contained his prescriptions for a British West Indian University based on an historical analysis of West Indian society and a general survey of the development of university systems. This work was given the stamp of approval by no less an educator than John Dewey who provided a brief foreword. The study had actually been completed in 1946 before Williams had left the United States, and in the meantime the University College of the West Indies had already been established in Jamaica. Both the content of its major recommendations and the circumstances of its belated publication, however, were instrumental in beginning a collaboration between Williams and a group of local teachers and educators who had founded an organization known as T.E.C.A., the Teachers' Economic and Cultural Association, Ltd. It was T.E.C.A. which sponsored the publication of Williams' book on the university and in his introduction the Director General of the organization, D. W. Rogers, wrote that the undertaking was in accordance with general T.E.C.A. aims, which were described as ". . . the uplift of the people, the progress of the Teacher." Rogers' introduction, moreover, provides an indication of the prestige which Williams had already acquired in the community: "Dr. Williams is not an ivory tower intellectual or an academic snob. Since his return to Trinidad he has undertaken a vast program of public lectures and the writing of a series of newspaper articles in the field of adult education with emphasis on West Indian History. He is President of the Historical Society of Trinidad and Tobago . . . He is today what a prominent politician in Antigua has called him, 'the philosopher of West Indian Nationalism.' "[3] This was but the first major occasion on which T.E.C.A. served to boost the prestige of the scholar at the Caribbean Commission; more significant services would be given a few years later.

In his recommendations for the British West Indian University,

Williams had struck a strong nationalist note not only by urging that the plan of issuing an external degree from London University should be replaced by a local degree, but also by favoring locating the university in an urban area where it would be close to the everyday life of the community, and by insisting that students should be given the responsibility of making their own residential arrangements. The Oxonian argued for the establishment of an institution more along the lines of the pragmatic American university than according to the models of the traditional European centers of higher learning. "Education in the modern world is," he wrote in a preface which John Dewey heartily endorsed, "more than anything else, education of the people themselves as to the necessity of viewing their own education as a part of their democratic privileges and their democratic responsibilities."[4]

These sentiments also seem to have summarized well the basic aims of the T.E.C.A. educators, hence their affinity for Dr. Williams. On the basis of interviews with several of its early leaders – W. J. Alexander, D. W. Rogers, Donald Pierre – the following impressions of the organization's membership and objectives were gained: At the time of its foundation a number of younger teachers, who considered themselves to be more socially conscious than the average, came to the conclusion that the official teachers' union was moribund. A common complaint was that it had little support from the teachers and failed to give voice in a militant way to their grievances against the dual system of education. The system of dual control of church and state had produced, some felt, flagrant examples of the victimization of teachers who failed to toe the mark according to the wishes of the authorities, and, of course, there was always the question of attempting to raise salaries and improve working conditions. In addition, there were frequent conflicts between teachers and the denominational boards arising from diverging religious outlooks among teachers and administrators. White expatriate instructors and administrators, particularly in the Roman Catholic schools, were often alleged to discriminate against teachers and students on the basis of color. W. J. Alexander summarized their dissatisfaction with the system in this way: "We were the victims, *par excellence*, of colonialism. We wanted to organize the teachers effectively, to improve their lot economically while at the same time making a cultural contribution to the community." T.E.C.A. therefore included in its functions the encouragement of study groups and music festivals, and it even established a bookstore in Park Street in downtown Port of Spain. In a dingy little second-story loft of this store, according to a knowledgeable clerk, Dr. Williams and T.E.C.A. leaders had met to plot the strategy for the formation of the P.N.M.

In November of 1954, as the Legislative Council decided to take up the matter of further constitutional reform once again, Dr. Williams embarked on another series of lectures at the Public Library. The theme was a familiar one: "Some World Famous Educational Theories and Developments Relevant to West Indian Conditions." During the course of the lecture he quoted from Aristotle's *Politics* in defense of his main thesis, that state control of education was desirable. At question time, the noted local Catholic educator and Benedictine Monk, the Reverend Dom Basil Matthews – a tall, black, striking figure – rose to challenge Williams' citation of Aristotle in support of his argument. The distinguished Negro churchman, a Ph.D. from Fordham, took over the platform himself on November 9 to lecture on "Aristotle, Education and State Control" in rebuttal of the secular educator's argument. Given the longevity of the issue in Trinidad, its current repercussions in the teaching profession as just described, and the community stature of Dr. Williams and Dom Basil, the debate was clearly a major occasion in the intellectual life of the colony. The analogy to the Lincoln-Douglas debates seems curiously appropriate. Dom Basil unwittingly played Douglas to Williams' Lincoln in exchanges in which the institution of slavery figured prominently and which would elevate Williams, like Lincoln, to national political eminence.[5]

On November 17, Williams provided a rejoinder entitled "Some Misconceptions of Aristotle's Philosophy of Education" in which he charged, according to the *Guardian*, that Dom Basil's enthusiasm for Aristotle's ideal state concealed slavery, the exclusion of workers from citizenship, the subordination of women and imperialism! "Hundreds were storming the gates of the Public Library long before Dr. Williams was due . . .," the *Guardian* reporter noted. "When Dr. Williams arrived he had difficulty in getting through the hundreds who were pleading for admission to the already crowded Library. Some even suggested to Dr. Williams at the gates that he transfer the lecture to the Grand Stand at the Savannah or to Woodford Square."[6] Having initially cited Aristotle in support of his argument for state education, Dr. Williams appears to have nimbly turned the tables on Dom Basil by later attacking the philosopher. The following passage gives the flavor of the exchange:

> Dom Basil in his lecture said not so much as a whisper of the slave basis of Aristotle's state. I had to drag it out of him with a question. What was his reply? Listen to it as given in the Trinidad *Guardian*, 'slavery was sometimes necessary to the common good but that you could enslave men's bodies but not their minds' . . . The moral and religious

excellence of the life of the Greek citizen which Dom Basil so extolls is nothing more than the life of the slaveowner . . .[7]

While putting a spokesman of the Roman Catholic Church on the record as having publicly defended slavery must have created a sensation, there were some who were critical of what they regarded as Williams' casuistry and playing to the gallery. A letter published in the *Guardian* some months later voiced a common criticism made against Williams and his admirers. The writer accused Williams of descending ". . . to the most abysmal depths of cajolery in order to pander to the whims of his audience."

> Though at these lectures questions are invited, the honest questioner is somewhat chilled by the atmosphere which surrounds him. Who is so presumptuous as to question the 'Trinidad Oracle?' There is a sort of derisive tolerance which sometimes bristles into expressed irritation . . . This state of affairs was [so] pronounced during one of the Aristotle lectures that the Chairman, the Hon. Albert Gomes, had perforce, to threaten to end the series of lectures if questioners continued to be heckled . . . [As the audiences] leave the lecture hall they apostrophise him to the skies, 'Giant!, Master!' can be heard on all sides.[8]

Nonetheless, the writer of this letter conceded that Dr. Williams was responsible for "an intellectual awakening hitherto unknown," thus expressing an ambivalence toward Dr. Williams frequently encountered in Trinidad: wide approval of Williams' objectives coupled with hostility and even fear of what many viewed as his personal arrogance and ruthlessness and his encouragement of a fanatical following. In fairness to Williams, however, it should be pointed out that the celebrated Aristotle debates were closed by a suggestion from Williams that a collection be taken to purchase the philosopher's works for the library and that the chore be supervised by himself and Dom Basil.

A week later Williams gave the last lecture in the series, "Analysis of Recommendations of Education Commissions and Experts in Trinidad, 1869–1954," in which he once again presented the case for state control of education. As he wrote for the *Guardian* a few months later, "I see in the denominational school the breeding ground of disunity; I see in the state school the opportunity for cultivating a spirit of nationalism among West Indian people and eradicating the racial suspicions and antagonisms growing in our midst."[9] This final lecture was attended by 700 persons packed into the library, and a sizeable crowd, the first students in the yet-to-be-formed University, heard the proceedings relayed by loudspeakers to Woodford Square.

It seems probable that by this stage in his public appearances Dr.

Williams was contemplating some type of political action. In the midst of the debates his friend and T.E.C.A. leader, D. W. Rogers, wrote a letter to the *Guardian* in which he observed that a renaissance was taking place in Trinidad and the West Indies. "The apostle of this revival," he wrote, "is Dr. Eric Williams . . . people of all classes, professions, colours, races, flock to hear him." He congratulated the Gomes government for having recently consulted Williams on the problems of the sugar preference agreement and trade. "Yet," he continued, "this is not enough."

> Why not once a week lectures on problems facing our citizens on various aspects of what he calls the world cultural heritage? Why not a broad People's Education Movement centered around our Adult Education Forum for citizenship with Dr. Williams as its inspiration . . . This is not a panegyric, but a demand to make use of the man himself. When Dr. Winston Mahabir [a member, incidentally, of the *Bachacs* study group] made a similar demand at the library in moving a vote of thanks to him for his series of lectures, the audience left no one in doubt as to what it thought of the proposal.[10]

This was a straw in the wind. After his lecture the following evening, Dr. Williams was applauded when he suggested that members of voluntary organizations meet with him to discuss the formation of a nonpartisan committee for education in "Citizenship." "The Committee," Dr. Williams stated, "would undertake to promote further development of community consciousness, discussion of public affairs, and dispassionate inquiry by the people."[11] As a later-prominent P.N.M. official told the writer, "Anyone with eyes to see could deduce what was going on: they were preparing to form a political party."

Those preparations, however, would take another full year in coming to fruition. In the meantime, Williams rounded out his public speaking engagements in 1954 by addressing the Seaman and Waterfront Workers on the development of trade unionism, racial discrimination, and the need for workers to take part in government. Early in December the *Guardian* published a long, three-part letter from Williams in which he outlined his views on the formation of a British West Indies Federation. "I have," he observed, "since 1940, advocated publicly . . . the political Federation of the British West Indies as the first step towards the economic Federation of the entire Caribbean area." He recalled that, in an article published early in his career, he had envisaged a Pan-Antillean Federation based on a similar history, "racial origins," and the same economic curse. He had considered the possibility of two federations, one based on Trinidad, the other on Puerto Rico. He repeated his oft expressed conviction that "a Federation based on participation by the French, Spanish, English and Dutch including 15 million people would enable the economy of the whole area to be organized . . . Industrialization of Trinidad or Cuba or Haiti, each in isolation, is an absurdity . . ."[12] As for the desirability of an immediate federation of the British territories, he declared, citing Cipriani's slogan "Agitate, Educate, Confederate," ". . . any Federation is better than no Federation . . . *the Colonial Office should have imposed Federation on the West Indies*."[13] In December of 1954 also, Learie Constantine returned to Trinidad from his 30-year sojourn in the Mother Country. He came not to play cricket but to practice law, having just qualified for a barrister's degree, and thus to embark on a new career. He was employed by a petroleum firm and announced that he had no intention of entering politics. A year later he would be induced to become Chairman of the newly-founded P.N.M., having decided, as he said, "to lend a hand to an old friend who used to come down from Oxford to visit me."

During the first six months of 1955 there appears to have been something of a lull in this public build-up of Williams. In January the *Guardian* published a letter from the Anglican Canon J. D. Ramkeesoon (the very man whose eyes had moistened while standing beside C. L. R. James during a Cipriani speech), in which Williams was praised for an article he had written in commemoration of India's Republic Day. By stressing the common heritage of Indians and Negroes in the Caribbean, this respected East Indian churchman wrote, Dr. Williams had performed a valuable service to Trinidad. In January, too, there were important political developments in Jamaica as Norman W. Manley's People's National Party, perhaps *the* West Indian politician and party most admired by the Negro middle class in Trinidad, were victorous in general elections held in that colony, ousting the reluctant federationists of Bustamante's Jamaican Labour Party. In February, Princess Margaret visited Trinidad on an official tour and a few weeks later an era of British politics came to an end when Winston Churchill resigned as Prime Minister. In March, Williams made an appearance at a trade union conference in Trinidad in which he stressed the need for a comprehensive development plan for the entire Caribbean aimed especially toward raising standards of living in the Leeward and Windward Islands. This would, he asserted, ease the pressure for immigration to Trinidad when a federation with freedom of movement between the territories – a key issue in the federal talks which had been taking place – would be established. This proposal for raising the standards of life in poorer islands to approach that of the more advanced ones was repeated again a few years later in an important Trinidad government document, *The Economics of Nationhood*, in which the principle was again enunciated that the primary aim of centralized, federal economic planning (which Trinidad, in opposition to Jamaica, most strongly advocated) should be to raise the levels of poorer units to that of the better-off ones, rather than the latter attempting catch up with the standards of more advanced countries. How politically realistic this proposal might have proven to be, if a strongly centralized federation had materialized, is difficult to say, but it was, at the very least, an altruistic nationalist gesture on the part of the P.N.M. government which was naturally received with enthusiasm in the smaller islands – and totally unacceptable to Jamaican opinion.

Although things appeared quiet during these first months of 1955, an inner circle of political activists was crystallizing around Dr. Williams in the form of a secret Political Education Group (P.E.G.). Initially the P.E.G. was organized chiefly for the purpose of promoting Dr. Williams' personal candidacy for public office in Trinidad. However, on the basis of the phenomenal public reception he received over the Aristotle debate and from later evidence of growing public acclaim, its aspirations mounted by degrees from running a few candidates with him to hopes of forming a strong opposition party, and finally, riding the crest of popular enthusiasm and assisted by repeated delays in the holding of the next general elections, to the realization that it might actually sweep into power.

Two simultaneous processes of political organization were in fact taking place: the first consisted of gradually expanding the hand-picked membership of the P.E.G. cell; the second, of providing Dr. Williams with an ostensibly non-partisan forum to continue his public lectures and build his mass following. The latter function was served by the so-called People's Educational Movement (P.E.M.) which was simply a platform provided by T.E.C.A. for Dr. Williams, and which published his early speeches in pamphlet form. The professed aims of the People's Educational Movement were suitably vague. According to an old, dusty circular found on the floor of the old T.E.C.A. headquarters, "the Fatherhood of God, the Brotherhood of Man" were its ultimate goals, and sponsorship of the Williams lectures was represented as only one step in ". . . the widest possible diffusion of knowledge." When the P.N.M. was formed in January of 1956, the P.E.M. had outlived its purpose and passed quietly away. We shall return to the process by which the P.E.G. was organized in Chapter 8.

On the evening of June 21, 1955, Dr. Williams made his first appearance as a speaker for the P.E.M. from the bandstand at Woodford Square. The topic of his speech was nothing less that the career of Dr. Eric Williams, specifically, "My Relations With the Caribbean Commission, 1943–1955." These relations, as was noted earlier, had come to an end that very afternoon when his contract with the Commission had expired after the organization had declined to renew for another term of years their relations with the Trinidad scholar. Dr. Williams gave two reasons for relating the long story of his frequently troubled association with the Commission: "The first is to clear my name and reputation from any imputations of inefficiency or failure or factious opposition or disloyalty to which the termination of service of a public servant frequently gives rise. The second is that the issues are not personal but political; they involve not a single individual but the West Indian people."[14] The upshot of this autobiographical apologia, which filled 51 printed pages, was that life on the Caribbean Commission for a talented West Indian Negro reproduced in miniature the evils of colonial rule in general. West Indians were relegated to junior positions while incompetent white expatriates were given top jobs, intrigued against local persons, and reacted sharply to the slightest signs of criticism from the colonial ruling class while watching the junior local staff with suspicion lest they display any radical tendencies. Because of his published critiques of colonialism, most notably the democratic sentiments expressed in *The Negro in the Caribbean*, and because of his independent, nationalist outlook – including one peculiar, unexplained episode in which he carelessly let slip into an official document "some reference to the abolition of private property" – Williams complained that he was under continual suspicion of being a Communist.[15] But during his twelve year struggle with the colonial bureaucrats on the Commission he had fortunately received strong support from various influential sources: Norman Manley of Jamaica, the Puerto Rican members of the Commission, and various American Negroes who had served on the organization. Another powerful source of potential support which he held over the heads of his opponents, he went on, was the British Labour Party. The personal opposition to his appointment to the Commission held by the British Colonial Attaché in Washington at one point led the scholar to seek an interview with the Labour Secretary of State for the Colonies, Creech Jones (a Fabian socialist of long standing), but that official had left the U.S. before Williams could reach him. Williams placed great stress on the theme of his potential support and connections with persons of position and influence in this report to the people. Of this early episode, he stated:

> . . . I told the Colonial Attaché that I would have asked Mr. Creech Jones for an assurance that I would not be disqualified from making my contribution to the Commission merely because my views did not coincide with those hide-bound conservatives in the British Colonial service and were quite close to those of the Labour Party. He turned yellow

> and trembled in every limb. During the conference at which I was accused of being a Communist, I asked the British Co-Chairman what reply he would make to his boss, Mr. Creech Jones, if he were asked whether he did not know that the sentence held against me [i.e., 'some reference to the abolition of private property'] was not Communism at all, but very good Socialism. He remained silent. It was with Mr. Creech Jones that Norman Manley took up my case. When I was in London last year attending the London conference on G.A.T.T., I discussed the difficulties which had arisen in the Secretariat with one of the highest officials in the Labour Party. It is of the utmost significance that my successful struggle to save my job over *The Negro in the Caribbean* was fought in the context of the British Labour Party's victory in the 1945 elections, while I received the official notification of the Commission's decision not to renew my contract on the very day the Labour Party was defeated in the 1955 elections.[16]

This passage is also of interest because of the awareness it indicates, on the part of an aspiring nationalist politician, of a connection between the politics of the metropolitan power and the freedom of action of the colonial intellectual. It may not be too much to suggest that this perception of the direction in which the ideological currents were flowing in the Britain of the Fifties, including the neo-revisionism of the hapless Labour Party, partly inspired Eric Williams' later proclamation of the end of ideology in Trinidad.

Eric Williams boldly presented himself to his audience in Woodford Square that evening as a martyr in the anti-imperialist struggle. Though neither threatened with imprisonment nor compromised in his eligibility for other employment (rumors circulating at the time held that Manley had discussed with him the possibility of a post in the Jamaican government), his dramatic narrative of his vicissitudes within a quasi-colonial establishment nonetheless served to project the image of one who had suffered in the anti-colonial cause. He, too, as the T.E.C.A. leader quoted earlier said of his colleagues, was a victim *par excellence* of colonial discrimination and inefficiency. For some of his middle class supporters this cavalier treatment at the hands of an expatriate white elite must have aroused strong sympathies; for the black lower class the image of a scrappy, apparently radical underdog doing battle with the big men was, and would continue to be, a highly satisfactory portrayal of how a leader in the tradition of Cipriani and Butler ought to behave. Eric Williams, whom some older heads remembered fondly as a diminutive but adroit football player during his student days at Q.R.C., was a man with an aggressive, often brusque, air about him; a man who, in the local argot, "met steel with steel" and could give "licks like fire" when the occasion demanded. It appeared from his account of his relations with the Caribbean Commission that he had outwitted and outmaneuvered his enemies at every turn. Here was not a dry recitation of services rendered but a lively, executive-suite drama in which the hero, in announcing his decision to stay in Trinidad and continue the struggle, invited his audience to participate in writing the final scenes. It was epic theatre, in the flesh.

Was it all a consciously contrived performance? No one really knows; not even Dr. Williams' closest advisors seemed certain. The political genius of Dr. Eric Williams to a large extent seems to have been based on his ability to communicate an authentic colonial *persona:* as a Negro, and as the citizen of a colony, he twice over occupied an inferior status in the larger international society of which he considered himself a member, and he was deeply resentful of that fact. If he had sustained what Lloyd Braithwaite called the "narcissistic wound," in his discussion of the all-pervasive color prejudice to which West Indians are exposed from birth, Williams responded not by adopting the inner identity of a black Englishman for whom the color of his skin was an unfortunate nuisance, but by setting out to change the system which accorded him, and others like him, a subordinate status. Throughout his career, indeed, Williams had attacked the two institutions which were the historical causes of his position of inferiority: slavery and colonialism. His was, in contrast to that of many other colored professional men in the West Indies, a truer perception of the objective conditions of social life in the West Indies. He rejected the long-standing, polite mutual conspiracy between the upper echelons of the colored community and the white elite which minimized the existence and significance of the social barriers dividing them. Moreover, Williams was apparently viewed by his white superiors not only as black but as red; it was a natural assumption to make at the time, and one which Williams, with his radical allusion to the abolition of private property, apparently did little to clarify. In the career which Dr. Eric Williams had carved out for himself he had risen far above the average social level of the West Indian middle class; he was in direct contact and, apparently, in competition with the senior staff of an expatriate, quasi-colonial organization, and into this situation of potential conflict he brought the temperament of an ambitious, industrious, irascible man of color sharply on the lookout for signs of condescension or discrimination.

Williams defended himself in a skillful manner during the buffetings which seemed to have dogged his association with the Commission. But in his narrative of those years one sometimes detects signs of what might be termed an element of fantasy. For example, when the nationalist sentiments he expressed in *The Negro in the Caribbean* led him to a conflict with a "Mr. X" at the Commission, Williams took notes on an encounter with this official, and he read an excerpt to his audience at Woodford Square:

> Throughout the discussion I was conscious of two impressions:
>
> (a) that Mr. X was literally flabbergasted. I doubt that he had ever expected any colonial to write or speak to him like that; (b) that morally and physically I was his superior. That he should be evasive and apologetic I fully expected. But he was more than that. At times he was quite incoherent, and I had to ask him at least twice to explain what he meant. He placed the blame on fatigue. When we were through he had had enough; I could have gone on for three hours. On one occasion he conceded that I was fundamentally right. I replied that I was fundamentally, legally, morally, intellectually right. I refused to yield one millimetre of ground.[17]

One cannot help but notice in this and other passages, that Eric Williams was always fundamentally, legally, morally and intellectually right, while his Commission opponents were usually incompetent, malicious, and weak-willed creatures who "turn yellow and tremble in every limb" or, as in the passage just quoted, are reduced to an incoherent blubbering as the omnipotent young black colonial reduces their arguments to ashes. Aside from his victorious direct encounters, Williams indicated that he was always on his guard against plots. The lesson he drew from the above episode was: "The snake has been scotched, not killed. But it has been scotched very badly." And then he added, "I forgot that a snake sheds his skin."[18]

It is not my intention here to embark on that favorite Trinidad cocktail hour past-time: the psychoanalysis of Eric Williams. No new contribution to psychological insight into the complex character of the Prime Minister of Trinidad & Tobago will be achieved by observing that he often displayed signs of a highly suspicious, authoritarian disposition. (He could likewise be a witty, charming, and always intelligent conversationalist when the signs of the Zodiac, or whatever forces determined his moods, were in the proper conjunction.) Ashford Sinanan of the opposition party in the Legislative Council once even went so far as to read into *Hansard* the clinical definition of paranoia in order to impress on the nation the perverted mentality of the leader who was taking them down the path to perdition. But Williams' charisma was based on other factors: he had verve and flair; he had that all-important quality identified by Vidia Naipaul as the personal trait which Trinidadians most highly value – *style*. With his dignified bearing, sharp tongue, his ever-present trinity of props – hearing aid, dark glasses and cigaret drooping from his lips – "The Doc" was a sharply-etched, unique public personality. With this capacity for projecting an original style Williams combined his reputation for unsurpassed intelligence and diligence, and his reknown as battler for the cause of the people, the colony, and the emerging West Indian nation. Eric Williams, that is to say, had the social, intellectual, and temperamental endowments which Creole Trinidad highly valued. It is idle to speculate about the course of the island's development if Williams, like so many other gifted West Indian intellectuals, had not returned home, but had pursued a career in Britain or the United States. It seems unlikely, however, that any other man then contemplating a political career in Trinidad would have had such an electric effect on the Creole masses or would have wielded so much power as an elected politician as did Williams.

Williams' basic programs were outlined during the middle and latter months of 1955 in a series of speeches made under the auspices of the People's Educational Movement in Woodford Square and other locales in the island. In July, in introducing a lecture on "Constitution Reform in Trinidad & Tobago," a subject once again under debate in the Legislative Council, he hit upon the idea of founding the University of Woodford Square:

> Somebody once said that all that was needed for a university was a book and the branch of a tree; someone else went further and said that a university should be a university in overalls. With a bandstand, a microphone, a large audience and slacks and hot shirts, a topical subject for discussion, the open air and a beautifully tropical night, we have all the essentials of a university.[19]

Thus Dr. Williams created his own West Indian university after the criteria he had laid down for such an institution: it was in the heart of the city, it had a mass enrollment, and its curriculum was geared to the needs of the society. It had one further feature, however, which might make its accreditation as a bona fide institution of higher learning questionable: the staff, aside from an occasional visiting foreign dignitary or visiting academician, contained but one full professor. Nonetheless, the University was surely a political *tour de force* of the first magnitude; the Doctor did not so much descend into mass partisan politics as he attempted to elevate mass politics to the status of adult education. The "tutelary democracy" that was colonial Trinidad received, in effect, a new indigenous tutor. Williams would not only lecture the local population on the steps required to modernize Trinidad, but would also give some lessons to the former colonial tutors.

The speech on constitutional reform ended with an appeal to mass action. Williams had prepared a set of constitutional recommendations for which he invited public signatures. This was the first real test of the organizational ability and dedication of his coterie of middle class followers, and they proved their mettle. For the signature campaign he had a few days earlier recruited a local bank official and amateur anthropologist, Andrew Carr. A public-spirited, active figure in the life of the colony, Carr later wrote a vivid portrayal of how the mass movement created at the University literally engulfed the faculty after Williams' call to action on constitutional reform:

> I shall never forget the rostrum and its precincts after the meeting as hundreds of people rushed up for the documents. They climbed over the bandstand rails and packed the rostrum so that movement was about impossible . . . [Dr. Williams'] coat was nearly torn off him. For some moments I stood flabbergasted and defeated. I had failed to get a single name. In the melee around me I had not enlisted a single volunteer. I moved around the bandstand as best I could addressing kindly and interested faces which I had never seen before . . . The response was quick and good. Soon I had a staff of ten men and women who were willing to come in at 8:15 the following morning for as long as they were needed.[20]
>
> I tried to find the Doctor that night, [Carr continues] I went from group to group . . . in what was still a concentrated mass of people. Presently I came to a large group. 'The Doctor inside there?' I asked a man on the fringe. 'Yes man, the Doctor inside there,' he replied. Some fifty or sixty people surrounded him, and . . . with his height around 5′5″ he could not be seen . . . It was several minutes before I could rescue him.[21]

During the following weeks and months as Williams lectured around the island almost nightly on constitutional reform, race relations in the Caribbean, and the need to establish genuine party politics in the colony, Carr and his volunteer staff kept the vigil for signatures at the bandstand in Woodford Square. Over 700 volunteers were engaged in collecting signatures, and the bandstand became so much the recognized office of the movement that mail began to arrive addressed simply to "Eric Williams, University of Woodford Square." Williams' reception was not everywhere as overwhelmingly favorable as in Port of Spain; in some areas he was encroaching on the traditional bailiwicks of other politicians, but his reception in the industrial south appears to have been quite strong from the outset. His hard working advance men included the T.E.C.A. leaders, D. W. Rogers and John Donaldson, as well as others in the inner circle of the Political Education Group. By October 6, Williams could present Governor Beetham with six bound volumes containing almost 28,000 signatures to the memorial on constitutional reform. Two days later he left the island for over two months

The People's National Movement: first government, 1956–61.

Governor Beetham arriving in Port of Spain in June, 1955. *Guardian* photo.

Bhadase Maraj in an informal pose in the 1950's. *Guardian* photo.

C. L. R. James, center, returns to Trinidad in 1958. His brother, Mr. Eric James, at left, and Mr. Carlton Comma, Port of Spain librarian, is at right. *Guardian* photo.

George Padmore of Trinidad. *Courtesy Dennis Dobson.*

Sir Grantley Adams, federal Prime Minister, replies to inaugural speech by Princess Margaret in 1958. *Guardian* photo.

The March in the Rain to demand the return of Chaguaramas. From left, in front row: W. J. Alexander, Dr. Williams, Learie Constantine, Dr. Patrick Solomon, Ulric Lee. *Courtesy Sampson Studios.*

Dr. Williams relaxes at the races in 1962 with close advisors: Dr. Patrick Solomon, John O'Halloran, and Donald Grenado. *Guardian* photo.

As Dr. Williams calculates 1961 General Election returns, friends engage in an old-time Creole bacchanal. Daughter Erika yawns while Mrs. Andrew Carr embraces biscuit manufacturer and successful P.N.M. candidate Alfredo Bermudez. Mrs. Harold Despres, wife of early Williams supporter, has Andrew Carr standing behind her and Dr. Solomon on her left. *Guardian* photo.

Dr. Rudranath Capildeo, at right, leaves Queen's Hall constitutional talks in 1962, preceded by Ashford Ainanan, at right, and H. P. Singh, center. *Guardian* photo.

YOUR FREEDOM IS IN DANGER

THE

D. L. P.

ANNOUNCES ITS

MASS MEETING

TO BE HELD AT THE

GRAND SAVANNAH

(OPPOSITE GOVERNOR-GENERAL'S HOUSE)

ON

SUNDAY 15th OCTOBER, 1961

at 3 p.m.

WHERE

Our Candidates Will Be Presented

AND YOU WILL LEARN THE TRUTH ABOUT

- OUR BANKRUPT TREASURY
- THE SEWERAGE SCHEME SCANDAL
- THE VOTING MACHINES
- THE REPRESENTATION OF THE PEOPLE, 1961.
- GOVERNMENT'S ATTEMPT TO SILENCE THE VOICE OF THE D.L.P.
- HOW YOUR LIBERTY IS IN DANGER.

Listen First-Judge Later

Main Speaker: DR. R. CAPILDEO

Chairman: ***Dr. M.A. FORRESTER***

MOST IMPORTANT

WE ARE ASKING ALL OUR PARTY SUPPORTERS FROM ALL OVER TRINIDAD TO MAKE EVERY EFFORT TO ATTEND THIS MEETING.

At mass meeting on the savannah, Dr. Capildeo cried out to followers to "arm yourselves with weapons and get ready to take over the government of this country."

in connection with duties as an adviser to a conference on plantation labor being held in Geneva by the International Confederation of Free Trade Unions. Before his departure, however, the course of future action had been firmly decided. "We will," he told his associates, "postpone *formal* launching of a party until my return."

The hundreds who attended P.N.M.'s inaugural conference in the Good Samaritan Friendly Society Hall on January 15, 1956, assembled to endorse a very general political program, and above all, a man. The program was a more or less standard West Indian document of the period stressing: a) the elimination of colonialism; b) the promotion of progress in all fields, with special emphasis on political education of the people, racial and class unity, equality of opportunity, encouragement of democratic trade unions, a higher standard of living "both material and moral," encouragement of "Caribbean Culture;" c) Dominion status for a British Caribbean Federation within five years after its establishment; d) collaboration with all Caribbean countries to promote more effective use of Caribbean resources; e) collaboration with progressive people everywhere to achieve the abolition of colonialism and racialism. The constitution of the movement was, as a homely back-cover notation indicated, "Printed and Published for the People's National Movement, c/o Dr. Eric Williams, 22b Cornelio Street, Port of Spain."[22] The party had at last been formed and, thanks to another postponement of elections due to the slow progress of constitutional reforms underway, it would have another eight months to build up its following in the colony. During these months Dr. Williams continued the speech-making marathon he had begun during the previous year, and as the prospects for success improved he persuaded several local politicians and businessmen to stand for office on the P.N.M. ticket. One was Gerard Montano, a popular San Fernando businessman and former member of the *Bachacs* study group; another was Dr. Patrick Solomon who was persuaded to re-enter politics after his withdrawal from public life following his defeat five years before. Dr. Winston Mahabir, an East Indian physician, "silver-tongued" orator, and also a *Bachacs* veteran, joined the ticket. Both Solomon and Mahabir, like Williams, were Island Scholars.

In the elections held in September, 1956, only the P.N.M., of the seven parties contesting, mustered candidates for all 24 constituencies. In an exciting, suspenseful contest the P.N.M. polled 39% of the vote and won 13 seats (which later rose to 14 when a successful independent candidate joined forces with the party). This, however, was not sufficient to give the P.N.M. the status of the long-sought parliamentary majority, because the LegCo would also contain four members nominated by Governor Beetham. If these were selected from the ranks of those vested interests who saw in Williams a black Hitler, the P.N.M., with or without its 14th elected member, faced the possibility of parliamentary stalemate. It was a momentous hour in the political life of the colony, and the Colonial Office did not miss the opportunity to use its power to cooperate in the creation of a party government on the British model. Over the angry protests of the opposition politicians and the white commercial elite, the Colonial Office allowed the P.N.M. to name two of its four nominated members, thus conferring on the party a clear majority.

The P.N.M. victories were scored in the predominantly Negro urban areas in and around Port of Spain and San Fernando. Its closest rival was the People's Democratic Party of Bhadase Maraj which polled 20% of the vote, mainly in the sugar belt, and placed five candidates out of the 14 seats it had contested. The fading Butler party, while contesting 20 seats, managed to elect only the Chief Servant himself and Stephen Maharaj, an East Indian sugar belt druggist, while polling only 11% of the votes cast. The electorate's rejection of the old regime was most evident in the defeat of all nine candidates in Albert Gomes' Party of Political Progress Groups, Gomes himself being upset by the young P.N.M. trade unionist, Ulric Lee. Thus a party which was widely regarded in P.N.M. circles as the party of "big business" and a stronghold of "bigoted" Roman Catholics and local whites passed from the scene as a separately-organized political faction. The smaller splinter parties all met with disaster at the polls.[23]

Magnum Est P.N.M. Et Pravalebit – Great is the P.N.M. and It Shall Prevail. The old school spirit, complete with inspirational Latin motto, party neckties, three Island Scholars, a world-renowned cricketer, and a new University had arrived in Trinidad politics. The question was, where were they headed?

CHAPTER 7 A Red Star over Trinidad

In my stay here I have "discussed" socialism with Dr. Williams for at most three minutes.

– C. L. R. James[1]

In 1928 the sea off the south coast of Trinidad began to churn and bubble as an underwater mud volcano, created by gas pressure on the marine oil sands, pushed a new five-acre island into existence. This spectacular geological phenomenon spread great fear and consternation among the simple village folk in the region, but loyal British subjects, including the Governor dressed in full regalia, rushed to the scene, went out in a little boat to the island and planted a flag, it is reported, to the strains of *God Save the King*. Unfortunately, the new island in Erin Bay soon sank back into the deep, flag and all. (It reappears now and then, however.) Aside from its administrative merger with Tobago at the close of the nineteenth century, this was the only addition to the boundaries of Trinidad & Tobago since its capture by the British.

While during the nineteenth and twentieth century great expanses of the world were divided and redivided along imperial or national boundaries, the placid West Indian islands remained territorially secure and unaltered. The low rate of trade and inter-migration among many of them, particularly to and from the remote northwest island of Jamaica, fostered an acute insular consciousness. Each island complacently accepted the existence of the others and acquired little interest or knowledge about developments in the other West Indian territories; it was Britain and North America that counted. Some islands, however, were more insular than others. The steady immigration of Negroes into Trinidad from the Leeward and Windward Islands, combined with a natural, if tenuous, affinity between East Indians in British Guiana and Trinidad, made the latter into something of a regional center. British Guiana produced a few of its own calypsonians, and the steelband movement radiated out from Port of Spain to encompass the entire eastern Caribbean.[2]

One of the major obstacles in the way of creating a pan-island West Indies nation was the virtual absence of a unifying sense of hostility toward the metropolitan country. The federal movement in the area did not have to stimulate a popular demand for higher standards of living; rather it had to convince the local populations – particularly in Jamaica and Trinidad – that political independence under federation would enhance rather than endanger the realization of that objective. The poorer, grant-aided islands in the Eastern Caribbean were fearful lest the proposed federal government should fail to provide them with the subsidies they were accustomed to receiving from the Colonial Office; Jamaicans were apprehensive about the cost of the federal establishment and leery about the degree to which it would interfere with development plans already in progress in that island. British Guiana decided to have nothing to do with the federation. Dr. Williams and the P.N.M. would become the most consistent champions of a strongly centralized federal system, but their concessions to Jamaican opinion proved to have been fruitless anyway when Jamaica's Premier, Norman Manley, under perpetual anti-federation pressure from Sir Alexander Bustamante's opposition party, and in view of serious reservations over the desirability of the federal union within his own party, decided to hold the 1961 referendum in which the Jamaican voters selected the Freedom Bell and voted "No" to continued federation. In the meantime, a concerted effort had been made to show by economic argument, by appeals to a regional "West Indian" versus local, insular consciousness, by the introduction of regional quasi-national services like the University College of the West Indies in Jamaica – and even of the provisional West Indies Federation itself – that West Indian nationhood could be a socially progressive reality, and not an expensive and risky undertaking even worse than the paternalistic British-led administration. The economic argument was not always persuasive; the appeals to a national, regional consciousness were felt more strongly in the cosmopolitan outlook of the educated, liberal middle classes than in the narrower confines of the rural folk. The impact of the weak, newly-established federal government was not sufficient to promote confidence that a merged rather than a separate path to independence would be most feasible. Thus Trinidad's progress toward independence, when the P.N.M. came to office, was already entangled in the federal question, and this must be briefly related.

After the civil disorders of the late 1930's had led to the rise of mass labor-based political parties in the West Indies, parties which were founded, like Uriah Butler's, on the principles of social melioration and self-government; and after the Labour Party came to power in Britain after World War II, the Colonial Office had decided that the West Indian demands for independence should be seriously entertained. During a 1947 meeting in Jamaica's plush resort town, Montego Bay, to which had been summoned representatives from the major political parties of all British possessions in the area, tentative agreement subject to the ratification of the various local legislatures was reached in favor of obtaining Dominion status once the various territories could come to agreement over a federal formula.[3]

The political history of the British West Indian islands as a whole from 1947 to 1962 is chiefly the history of this protracted, faltering, briefly implemented, but ultimately unsuccessful, quest for a federal nationhood. The British had sporadically attempted various forms of unified administration over parts of the area since the seventeenth century. During the nineteenth century the attempt to make Barbados a part of a Windward Islands Federation led to the famous "Federation Riots" on that island. Having had its fingers burnt in a number of feeble federal experiments, the Colonial Office left the job of assembling all the pieces largely in the hands of the West Indian politicians themselves. This task was complicated by the fact that the various administrative units had already achieved not only long traditions of a separate special relationship to the Colonial Office, but had also been moving at very different rates toward semirepresentative local legislatures. From the Montego Bay Conference onward, deliberations over the federal constitution took place simultaneously with the process of constitutional reforms in the local legislatures. The Colonial Office found itself in the position of a dilatory master chef who had allowed a number of different constitutional dishes to get into different stages of preparation for independence, but which had somehow to be brought to completion simultaneously in order to serve up a unified, self-governing West Indies Federation. The questions of rate and timing of the various constitutional changes leading toward greater local self-determination, therefore, shared the stage with deliberations over federation. By 1955 Jamaica and Barbados were ready; but the rest of the Eastern Caribbean, especially Trinidad, was still unprepared, a fact which Trinidadians themselves realized, and from which plight Dr. Williams and the P.N.M. extricated the colony. Thus the P.N.M. appeared, relatively speaking, quite late on the scene of West Indian nationalism. In the final and critical stages of federal negotiations from 1956 onward, conflicting economic interests, local political exigencies, insular chauvinisms, personal feuds, and diverging political philosophies and methods came to a head. Dr. Williams announced before the 1961 Lancaster House conference, which drafted the final constitution by which federal sovereignty was to have been conferred, that if a "P.N.M.-type," strongly centralized federation was not obtained, Trinidad & Tobago would withdraw from the experiment. The Lancaster House constitution did not result in such a federation; the Colonial Office, according to a candid high-ranking Jamaican official who attended the conference, made every effort to placate the decentralizing "con-federationist" demands of the Jamaican delegation.

But even this could not check the secessionist tide in Jamaica. After the results of the September, 1961, Jamaican referendum were in, and after it was virtually certain that Trinidad would not be prepared to shoulder the responsibility involved in remaining in a federation with the poorer Leeward and Windward Islands (in Dr. Williams' mathematics of nationhood, "Ten minus one equals zero"), Mighty Sparrow, while assigning chief blame to "Jamaica" for smashing the federation, angrily attacked the failure of the West Indian nationalists to come to agreement. In the *Federation Calypso* which swept through the islands after the Jamaican referendum, Sparrow charged that:

> *Federation boil down to simply this,*
> *It's dog eat dog and survival of the fittest.*

In its final stages, therefore, the West Indian independence movement as a whole can hardly be characterized as a unified, militant nationalism taking to the barricades against an intransigent imperialism. Moreover, as local autonomy increased in the various territories, and even long after it was obvious that the British were determined to be rid of their West Indian possessions (as cheaply and tidily as possible, of course); and long after it was evident that the chief obstacle to self-government was the snarled negotiations over a formula for federation, there was no corresponding departure from the mildly Fabian perspectives and assumptions favored during the earlier stages of nationalist agitation when local elected leaders had enjoyed much more limited sway.[4] Instead, almost the reverse trend took place. The "Marxist" faction of Manley's People's National Party was expelled in 1952. Some of the individual radicals of the earlier period of left-wing ferment in Trinidad had speculated that Dr. Williams might continue in the political orientation which they had advocated, not stopping short of nationalization of major industries. These expectations would eventually be seen as having been very wide of the mark, but the P.N.M. and Williams himself seemed, during these early years, to be torn by contradictory aspirations – by the desire to assert national sovereignty while at the same time accommodating to a neo-colonial economic dispensation.

As early as the middle of 1956, when the P.N.M. was gaining increased confidence in its chances for an electoral victory in September, the economist and historian who was leading the party wrote a series of articles for the *P.N.M. Weekly* in which he traced for his readers imperial policy with respect to petroleum and the recently concluded sale of much of Trinidad's petroleum resources to the Texas Company. The story of Trinidad oil, which he noted had never been Trinidadian, had begun with the slogan of "Oil From The Empire For The Empire" inaugurated when the British Navy went over to oil before World War I, and had been a cardinal principle of British policy ever after. But, he added, "The old order changeth, yielding place to the new deal. Trinidad's oil will still be oil for the Empire from the Empire, but United States capital will hereafter share the responsibility for the development of Trinidad's resources."[5]

The Trinidad oil deal, he asserted, was merely one episode in the dramatic decline of Britain's ability to maintain adequate rates of investment in its overseas dependencies, and this had inevitably led to a breakdown of the traditional imperial policy of protecting the Empire for metropolitan investment only.

> In terms of statistics, the oil deal marks only one further stage in the decline of British financial supremacy stressed by the Secretary of State for the Colonies, Mr. Lennox-Boyd, in the debate on the transaction in the House of Commons on June 20, 1956: a British surplus of $16,800 m. before World War II had become converted at the end of the war into a deficit of $11,600 million.[6]

In view of this problem, he went on, the Chancellor of the Exchequer, Mr. Harold MacMillan, not only defended the oil deal, but championed the policy of American investment in the sterling area. MacMillan had told the Commons that foreign investment ought to be welcomed where it brought no "positive disadvantage" to either the U.K. economy or to the country in which the investment was made. Laying down the criteria by which the British government favored such transactions as that represented in the Trinidad oil deal, MacMillan stated:

> . . . This means that in considering an application for investment, including the transfer of ownership, we should give permission where the proposal promises to a significant extent to save imports, to promote exports, and to introduce valuable new techniques; and we should allow investment in a sterling area country outside the United Kingdom if it promises to contribute to the economic well-being of that country.[7]

Thereby, stated Dr. Williams, hung "a British tale of woe, of inability to invest in the colonies." He quoted a number of British newspapers and politicians of various political persuasions, all of whom had arrived at the same sad conclusion. The *Financial Times* comment was typical: "This sale was symptomatic of a real and serious failure. In the last decade Britain has been unable to make adequate investment in the Commonwealth . . ." The *Daily Telegraph* noted: "The whole reason for the sale is that the Americans have the resources to finance the development that is possible which the British company has not. This is a symptom of the underlying weakness of this country which is generally conceded."[8] And Walter Elliot, a former Cabinet Minister, put the matter in its broadest perspective when he told the Commons:

> We are faced with a general capital shortage. We have to accustom ourselves to the fact that this country, which during the whole of the nineteenth century was a capital exporting country, is now the centre of a large developing area which it is impossible to finance solely from the savings of this country, however great they may be . . . I do not think that we should accept the dog-in-the-manger attitude that if we cannot develop some portions of the Empire no one else shall.[9]

In summarizing these views, however, the P.N.M. leader noted quickly that ". . . if it is right now to permit others to develop the Empire it was right up to now to prevent others from doing so . . . That is exactly what Mr. Lennox-Boyd and his predecessors have laid down for generations." The P.N.M., he stated, welcomed this transfer of ownership not only because it augured expansion of the Trinidad petroleum industry, but because it corresponded with the P.N.M. policy of attracting maximum foreign capital of whatever nationality. This approach, he asserted, had been wrongly labelled anti-British by some of his political opponents. "The British Government itself now acknowledges its inability to provide the necessary capital. Britain itself has become anti-British in the eyes of P.N.M.'s opponents."[10]

Dr. Williams then went on to an analysis of Britain's general level of investment in the colonies. Characterizing these as a "flea-bite," he noted that the Secretary of State for the Colonies had acknowledged that by 1955 average per capita investment by Britain in the colonies had fallen to under $7. "The Caribbean," Dr. Williams added, "occupies only a very small place in this picture. It is Nigeria, Gold Coast, Malaya which matter." And he cited the "brutal frankness" of one speaker in the Commons who admitted that a very low priority would have to be accorded investment in the Caribbean in light of the difficulties encountered in capitalizing such great African projects as the Volta River scheme. During the debate, Mr. Walter Elliot observed: ". . . I can see every reason for such a switch as is proposed, if foreign investment in the Caribbean area results in giving us greater freedom to develop the less developed portions of the Empire."[11] The lesson to be drawn from this observation seemed perfectly clear to the P.N.M. Political Leader:

> So Trinidad and Tobago have become a developed portion of the Empire! And the band played! The tune? *Britain has written off the Caribbean.*[12]

Defending this "harsh" conclusion, Dr. Williams delved further into the precarious shortage of investment capital in Britain, a situation which dictated that Britain must first attend to its indigenous investment and modernization needs before it could consider diverting requisite sums for colonial development. And the Trinidad scholar looked skeptically upon the Labour Party spokesman, Harold Wilson, and his arguments that assistance to colonial territories could be continued at an adequate rate, adequate enough, that is, to "answer the Communist challenge," if the British population made sacrifices in the rate of its own rising standard of living. This view struck Dr. Williams as "infinitely stale" and "academic," and he quoted with apparent agreement from a rebuttal made by a Tory speaker:

> If he [Wilson] is holding out for a standstill in this country of the continually rising wage demands so that money may be available for investment overseas, he will find a great deal of cooperation . . . but not in the quarters which usually support him and his party.[13]

The decline of British investment and the ascendancy of America's manifest economic destiny in the Caribbean was thus, Dr. Williams felt, not only inevitable but overdue, and the Conservatives were simply following the dismal dictates of political economy in opening the development of Trinidad petroleum, chiefly by off-shore drilling and a great expansion and diversification in the refining of imported crude oil, to American capital and thereby "writing off the Caribbean." Thus the author of *Capitalism and Slavery* could see that the liberation of capital for the further exploitation of Trinidad oil in 1956 resulted from the same factor which had led to the liberation of the slaves in the Caribbean in 1833: from the paramount economic interest of the metropolitan country. And there was a strong presumption that, having lost its major economic stake in the colony, the British would view with considerable equanimity losing the responsibility for political administration of the territory. But Britain's loss would be, Williams correctly predicted, Trinidad's gain. Greatly expanded production, revenues, and wages would develop out of Trinidad petroleum, not under the red banner of nationalization, as earlier radicals had urged, but under the red star of the Texas Company.

Dramatic consequences of this expansion in petroleum were not long in coming. A P.N.M. economic analyst, writing in the *Nation* at the end of 1960 under the modest pen name of "Ricardo," observed that during the preceding four years ". . . the principle contributor to the rapid growth of the Gross Domestic Product has been the oil industry."

> . . . The contribution of the Petroleum and Asphalt sector to the Gross Domestic Product at Factor Cost rose from $187.2 mn. in 1956 to $238.0 mn. in 1959. This increase, in turn, led to the increases in many other sectors of the economy, for example, Wholesale and Retail distribution, which is included under "Other Industries" . . . Finally, the net output of construction rose from $17.0 mn. in 1956 to $33.0 mn. in 1959. This increase largely reflects the building boom initiated by the Government's Five Year Development Programme.[14]

Despite this early demonstration of a positive attitude toward the shift of investment in Trinidad petroleum from Britain to the United States, Williams and the P.N.M. were suspected by many local businessmen of harboring Communist sympathies. This image, apparently fixed for all time in the thinking of some members of Trinidad's more reactionary and know-nothing white commercial elite, Williams attempted to scotch over the years in a variety of contexts. A notable example was a speech he gave during the campaign for the federal elections delivered in January of 1958. In a lengthy analysis of world political and ideological trends, Dr. Williams outlined his basic political and economic categories and reasoning, and he dwelt on what he termed the alleged conflict between the doctrines of socialism and free enterprise:

> Let us first look at private enterprise in the modern world, or free enterprise as it is sometimes called. The first and most obvious feature is that it is not free. The distinctive characteristic of modern economy is centralized control — either by the government or by the large privately-owned corporation.[15]

He then quoted not a Marxist, but rather *Fortune* magazine, on the size of modern U.S. corporations and noted that General Motors employs 600,000 workers, which was just a little less than the total population of Trinidad. He also cited Justice Brandeis of the U.S. Supreme Court, who in a 1931 antimonopolist statement had referred to the "Frankenstein monster" which states had created by their corporation laws. Noting that this was no Socialist speaking, but a judge of the United States Supreme Court, Williams went on to explain other U.S. official commentaries on the menace of the giant corporations.

> This, Ladies and Gentlemen, is free enterprise, this is private enterprise in the modern world . . . And what is free or private enterprise in our

West Indian society? Historically it has meant slavery and indenture – in other words, the freedom of enterprise has meant lack of freedom for the worker. In our own generation it has steadily come to mean the same concentration of economic power in the hands of a single large corporation, with the attendant political dilemma, economic problems and social disabilities.

The best West Indian example is Bookers, whose commanding position in British Guiana is brought out in the colloquialism that the letters B.G. stand for Bookers' Guiana. Bookers control 60% of the sugar production of British Guiana, own hotels, drugstores, steamships, dry goods stores, some of them in Trinidad, operate a taxi service, [are] interested in insurance, oil marketing and other activities.

Dr. Williams then posed a crucial rhetorical question to his Woodford Square audience:

What is Socialism? Even Socialists are not agreed about the answer. The most popular and general definition would probably be some vague sort of equality. But don't press a European Socialist too far on that. Do not ask him if he means equality between the European and the colonial . . . Socialists are no longer as sure as they once were about public ownership and central planning, . . . There is disagreement from time to time as to the priority to be given to their two principle themes – the inefficiency of capitalist production and the inequity of capitalist distribution.

He demanded of those in opposition who had insisted on the dangerously radical character of the P.N.M.:

What, then, is the Trinidad Opposition talking about? Do they oppose Government ownership in India of the telephone system which in Trinidad is controlled by private enterprise? Do they oppose progressive Government ownership in India of the fertilizer industry which is now to be started in Trinidad purely by private enterprise? Do they oppose in India progressive government ownership of road transport which is entirely controlled by private enterprise in Trinidad? . . . If they damn the Socialists, they damn Nehru. If they condemn Socialism, they condemn India. But this Government ownership of public utilities or government intervention in the economic life of the country is not confined to Socialist India. We find it also in the capitalist United Kingdom and in the capitalist U.S.A. under the Republicans.

After citing instances of government control of industries in the U.S.A. and the United Kingdom, he stated:

The issue, therefore, in objective economic terms, is not, as the Opposition in its simplicity believes, Socialism versus free enterprise, but private centralized control versus public centralized control. Let it be understood, Ladies and Gentlemen, from the standpoint of the workers it is six of one and half a dozen of the other.

Dr. Williams indicated that nationalization of industries in Britain had produced no changes from the workers' standpoint. He quoted the miner in England who had characterized the nationalized Coal Board as "the old faces at the top of a new suit of clothes," and he noted that strikes are not unknown in nationalized industries. He then turned to the second aspect of socialism, "distributive justice," and gave more examples from the case of India, which led him to the conclusion that:

> If this is Socialism, we are all Socialists nowadays. *Nehru calls it Socialism, the late Franklin D. Roosevelt called it democracy.* In his message to Congress of January 6, 1941, he said: 'There is nothing mysterious about the foundations of a healthy and strong democracy. The basic things expected by our people of their political and economic system are simple. They are: Equality of opportunity for youth and others. Jobs for those who can work, Security for those who need it. The ending of special privileges for the few. The preservation of civil liberties for all. The enjoyment of the fruits of scientific progress in a wider and constantly rising standard of living.'

The Political Leader observed in his peroration:

> All of this is similar to P.N.M.'s programme, which is non-Socialist, and to the programs of Manley and Adams who confess to being Socialist. For years the International Labour Organization, representative of Governments, employers and workers, has prescribed in its Conventions and Recommendations a pattern of social justice accepted today all over the civilized world, whatever the form of Government, Socialist or non-Socialist – minimum wages, prescribed working day, overtime wages, a weekly day of rest, protection of young women and children, protection of workers in unhealthy surroundings or from dangerous machinery, sick leave with pay, paid maternity leave, social security in old age and against unemployment. The United States has developed the most comprehensive system of social security the world has ever known. The Conservative Party in the United Kingdom has left untouched the welfare state organized by the Labour Party when in office.
>
> The West Indian Government of today equally interferes in the economic life of the country. Here in Trinidad it still runs the Railway and the steamer service between Trinidad and Tobago. It owns a stock-feed factory and a ground provisions depot and operates a statutory Marketing Board. It owns a number of houses and flats through the Planning and Housing Commission. It controls water and electricity through other Statutory Boards. It owns and operates a slip way at the wharves, it owns warehouses and jetties and it owns two banks – the Agriculture Credit Bank and the Post Office Savings Bank . . . The very vested interests who condemn Socialism have for years been agitating for the Government to build and own a luxury hotel because private enterprise will not do so, and to establish another statutory body, an Industrial

> Development Corporation to promote industrial development in various ways, including the construction by the Government of factories for lease to private enterprise....
>
> This pattern of Government ownership, of Government intervention in the economic life of the country, is broadly speaking, a West Indian pattern. Thus, for example, marketing in all the West Indian territories is very largely a government responsibility, involving even export crops – rice in British Guiana, bananas in Jamaica. The Government of Antigua operates an arrowroot factory; the Government of Jamaica operates an ice factory. The Jamaica and British Guiana Railways are government-owned and operated.
>
> Thus, Ladies, and Gentlemen, when the Opposition denounced Socialism ... we are entitled to an explanation from the present admirers of India, former admirers of the British Labour Party, former admirers even of the Soviet system and the Red Army, as well as from those of its members who, as the People's Democratic Party [headed by Bhadase Maraj] in our 1956 General Elections included in their manifesto the nationalization of basic industries and the conventional Socialist formula for a more equitable share of the wealth they produce. They are either ignoramuses themselves or they think us fools.

What did all this signify? The argument can be summarized as follows: Socialism means government intervention, control and ownership in the economy. All non-Communist governments including such diverse nations as Eisenhower's United States and Nehru's India practice intervention, control and ownership of the economy. Therefore, the term "socialism," aside from its mass welfare connotations which can equally well be called "democracy," is a mischievous and misleading label which might as well be dispensed with altogether. In fine, there is no real distinction between modern capitalist welfare state politics and socialism.[16] From the standpoint of some propertied interests in Trinidad, if they paid any attention to it this argument may have been received with some relief; but did it not contain a high degree of ambiguity? While Dr. Williams disavowed the name of socialist, he left unspecified the actual degree and type of government economic intervention which the P.N.M. might countenance under a latter-day New Deal "democracy." To a nervous Trinidad business community it could have made little difference under what ideological label government measures inhibiting what they viewed as the traditional economic order of things might be introduced.

These fears were dramatically reinforced a few months later when Williams installed none other than C. L. R. James as editor of the party weekly newspaper. As one of the most eminent of self-exiled West Indians, James, who had again been living in London since his expulsion from the U.S. six years earlier, was invited to Port of Spain to attend the inauguration of the federal parliament in May, 1958. It was his first extended visit in 25 years, and he was amazed at the mass following which Williams had acquired at the University of Woodford Square. "With a movement like this," he told his former student, "you can do anything." He began to renew old acquaintances in the West Indies and soon sized up the situation: there was little prospect for a radical movement in the area, but he was willing, at Williams' request, to assist in improving the party press and to give his advice on the problems of building up the party organization.

Intimate acquaintances were astounded, and many were disturbed, by the deference Williams began to display toward "Nello" (his Trinidad nickname) James. As one close associate of Williams put it: "For over a year Nello was number two in the party. In fact, there were times when we thought he might be number one." This apparent turning leftward by a Political Leader who had just gone out of his way to provide assurances to local and foreign propertied interests coincided with the one great nationalist adventure embarked on by the P.N.M. before independence: the agitation for the return of the U.S. naval base at Chaguaramas in which conflicting attitudes toward West Indian national autonomy became involved. To capture the militant spirit of those months, here is Dr. Williams speaking to the fourth annual P.N.M. convention in 1960:

> There is one and only one political method I know of – the education of the people, their education particularly in the intrigues which have saddled them with those monstrous burdens to whose removal I have dedicated myself. That is my code of political morality . . . We of the P.N.M. are the voice of West Indian Independence. We are the writers of the new West Indian history . . . We are, and we set out to be, a living protest against colonialism and all its works, a living symbol that, notwithstanding our slave past, we too want a place in the sun, we too belong to the new political aspirations of the twentieth century.[17]

It was a typical utterance for him during this period. The federal negotiations had been going very badly. Manley in Jamaica was no longer highly regarded in the P.N.M. because it was becoming increasingly evident that P.N.M. proposals for a highly centralized federal government were not going to be acceded to by the Jamaicans. Williams' general approach to the problem of power in the federation had in fact been very similar to the approach he had begun to instigate in Trinidad: a rationalized system of party government and more efficient administration. If he had sarcastically condemned the proliferation of political parties in Trinidad, he was equally keen on putting an end to what he viewed as the silly spectacle of the Leeward and Windward Islands operating separate legislatures and administrative establishments. He preferred to see a unitary state for the entire area, or at second best, a strongly centralized federation. The first preference had been out of the question entirely, and it soon became evident that "second best" was not likely either. Assisting in building a climate of acrimony among the federal leaders from the various islands was the Chaguaramas dispute.

In 1956 the P.N.M. program included a clause which stated that the party would honor all international treaties and obligations to which the colony had been made subject in the past. There was no specific mention of Chaguaramas; but none was required, because at that time the American occupation of the northwest peninsula and other deactivated areas was a simple fact of life in Trinidad which no one challenged. Officers from "the base" were active in the elite social whirl of the colony; the Caribbean fleet had acquired a steelband by virtue of its exposure to the Trinidad urban folk culture; the bases still provided some slight employment in the colony.

The entire issue might not have arisen at all but for the fact that, after first deciding that Trinidad was unfit to be the capital of the West Indies Federation owing to the notorious corruption in its public life, the Standing Federation Committee had reversed itself and had specified the Chaguaramas area as an ideal site for the capital![18] Dr. Williams and the P.N.M. had no part in this decision, which was viewed quite coldly in the party newspaper, where it was pointed out that Trinidad had committed itself to observe previous treaties. But ten months after the first P.N.M. electoral victory in 1956, in July of 1957, Dr. Williams set off as a reluctant observer to a conference on the subject, which had been arranged in London between representatives of the U.S., U.K., and West Indies governments.

In London Williams reversed his entire attitude on the issue. He had begun reading the Trinidad government files on the manner in which the original Anglo-American treaty had been granted, and what he found was that the British Governor of the day had strenuously objected to the ceding of so much Trinidad territory to the U.S. military. He had argued that the base should be constructed in an area where it would contribute to the development of the colony, perhaps in the Caroni swamp region. Williams pored over these documents, and when he entered the conference room he was a changed man.

The files which reached Williams – some were flown to him a bare fifteen hours before the conference began – convinced him that the original agreement, insofar as it had been reached over the strenuous objection of the Trinidad Governor and Legislative Council was, by his historians' retroactive nationalist logic, morally null and void. While other West Indian leaders tended to approach the question of release of the area as a *concession* on the part of the United States, Williams would have none of that line of reasoning; he insisted that return of the territory was a matter of Trinidad's *right* to dispose of its own territory.[19]

Even at this early stage of the negotiations, a P.N.M. editorialist was quick to seize on the possible implications of the issue in determining the global alignment of Trinidad and the West Indies in the Cold War:

> During the last war, India was used expediently to wage war on Japan. Indian leaders were put in gaol for demanding freedom for India. Today many Western peoples are annoyed at India's neutralism, but again – the reasons for India's neutralism can be traced to the feeling of Indians at the time of Partition and Independence. Within the next ten years (we hope in five) we will be making our own decisions as to the role the West Indies will play. Will the role be one of neutralism and abrogation of the treaty that makes us a target of the enemy? Or will our role be one of cooperation with the West? The struggle for the Capital Site is already a struggle that begins the shaping of our future attitude to our neighbor.[20]

This was the first statement of a line which would be reiterated over and over again during the following three years as the issue sputtered and smoldered, fitfully died down after a presumed settlement in 1960, and then flared back to life a year later and showed signs of continuing indefinitely, like a fire in a mattress. What happened during that period was that the issue got redefined at least three times, and the causes of Dr. Williams' displeasure moved from defense of national sovereignty to implementation of an agreement in which promises of U.S. aid figured prominently.

But the first stage of the Chaguaramas dispute arose in London in 1957. Dr. Williams and the P.N.M. sought to have Chaguaramas returned to the West Indies for use as a capital site. In this he was in agreement with the other members of the West Indies delegation, and a joint U.S., U.K., and West Indies committee was established to investigate the matter further. This committee probed the issue for almost a year and, with exquisite timing, released its report just as the federal parliament was established in its "temporary" building in Port of Spain. Their findings stated, in effect, that insofar as all parties were agreed that the United States should have a naval base in the Eastern Caribbean, Chaguaramas was by far the best location, particularly in that it would be prohibitively expensive to construct one elsewhere on the island.[21]

Along with this report the Colonial Office issued a communiqué in order to leave no doubt what its position was on the matter:

> . . . H.M.G. could not reasonably ask the United States Government either to relinquish part of the base or to meet the very considerable costs of moving the whole of it . . . Nor could H.M.G. entertain the possibility of themselves contributing towards the cost of such an operation.[22]

The immediate response to this report in the West Indies was highly mixed. The *Guardian*, at that time a voice of the Trinidad commercial community, philosophically assumed that that was the end of the matter and pointed out that the Australian government had waited "long and patiently" for 24 years before establishing its permanent capital at Canberra. However, Jamaican Chief Minister Manley did not take such a relaxed view of the matter and immediately flew to Trinidad for consultations on the issue. When he arrived at Piarco airport the following exchange occurred:

> Asked to comment on a statement by an economist that the West Indies should wait 82 years for Chaguaramas, Mr. Manley replied, 'An economist said that? It sounds more like a geologist.'[23]

Initially Manley seems to have given backing to Williams' insistence that the matter could not rest there, but the conservative, aging federal Premier, Sir Grantley Adams of Barbados, after some vacillation on the issue, announced in the federal House a few weeks later that he had been in communication with the American authorities and had received assurances that they would be prepared to renew the issue "in, say ten years' time, in the light of any changes in methods which might make it unnecessary to retain Chaguaramas as a naval base."[24] In the meantime, on the very eve of the debate over the issue in the federal government, the United States Consul General in Trinidad attempted to snuff out any hopes for a surrender of the base. A statement he made held that the United States considered the issue a "domestic British matter" and maintained that no formal or informal agreement had been reached in London to consider the issue further, once the committee of experts had made its report.[25]

This was too much for the P.N.M. A P.N.M. editorialist, wondering if the "evil shadow of Jim Crow" had fallen across United States policy toward the area, and lamenting the fact that the P.N.M. had not been able to "open the hearts" of other West Indian leaders to the spirit of nationalism which was swelling in the area, concluded:

> Still, although we are but a fledgling nation striving to find our feet, we say emphatically: NO SURRENDER . . . WE HAVE A RIGHT TO BE HEARD IN OUR OWN CAUSE . . . DOWN WITH COLONIALISM AND ALL ITS WORKS . . . We are DAVID![26]

This was the opening broadside in a struggle which continued for just over two years. In December of 1958 the Trinidadian "David" installed James as editor of the party press. A witty, withering barrage of propaganda over the issue was forthcoming from the paper as James almost single-handedly built up a publishing plant for the party and greatly augmented the paper's quality, circulation, and prestige throughout the West Indies. But in re-reading the polemics and heated words from those exciting days, one has to ask, what was really the issue? Did Trinidad, by itself or by exerting its influence within the Federation, aim at putting the area in some kind of formal league with the neutralist nations or even the Communist bloc? So Dr. Solomon, the P.N.M. Deputy Political Leader, hinted in London in the autumn of 1958. He was reported as declaring during a meeting at Trafalgar Square:

> We have got used to Western democracy, but if you and America slap us in the face, which way do you want us to turn – to the East; or do you want us to form a third force?[27]

One thing stands out during this period of militant Trinidad nationalism: at no time was the suggestion made publicly that the United States military presence be driven out of the West Indies altogether. Not even James, in his press campaign, suggested that this was the end in view of the agitation, which was described as the policy of "pin-pricking" the Americans, of making life at the base unpleasant. During 1959, when the agitation over the issue was building to its climax, James repeatedly published an outline of Trinidad's demands, which included:

> (1) The United States must give up Chaguaramas, preferably by discussion.
> (2) If the United States Government does not give up Chaguaramas, then steps will be taken to make life impossible for them there. These steps are legal and constitutional. The United States Government, the United Kingdom Government, have been warned about them.[28]

The United States had to give up Chaguaramas and move elsewhere – but when? That became the key question. The issue, as we have seen, had not arisen as a result of an ideological commitment to neutralism; what was at stake was chiefly the attempt to compel the Goliath of Big Power chauvinism to *negotiate* the matter with the Trinidad nationalist movement. The references to neutralism, while they were taken seriously by some in the party and even by United States officials in the area, were used in this context as largely a tactic aimed at compelling the intransigent State Department into taking cognizance of

Trinidad's assertion of territorial sovereignty over its own land. It was a tactic, and something more; it was a didactic occasion by which Dr. Williams, strongly supported by James but with the uneasy acquiescence of other close associates, attempted to educate Trinidad and the West Indies in the worldwide movement for independence of which many in the West Indies and the P.N.M. saw themselves as a part. Sentimental and ideological affinity in the West Indies for the Afro-Asian bloc was certainly very strong, particularly in the P.N.M. where a long series of articles on the meaning of the Bandung Conference had accompanied the establishment of the party newspaper in 1956. Thus Chaguaramas was a part of the international temper of the times. But as a matter of practical politics, an acrimonious ousting of the American military interests was, as opposition politicians charged and some of his own followers privately conceded, in apparent contradiction to the P.N.M. policy of attempting to create maximum American investor confidence in the territory. How much nationalist sovereignty could a tiny Caribbean territory afford? As it turned out, not very much.

By 1960 an impasse had been reached and the Chaguaramas issue had helped aggravate Trinidad's relations with the federal government. In March Dr. Williams stated in a radio broadcast, ". . . Trinidad is the champion of West Indian independence and Trinidad & Tobago is not going to support any West Indian Federal Government which starts off by being a stooge for the Colonial Office."[29] The breach with the federal government on the issue, and the climax of P.N.M. agitation, came on April 22, 1960, when, as Sir Grantley Adams prepared to visit the U.K. for Princess Margaret's wedding, Williams called a mass daytime meeting at Woodford Square and ceremonially burned The Seven Deadly Sins of Colonialism (including the U.S.-U.K. Bases agreement). Speakers at the rally were apparently selected with an eye to their shock value and included a well-known Trinidad Marxist, Lennox Pierre, and Mrs. Janet Jagan, wife of B.G.'s Marxist Premier. Afterwards, Dr. Williams led a peaceful March in the Rain to the United States Consulate where demands for the return of Chaguaramas were read to obliging United States officials at the entrance of the building.

The March in the Rain was, perhaps, the militant high point of Trinidad nationalism. But a settlement of the issue was already blowing in the wind. As spring came and Princess Margaret was wed to a high society photographer (or, as a baffled Sparrow told his audiences, "a camera man"), Iain Macleod, who had been made Colonial Secretary the preceding October, prepared to pay a historic visit to the West Indies, apparently determined to iron-out the seemingly interminable delays in the area's faltering progress toward independence. When he reached Trinidad he held interviews with senior civil servants, members of the business community, the Opposition, and then, as a P.N.M. spokesman recalled wonderingly, "he agreed to everything." Not only were certain longstanding constitutional issues composed, not only did Macleod assure the Trinidad government, with typical British understatement, that he would "speak to the Americans" about negotiating the Chaguaramas issue, but he issued the cheerful admonition that the area should "hurry up" towards independence.[30] If the West Indies were not in a hurry, some sage cynics suspected, Britain was. The racially-biased Commonwealth Immigration Bill was being prepared, and it might well be easier to justify if the West Indies were an independent nation than if they remained colonies.

The exact sequence of communications that finally led to the American willingness to enter into negotiations which would include the Trinidad government as well as the federal government is obscure. In May, Williams had made a speech at a meeting in San Fernando in which he stated unequivocally for the first time, having presumably been mugging-up his political geography, that Trinidad regarded itself as "West" of the Iron Curtain.[31] During this period, it is apparent from C. L. R. James's account of the events, Williams was turning away from close personal contact with his old mentor.[32] A United States official who was in Trinidad at the time later remarked to the present writer that it was after this speech that he had regarded the issue as negotiable: "The San Fernando speech marked Williams' break with James. It is a part of Williams' political style to telegraph his punches. After that speech we knew we could do business with him."

Whatever the details of the process by which negotiations were begun (and it seemed that a previous turnover in personnel at the United States Consulate may have been an important factor), the following months saw the crystallization of the P.N.M.'s general position on the question of global alignment. Once the United States had simply recognized Trinidad's right to negotiate the issue, several important changes took place in the P.N.M.: James was entirely frozen out from the position of easy access to Williams which he had enjoyed for over a year. Over the telephone he was bluntly told they had "nothing to discuss." The P.N.M. political leader took the position that the nationalist principle had been recognized because United States recognition of Trinidad's separate representation in negotiations had been obtained. The ambiguous references to neutralism vanished overnight.

Instead, there was a trip to London during the summer of 1960 to begin the process of bargaining in which the length of the United States lease to Chaguaramas would be cut down, and the question of

American aid to the colony became intimately linked to the resolution of the question. By November talks had begun in Tobago, where the Crown Point Hotel had been refurbished for the occasion and cabañas were placed in readiness to soothe the visitors between bargaining sessions. Williams left no question as to the position he had arrived at:

> I am for the West Indies taking their place in the Western Hemisphere and for membership in the Organization of American States, without any loosening of ties with the Commonwealth.[33]

And during the same statement he added a red-baiting remark of the sort which would become standard P.N.M. rhetoric from then on. As the P.N.M. *Nation* paraphrased him: ". . . if the world were divided into two camps, the West Indies which was historically, geographically and economically in the Western Hemisphere, could not claim it was going to be in the middle. If the Communists and fellow travellers were counting on him to pull their chestnuts out of the fire they would be disappointed."[34]

The Tobago conference, therefore, took place largely on a *quid pro quo* basis. Dr. Williams, who had been defended in the Legislative Council three years earlier against opposition insinuations that he was using Chaguaramas as a method of extracting aid from the United States, returned to the same chamber in late 1960, after the Tobago conference, and confessed to the assembly that the Trinidad delegation had gone to the conference with "*the problem of the economic needs of Trinidad & Tobago dominant* . . ."[35] What the settlement actually had been remained something of a mystery for several days, and the amount and type of economic assistance which the territory would receive involved a long, drawn-out series of further discussions with United States officials. In essence, however, the United States agreed to retain its hold on Chaguaramas until 1977 at the latest, and other United States facilities in the area would be surrendered unconditionally with the exception of 1,400 acres at Waller Field in the center of the island which would be made available to the United States in case of hostilities. In return for retaining Chaguaramas, sections of which would be under joint United States, West Indian, and Trinidad jurisdiction, the American team agreed that the United States would participate in certain specified development projects. Dr. Williams later stated that he had been misled as to the type and degree of assistance the United States would offer in these projects, and it was around this issue that the third and final stage of the Chaguaramas affair would revolve for several years until the base was finally abandoned in 1967.

Thus, in Trinidad a militant nationalism on an issue involving national sovereignty and global alignment contributed to the split in the ranks of West Indian nationalism. Just as Jamaica had not been prepared to hand over the formulation of economic policy to the federal center, neither was the P.N.M., once it divined that the attitude of federal leaders was at variance with its own, willing to relegate what it viewed as primarily a local dispute with area-wide implications to the federal government. Eric Williams and the P.N.M. attempted to shape West Indian nationalism after their own image, with very limited success.

Alone of the major federal leaders, Eric Williams had made a sustained attempt to promote federal nationhood and to resist metropolitan chauvinism and insensitivity on the Chaguaramas question. Strangely enough, however, this is not the interpretation of his behavior favored by some of the younger, more radical nationalists. Chaguaramas and the break with C. L. R. James tend to be remembered today as the big betrayal of West Indian nationalism. This interpretation, which rests implicitly on the premise that David can unaided slay Goliath, overlooks the contradiction between the P.N.M.'s previous definition of economic realities and the implications which surrounded the Chaguaramas struggle. The estrangement which developed between James and Williams partly resulted from the fact that each man had placed himself in a false position. For all his early personal regard for Nello James, Eric Williams was no revolutionary; and James, although he had curbed his radical instincts, was no bourgeois reformist.

There was, however, more to the Williams-James split than that. Chaguaramas was the central crisis which both brought them together and divided them. Beneath the surface, however, as James would document in his *Party Politics in the West Indies*, cross-currents within the P.N.M. were at work to erode their partnership. James's presence in the inner circle of advisors was tolerated because of Williams' sponsorship but, like the Old Bolsheviks who in 1917 resented the sudden rise to Lenin's favor by the upstart Trotsky, the old P.E.G. group was likewise disrupted by James's sudden claim to influence. Political parties are sociological phenomena, groups in process, and the surface drama of the Williams-James estrangement had a structural cause.

CHAPTER 8 The Structure and Problems of Power

This P.N.M. remind me of when two steelbands meet on the road. One band move over to the side to let the other pass. All the time they making a lot of noise and confusion — but they ain't going nowhere at all.

— From an interview with a P.N.M. militant.

When the People's Educational Movement in 1956 became the People's National Movement, more was changed than just one word in the name of the organization, but much in the way of policy and key personnel had already emerged. The period of pre-party activity not only established the dominant themes on which the party platform would be based, but had also been a time in which the norms of leadership and influence within the organization took shape. Not that the party was ever really at peace with itself, for all sorts of strains in the relationship of the leadership to the rank-and-file developed. The alleged isolation of the parliamentary group from the party organization itself was a frequent criticism leveled by lower echelon party workers at the leadership. But throughout its six-year gestation period to the time of independence, the party leadership structure retained a strong continuity in terms of personnel and the actual locus of decision-making. Dr. Williams, sometimes alone, sometimes in collaboration with an inner circle of policy advisors (most of whom were Ministers of the government), drafted major policies which were then put before formal party organs for discussion and ratification. There is, of course, nothing remarkable or unusual in this from the standpoint of the normal pattern of policy formation in democratically-organized political parties, and that is what the P.N.M., despite some major contradictory tendencies, was intended to be.[1]

The party was, in fact, organized by men of considerable organizational sophistication: some able British-trained lawyers participated in drafting the constitution; Dr. Williams, during his visit to England in connection with his trip to Geneva in the autumn of 1955, is said to have consulted C. L. R. James and George Padmore about it; the party chairman, Learie Constantine, had had personal experience in observing the inner workings of the British Labour Party; and the constitution of Manley's Jamaican P.N.P. which was, in turn, modeled after the British Labour Party, had been consulted as well. From the published reports of the P.N.M. General Council covering the years 1958 through 1960, and on the basis of observations obtained during the course of a year spent in close study of the operations of the party, I came to the conclusion that, despite the chronic problems of maintaining efficiency at the Central Office, the tendency of special party committees to evaporate into thin air, poor attendance by some members at party meetings, in short, the usual shortcomings of voluntary organizations, the P.N.M. was a functioning organization blessed with a considerable degree of internal squabbling and complaining, but withal enjoying a high level of general morale.

Associated with this general atmosphere of enthusiasm and satisfaction with the party, however, were strong tendencies toward oligarchy, verging on an autocratic leadership style. These tendencies can be traced to the organizational assumptions and structure which were adopted during the formative period of the P.E.G., the Political Education Group – the coterie of early middle class supporters which met secretly with Dr. Williams to plan the formation of a political party with him at its head. Dr. Williams, it must be remembered, had already attained the status of a great moral authority within this group by virtue of his learning and expertise, traits which had been more fully developed in his long research experience with the Caribbean Commission. The P.E.G. was formed primarily with the intention of advancing *his* career in politics; its *raison d'etre* was Williams' own mass appeal. Many of those associated with Williams in this period were not themselves particularly well known in Trinidad generally, although some were men of substantial reputations within their own professions or communities. But Williams was the stellar attraction, the only member of this group to generate a charismatic following. This would always be true. His associates, many of them able, dedicated men, would often have to content themselves with shining in the public eye by reflected light beamed from the Political Leader. When on a few occasions, notably in the career of C. L. R. James in P.N.M. politics, the sun of Williams' favor abruptly went out, the unfortunate associate vanished from the P.N.M. firmament almost as if he had never existed. James undoubtedly could have developed an independent following but, true to the terms of his contract, he apparently never really tried.

Williams began with a fairly tight-knit coterie of admirers. But to begin building an island-wide political organization, as the group soon determined to do, required the recruitment of additional members and the drafting of a political platform which would require ratification by a relatively large number of persons. This immediately raised the problem of how to maintain the general integrity and aims of the organization intact in the face of an ever-greater probability that, as more diverse elements were brought in, competing and conflicting viewpoints and cliques might emerge, possibly even inundating the original leadership. This functional problem, inherent in the formation and maintenance of any voluntary organization with objectives which might become redefined over time, was "solved" in the P.N.M. from the outset by three principal working rules: a) admission to membership was contingent upon obtaining the personal endorsement and sponsorship of an already trusted member; b) insofar as possible the precise method of implementing party objectives was kept vague and fluid, defined largely as the province of the Political Leader; c) every party member was expected to be personally loyal to Dr. Williams, and the development of an organized point of view within the party contrary to his current thinking tended to be viewed as presumptive evidence of disloyalty. These principles, largely implicit and emergent, were not consistently or rigorously enforced, for the P.N.M. was not as tightly organized as that; but they were very important in maintaining the continuity of authority in the party for a number of years. Moreover, the control which Williams exercised over the party served to discourage many who might otherwise have been inclined to enter the P.N.M. in later years; after the leadership structure had established itself there was no appreciable influx into the party leadership of new middle class elements. There was a pervasive feeling that the positions of responsibility and decision in the P.N.M. were already monopolized by the older members of the club, so that such new middle class participants as emerged were drawn into the decision process largely from the official, government side. From its inception there were only a few cases of an important increase in mobility within the party itself. Some of these were the recipients of the co-optation which Williams employed to mend sagging political fences in the "radical" south where some party members, stimulated by the intense partisanship and radical atmosphere prevalent before the settlement of the Chaguaramas issue, had begun, without invitation, to look to Mr. C. L. R. James as a possible senior partner in the firm of Williams & James.[2]

At the meeting of the P.E.G. steering committee on July 3, 1955, held just two weeks after Dr. Williams had delivered his famous autobiographical apologia in Woodford Square, a formal list of criteria for expanding the membership of the group was drafted. The group, which at that time numbered just thirteen members, defined the following qualifications:

1. Men and women of sincerity and integrity in broad agreement with our views.
2. They must in general have no affiliation or political past. The Executive Committee is empowered to make necessary exceptions to this rule.
3. They must be opposed and be prepared actively to oppose racial discrimination or bias.
4. They must be persons regarded as likely and willing to accept the discipline of the Party.
5. They must be willing to work, make sacrifices, do the necessary study, and organize.
6. *Ceteris paribus,* priority will at this stage be given to persons with a following and influence in the community.
7. Selection will be made with the view to achieving, in so far as possible, a balanced racial representation, so long as this does not involve compromise with basic aims, principles and objectives of the party.

The first of these criteria, so far as "sincerity and integrity" is concerned, is plain enough, but what did "broad agreement with our views" mean? At this early stage of the party it appears that the question of whether or not to adopt one of the standard ideological labels – "labor" or "socialist" – attached to West Indian parties was being debated because, among the P.E.G. documents examined by the writer, there were in fact two separate versions of the criteria for membership: the two were identical except that one contained the phrase "in agreement with broadly socialist views," rather than "our views." The meaning of "our views," therefore, seems to have been regarded by at least some members as more or less synonymous with "socialist views." But in that case, since the term had favorable connotations in West Indian mass politics, why not simply call the party "socialist"? The answer, as we have already seen, was that the charismatic leader himself – despite his Marxist historical methodology, his anti-colonial writings, his espousal of the cause of the laboring man, his indiscreet reference to "the abolition of private property" which had jeopardized his post with the Caribbean Commission, his readiness to collaborate with other West Indian politicians who considered themselves to be "socialists," his willingness to call upon British socialists in defense of his career on the Commission, *and* his eventual summoning of C. L. R. James to act as P.N.M. ideologue – despite all these apparent signs of a socialist political identity, Eric Williams did not regard himself as a socialist, nor would he lead a socialist party. Some of his closest associates and admirers, however, had considered themselves to be "socialists." It could hardly have been otherwise, given the traditional link in West Indian politics between the cause of labor and the cause of self-government, and labor was usually defined as synonymous with socialist. What Eric Williams did in Trinidad was to sever that link and create a unique type of mass political organization in the area: a nationalist party without a strong, formally-affiliated trade union wing. *The party, with him holding the reins, had, as he saw it, to rise above the major interest groups of a divided society: it had to rise above disputes between capital and labor, between East Indian and Negro, in order to create, for the first time in the history of the colony, a secure center of elective political power with sufficient authority to arbitrate between the contending ethnic and economic factions within the society.* This, at any rate, is my interpretation of the central feature of the system which Williams envisaged, created, and in fact manipulated for a decade after his entry into politics. The P.N.M. was able to dispense with potentially entangling alliances with the Trinidad labor movement because of the lack of political cohesiveness of the latter, and of equal importance, because Williams' charisma had created an ethnic following and movement largely independent of other institutional sources of support. In 1956 the head of the Oil Worker's Trade Union had himself run for office against the P.N.M., but it appears that the rank-and-file union member in that election voted heavily for the party headed by the exciting new intellectual-politician. By the 1961 elections most of the major trade unions had gotten on the P.N.M. bandwagon, but the party organs at no time included what could be called a powerful trade union wing.

Another cause of this centralization of organizational authority in the hands of Eric Williams and his earliest collaborators can be traced back to the criteria for membership in the P.E.G. listed above. The reference to "no affiliations or political past" and the necessity of members being "likely and willing to accept discipline" were reflections of a certain apprehensiveness about the presumed dangers of organizing a political party in Trinidad, apprehensions based on observation of the factionalism – and what Dr. Williams viewed as the incorrigible "individualism" of Trinidadians – of previous parties. These, it was widely believed, had been torn by plots and counterplots; thus, under the slogan of "No Deals" the P.E.G. leaders sought to organize a party unsullied by the corruption and opportunism which they felt characterized many politicians and parties already in the political arena. But if the group was to be limited to the inexperienced new men, to untainted political virgins, it could not at the same time really hope to establish a fully multi-racial party because many East Indian voters already felt a debt of gratitude to Bhadase Maraj. This is probably the reason for the inclusion, in the membership criterion stating the desirability of a "balanced racial representation," of the qualifier, "so long as this does not involve compromise with basic aims, etc." Maraj, to put it mildly, was at that time regarded in the Creole community as something less than a model of Hindu piety; indeed, he was for many years regarded as a kind of bogeyman. For a group of respectable middle class reformers to approach Bhadase Maraj for the purpose of forming a coalition party, therefore, probably seemed to stretch the principles of the reform-oriented P.N.M. beyond toleration. Nonetheless, there had been some discussion of this possibility, for, since Bhadase Maraj had acquired and controlled a substantial bloc vote among many East Indians of the sugar belt, there was little possibility that a fully multi-racial national party could be formed without him, or without bringing into the party leadership East Indians of wide influence in the Hindu community. Here the P.N.M. was caught in a genuine dilemma, in a contradiction between an ideal and a practical political reality. It embraced the ideal and then proceeded to insist that the ideal reflected political reality, which it did not. The P.N.M. leadership tended to take the position that since it was a "national" party, and because it was genuine in its espousals of racial harmony, the dominantly East Indian opposition party was a kind of mirage which did not really exist, or which would vanish if only opportunistic East Indian politicians would not exploit the ignorant country Indians by "preaching race."

The growth of the P.E.G. took place on a "by-invitation-only-basis," stressing personal acquaintance and character endorsement by those already within the group. *This was a highly significant feature of the recruitment process because it meant, in effect, that early membership, and thereby a high chance of attaining a leadership position in the group, would proceed along a network of personal relationships, the sociometric lines radiating out from the nucleus of the initial members into the community at large.* When that process of selection was conditioned by the over-riding criterion stressed in rule six, the "priority" to be given to persons with a following and influence in the community, it meant that initial recruitment of party leaders would be directed mainly into the Trinidad Negro middle class. Furthermore, a "voluntary association" being precisely voluntary reflects in its membership a high degree of self-selection in individual and group backgrounds. Most white, French Creole, Trinidad businessmen would probably not, even after receiving an invitation, have joined Eric Williams' party.

I could not attempt to trace out the full chain of these early nominations, but a few examples may suffice to show what probably took place. Late in 1955 a member of the P.E.G., a Port of Spain physician, approached his cousin, a suburban druggist (later to become

Minister of Labour), to ask him to join the group. The druggist, who had been tutored by C. L. R. James when a pharmacy student in the Twenties, had been a candidate in County Council elections against a Moslem proprietor, publicist and volunteer social worker who had in turn been an early admirer of Dr. Williams, and who would himself become Minister of Agriculture in the P.N.M. government. And so on . . . the number of overlapping acquaintances, including kinship ties, in a small society like that of Trinidad was very extensive, particularly given the class bias injected into the recruitment process. In all this there was, however, a characteristically West Indian element of chance; to some extent, apparently, recruitment depended on whom the P.E.G. member happened to run into on the street. Andrew Carr had been an old neighbor of Dr. Williams and had just happened to drop in to see him a few days before the memorial on constitution reform was to be launched. A. N. R. Robinson, the Tobago-born barrister who would become Williams' understudy in the Ministry of Finance, had just returned to Trinidad from his studies in England when the party was being started and had dropped in to see Dr. Williams about contributing an article to a magazine he wanted to begin, when Williams invited him to participate in forming the party. Ulric Lee's recruitment appears to have been just as accidental; the ex-T.E.C.A.-leader-turned-barrister, W. J. Alexander (one of the closest and most durable advisors of Williams), happened to have been the attorney for Lee's trade union, and he mentioned the formation of the party to the young organizer. The process, then, was somewhat random, but concentrated in the middle class; and in several instances a special effort was made to recruit men who by their non-Negro background would give the leadership a more "balanced" appearance.

Further evidence for the hypothesis that the first members of the group became the nucleus of a party policy clique can be adduced from the eventual political careers of those few persons named in the July 3, 1955 memorandum just cited, written *a full six months before the party was even inaugurated.* One member would become Minister of Labour from 1956–62, and Minister of Health in the second P.N.M. government; another would be Minister of Health in the first P.N.M. term in office; still another became a nominated member to the Legislative Council for the P.N.M. and was named Senator and Minister Without Portfolio and Special Advisor to the Premier in 1962; a fourth member was a P.N.M. representative in the federal government and later became a key government Minister; a fifth served as Minister of Agriculture and later of Public Utilities; a sixth was eventually appointed government public relations officer; a seventh would serve continuously as Vice Chairman of the party; an eighth was appointed to the Trinidad Senate in 1962; a ninth member would be head of the P.N.M.'s Women's League and elected to the legislature in 1961; a tenth served for several years as General Secretary of the party. One member, a reporter for the Trinidad *Guardian*, did not remain in the group long enough to reap the reward that was undoubtedly in store for him, but which must then have seemed a rather uncertain and distant prospect. Instead, he took a public relations position offered him by the Gomes government and by this startling turn-coat behavior reinforced the tendency to place a premium on recruiting persons of known trustworthiness. A continual stress on "loyalty" would be heard within the P.N.M.; and this, by virtue of Dr. Williams' preëminence, tended to become equated with personal loyalty to the Political Leader himself.

Because of the intimate, personal nature of the recruitment process and the small size of the community, Dr. Williams, although firmly committed to putting an end to corruption and graft in the political life of the colony, found himself presiding over a party and a society with much of the character of a *Gemeinschaft* community in which bureaucratic regulations, stress on merit over personal connections as a basis for status and rewards, and the other structural concomitants of a large-scale, industrialized society were at a relatively low stage of development. This factor, perhaps more than any other, was responsible for the split-image which the investigation of P.N.M. influence structure often produced. The fact that Trinidad was really a very small place in which every individual enjoyed some, often ambiguous, degree of acquaintance with a relatively large percentage of the members of his milieu or class always threatened to make a fiction of the belief that public institutions were organized mainly along impersonal, bureaucratic lines. Trinidad's long tradition of corruption in public life and in business – the notorious *bobol* syndrome which had initially prevented it from becoming the federal capital – was a phenomenon against which the internal P.N.M. crusade was to a large extent directed. The weight of this tradition of wire-pulling and light-hearted, petty grafting descended with full force on the P.N.M. Political Leader. Given his predisposition toward personal aloofness, Williams responded to this situation by adopting the role of an olympian and incorruptible leader. He publicly professed intense distaste for the patronage and socializing side of politics. The latter he found particularly disagreeable because, as he frequently complained, Trinidad was full of people trying to play "big shot," trying to curry favor or attempting to approach him informally on some business matter. Often one had the feeling, particularly surrounding Williams and one or two other Ministers, that social distance and interpersonal coldness were being maintained to compensate for the tendency of the small community to operate on a personal, informal level. But the dysfunctions of this posture were considerable as well and gave credence to the image of Williams as lonely, isolated and dictatorial.

This tendency on the part of P.N.M. Ministers to become remote from the citizenry and from the rank and file party member once led a hardworking party member to complain: "People in this country are used to *knowing* their politicians. A man used to come around and maybe give you a bob or go hunting with you. Now all that is finished. Now they drive by you in a big motor car. People asking – 'why can't they come and see us?' I think the break was too great." During the same conversation, another member said: "I was down in Strikers' Village once when they brought Williams down there for a speech. Man, those people were glad to see him. A few of those big Grenadians grabbed him and threw him up on their shoulders. I tell you, the man was frightened half to death. From then on I knew that Williams was afraid of the people." Similar comments and complaints were heard with fair frequency in some quarters of the P.N.M. To some extent, however, they may have been a reflection of the social class cut-off point discernible in the backgrounds of party activists below the parliamentary level and in the Party's Executive Committee, where professional status quickly trailed-off into much lesser occupations, generally of a lower middle class type.

Here again, in the generally solid middle class background of the P.N.M. leadership, is a basic structural pattern which can be traced to the formative period of the P.N.M. As the P.E.G. expanded, and as the need developed for rapidly increased numbers in order to provide the party with a substantial set of "Foundation Members," recruitment mushroomed to include members of a "First Hundred" and a "First Five Hundred." The documents dealing with this process show quite clearly the social composition of this initial stratum of low-echelon party activists: it was predominantly of a Negro lower middle class, artisan, character. This distinction between the social class backgrounds of the mass of the party delegates on the convention floor and the leaders on the platform – or between the parliamentary group, the top party officials, and the members of the General Council – remained with considerable consistency throughout the history of the party up to independence. There was some tension generated on this account; but on the whole, the lower-echelon party members seemed generally disposed to accede to the policies laid before them by the party leadership, which was better educated, higher statused, and most important, led by the revered Dr. Williams. Several knowledgeable party workers not otherwise prone to confirm Dr. Williams' diagnoses of the problems of the party told the writer that this stratum of "policy ratifiers" was usually more interested in attaining status in their local communities through participation in the General Council of the party than in preparing forceful, well-reasoned points of view at variance with those of the party's upper echelons. A position in even the lower councils of the party was, after all, something of a prestige-building activity in the local community; invitations to ceremonies and banquets, perhaps even at the new Hilton, were in store for the minor local party leader.

Two further features of the pre-party organization which was forming around Dr. Williams, and which foreshadow his personal authority for many aspects of party policy, come to light in the minutes of the P.E.G. meeting held on July 28, 1955, three weeks after the meeting which was the starting point of the above discussion. The first item bears out his positional prominence: six subcommittees of the newly formed Executive Committee are listed, and although the still small membership of the group at the time led to considerable overlapping memberships in the committees, Dr. Williams was the only member to be assigned to all of them. Secondly, under "Other Business" this notation occurs: "On the question of Dr. Williams' lectures, it was agreed that *he was free to accept or reject all* comments on said lectures, as they were his personal responsibility." This free scope, however, was not entirely accorded Williams after the formation of the party, but it is significant to note that he did hold such authority during the period when the general perspectives of the party were being shaped. Several high party members insisted that after the formation of the party, however, he did in fact amend his speeches in accordance with suggestions made by other leaders. "Sometimes he would hardly recognize them when they were finished with them," one associate boasted. It is not known how long or how regularly such group censorship prevailed; the major impression one has in attempting to reconstruct the internal history of the party was that Dr. Williams had on most issues said precisely what he wanted to say, sometimes without the foreknowledge and approval of even his closer associates. Rather, as the time of independence drew near it was they who had to take care in their public utterances lest they become the subject of a public reprimand from Dr. Williams. The writer vividly recalls an incident at Woodford Square just after the resounding victory of the P.N.M. in the 1961 elections. A high party associate speaking during the customary warm-up preceding Williams' appearance stated that with the bitterness and strife of the campaign behind them, the time had come to adopt a more conciliatory attitude toward the opposition. Dr. Williams did not let this breach of party discipline pass unnoticed a few minutes later, when he delivered a sharp verbal rebuke at the previous speaker stating that if he (the previous speaker) thought that the time to forgive and forget had arrived, then he (Dr. Williams) said "to hell" with the previous speaker. The reason supplied by bystanders for this public denunciation was, "Dr. Williams is the boss. The other fellow is a big fellow, too, but he's not the boss." Thus enlightened, we turned our attention back to the speaker who soon became engaged in a denunciation of the ingratitude of certain (predominantly East Indian) areas which, despite having received government projects, had stubbornly persisted in voting for the opposition candidates.

Through such incidents, the image of the P.N.M. as a party resting on Williams' charismatic autocracy within a sycophantic oligarchy became established in the minds of many Trinidadians. The secrecy surrounding party decisions, the closed party conventions, kept the public ignorant of the degree to which there were in fact avenues of formal discussion and dissent at all levels of the party organization. These avenues, however, would naturally be viewed by C. L. R. James – former I.L.P. member and radical populist that he was – as totally inadequate. During his months in favor he urged Williams to work for a democratization of the party; to increase rank-and-file participation and to expand party activities at the grass-roots.

Sincere in his desire to create an Educated Democracy, Williams listened, for a time, during the flux and excitement of the Chaguaramas campaign. But this produced a crisis in his relationship with some of his closest colleagues: W. J. Alexander and A. N. R. Robinson would refuse to attend conferences at which James was present. Former members of the P.E.G., who had stood by Williams for over three years, grew apprehensive about what their status would be if the upstart James were allowed to tamper with the organization. Thus, two pressures converged on Williams – the populist direction favored by James and the resistance of other close associates. We have already seen how this conflict would be resolved. Had James been in Trinidad in 1955 things might have gone differently, but by 1958–59 the charismatic leadership style, and the informal oligarchical norms, had hardened into group traditions and working principles. In addition, any radical departure from these principles was precluded by the broad policy assumptions on which the party was founded and by the original collective self-image of the leadership vis-a-vis the traditional elites.

While Dr. Williams went abroad for two months in the autumn of 1955, the P.E.G. undertook to organize the rapidly expanding membership on a preliminary geographical basis in preparation for establishing constituency and party groups. Furthermore, a panel of speakers selected from the group was, according to the group's minutes, ". . . charged with the responsibility of meeting members in different parts of the country to discuss, advise, lecture, and generally to make those members familiar with the aims and objects of the party being formed."

The degree of activity carried out by these panel members was not indicated by any accessible documents, but the contents of a briefing memorandum to the speakers is significant in that it indicates how, in Williams' absence, at least some members of the group interpreted its general ideology and objectives. The dominant theme of this document, which took the form of a political catechism, is vagueness, and above all, caution. Moreover, it reveals that despite a fair degree of homogeneity in the social backgrounds of the group, recruitment within the colored middle class had inevitably crossed religious lines, and efforts at composing differences between the more radical secularists in the group, including Dr. Williams, and the Roman Catholics, were already being contemplated. This would, for some in the party leadership, seem to be the better part of political wisdom, for opposition from the church was thought to have contributed to the defeat of some candidates in previous elections, and there remained a strong sensitivity to pressure from that quarter. Equally important, as the document indicates, was the fact that the group contained strongly religious Catholics who would oppose some types of policies as a matter of principle.

The first question which a panel member might be asked was phrased, "What is being done about the Party?" The answer: "A group of persons led by Dr. Williams have got together and agreed to form a political party for the purpose of giving the country good government in the interests of the people and to provide 'the key needed to open the door behind which the dynamic energies of the people are presently confined.'" Furthermore, the panel member was to instruct his questioners that a party program and constitution were already drafted "and awaiting ratification." An indication of the novelty of the group's pioneering effort in creating an organized party is indicated by the suggestion that the panel speaker should "state what a Party Programme means and the number of Sub-Committees involved in its preparation."

But the second question in this catechetical self image of the group specifically addressed the question of ideology, referring to the left-wing of Norman Manley's Jamaican party which had been expelled in 1952: "Is the party going to follow the Hills' P.N.P. program?" The answer: "Hill is no longer associated with the People's National Party, having been expelled because his views were not consistent with the aims and objectives of the P.N.P."

"Who are the members of the party?" was question three. The answer: "Except it is unavoidable, i.e., where it is necessary to convince listeners, names should not be mentioned . . . ," but panel members should assure their listeners that integrity and the elimination of graft were cardinal principles of the group. The reason for this secrecy was probably partly strategic, aimed at keeping potential opponents in the dark; and there may also have been some desire on the part of members to minimize the risk of possible pressure which might have been brought to bear on them from the established authorities. Question four asked, "What is the Party's attitude to: a) state schools, b) nationalization, c) birth control, d) trade unionism?" The answers are interesting. On state schools (the very issue which had projected Williams into political prominence), "The whole history of education in these parts is linked with denominationalism and it will be folly for anyone or any party to attempt to change that even if he wanted to." On nationalization: "We will want to encourage private capital in order to satisfy the country's greatest need – industrial development – and therefore the question of nationalization does not arise." But in the very next line: "If the situation demands it, Party will be prepared to consider it." As for birth control, this path to higher per capita income was dismissed in one line: "This is not included in our Programme." (Actually, it was widely believed that Dr. Williams did favor birth control, as well as state control of schools, but during the 1956 campaign he disavowed the former and, as we will see, eventually compromised on the latter issue.) The group's attitude toward trade unionism had a familiar ring: "We feel that trade unions in this country should be brought in line with those in the United Kingdom."

Question five came to grips with "What is the party's attitude toward Roman Catholicism?" The answer: "There are many practicing Roman Catholics in the Group who wouldn't remain in if there was any opposition to the faith." This was true enough, for about *one-half* of the top leadership of the P.N.M. would be Roman Catholics, but that designation, in Trinidad as elsewhere, did not define a political type. Some were more devout practicing Catholics than others, some more sensitive to pressures from more conservative Catholic authorities, and some had their ups and downs with the church during the following years. Dr. Williams himself was said to have been reared as a Catholic, but he was not a practicing member of the church. Question six: "Is the party socialist?" Answer: "Our party will be nationalist – we will work for the good of the country." Question seven returned to the population problem and asked what would be done about it. The answer was ingeniously simple and direct: "Raise the standard of living and education and the situation will even itself. We feel that the question in this country is not one of overpopulation but of underdevelopment." Finally, in a catch-all query the panel member was instructed how to answer, "Is Dr. Williams a) irreligious, b) intolerant, c) pro-Indian? [*sic*]" The answers: Dr. Williams was not a fool; and anyone who tried to remove religion from a people in whom it was so deeply rooted would be a fool; Dr. Williams consulted with many people, liked strong arguments, and was always prepared to bow to the will of the majority; neither he nor anyone associated with the group was racially biased, being only pro-West Indian.

This document has been quoted at some length because it strongly suggests that although Dr. Williams may have been regarded as a keeper of the nationalist keys by which the earthly city of democratic nationhood might be entered, his secular development programs at some points conflicted with the religious convictions of many of his adherents and therefore placed an important limitation on his charismatic authority within the group. Williams, despite his status as a black messiah, never claimed that God was on his side, nor that he represented anything more or less than the ideals of the Enlightenment and the Age of Progress as restated in the world anti-colonial movement. Those ideals, however, were not exhaustive of the ultimate values and beliefs of some of his adherents. These had at least to be tolerated because, aside from the question of official church pressure, it was obviously impossible to form a successful political party in the Negro community exclusive of Roman Catholics.

The significance for future political developments of the initial recruitment process can now be visualized in terms of the tri-peaked diagram of the Trinidad social structure presented in Figure 1, on pages 86–7. During the preceding six years executive power had been wielded chiefly by a representative of the middle minorities, the Portuguese Albert Gomes, in a politically-fragmented legislature where East Indians formed the largest ethnic bloc: Ranjit Kumar (engineer), Bhadase Maraj (businessman and cultural leader), Chanka Maharaj (wrestler), Stephen Maharaj (druggist), the Sinanan brothers, Mitra and Ashford (barristers), and Ajodhasingh (masseur). The Negro electorate was represented by such uneducated lower class types at Butler, A. P. T. James of Tobago, and Pope McLean. In order to achieve a greater balance and give representation to the Negro middle class, it had been necessary for the Governor to nominate two exemplars of the old Port of Spain middle class, Miss Audrey Jeffers and L. C. Hannays.

The social composition of P.N.M. leadership and its first cabinet would be entirely different: Dr. Williams (Political Leader), Dr. Solomon (Deputy Political Leader), and Learie Constantine (Party Chairman), all occupied a status at the pinnacle of the Negro community; Williams' closest associates in launching the party had been middle class Negroes – W. J. Alexander, D. W. Rogers, John Donaldson, Andrew Carr. These were among the men who would establish the image of the party for the Negro electorate as one securely in the hands of a Negro leadership. Not a single Hindu of renown nor a really eminent member of Port of Spain commercial elite was included. To balance the ticket there is, to be sure, a Christianized Hindu, Dr. Winston Mahabir, and the Moslem leader Kamalludin Mohammed.

The racial bias in the social backgrounds of the P.N.M. leadership was not, as already emphasized, a product of deliberate preference; rather, it was an emergent consequence of the early membership criteria and of the informal recruitment process which fanned-out through the links of personal acquaintances in the "educated" Negro middle class and its periphery. Indeed, the party leadership probably could not have been as diverse as it was, were it not for the emergence of a broader class awareness among the most educated of all ethnic groups, including detribalised East Indians, around the "cultural" events which swung into high gear after World War II. Before the war, from all accounts, the Trinidad middle classes, taking their cue from the European snobbery of the colonial elite, tended to view the local folk culture as something shameful. The mentality of the P.N.M. leadership was entirely different, the product of a major transformation in social consciousness. In the post-war period the educated Trinidad middle class discovered the *artistic validity and prestige* of local folk culture. The process by which this occurred is complex, but it had the dual significance of forming a congerie of patrons and publicists of local culture, and it helped pave the way psychologically for a middle class rapprochement with the masses. The history of this cultural movement cannot be detailed here, but two milestones can be cited: the establishment of *The Little Carib* modern folk dance theater by Beryl MacBurnie in the late 1940's and the middle class discovery of the steelband in the early 1950's. In the souvenir program marking the opening night of *The Little Carib* there is a long list of local supporters, a number of whom would be active in the formation of the P.N.M. Not surprisingly, Dr. Eric Williams, then newly returned to Trinidad after fifteen years in England and the United States, was called upon to write an introduction on the value and significance of the West Indian cultural movement. *The Little Carib* marks a major event in the beginning of the Negro elite's affirmation of a distinctive and worthwhile local artistic tradition which would lead to recognition for the steel-bandsmen, spawn folk choruses and dance groups, and culminate in the mass, island-wide village musical competitions in Queen's Hall during the independence period.

Coinciding with this Negro movement in the post-war years is the renaissance of East Indian middle class interest in Indian drama, music and dance. But this movement is largely independent of, and competitive with, the Creole cultural activity, and its political and social significance will be the exact reverse. Whereas the Negro middle class's embrace of the steelband and Carnival as valid art forms serves to stimulate an identification with the local society and thus support nationalist sentiments, the East Indian cultural renaissance, based as it is on a prestigious foreign tradition, can only serve to preserve or revitalize the nostalgia for Mother India. The Creole cultural movement, of which T.E.C.A. was a part, leads directly to the middle class nationalist political movement; the Indian cultural revival will serve to retard the creolization of that minority and will be used to reinforce an anti-nationalist ethnic solidarity.

The advent of the P.N.M. in 1956, then, did not represent an upsurge of either the trade unions or lower class leaders to political power. There was, rather, a delayed move by the Negro middle class into the seats of power at last being vacated. Although the social upheaval accompanying this historic political shift obscured the fact, it is perfectly evident from the stated policies and objectives of Dr. Williams and the P.N.M. that they meant the transition to be as smooth as possible. From the time of his initial public lectures at the University in the summer of 1955, it is clear that Dr. Williams had foreseen certain sources of internal conflict and was prepared to seek an accommodation in a number of important areas of policy with the traditional elite. There had been considerable public discussion in the press, for example, as to what the fate of white business interests would be under a fully elected legislature to which they could probably not hope to be elected as independent spokesmen for property. Williams attempted to deal with this issue by making the novel proposal that an upper house, a Senate, to be appointed by the government, should be provided so as to give the nation the advantage of the counsel of the elite of various institutional orders such as business, the churches, and the trade unions. By the standards of the time this constitutional proposal, implemented in the independence constitution, was decidedly accommodative in that an elective, unicameral legislature was most commonly envisaged.

Here is Andrew Carr's account of his initial reaction when Dr. Williams showed him the memorial on constitutional reform for which he would lead the signature campaign:

> I liked the idea of people at all levels of our cosmopolitan, multi-racial and multi-religious society coming together in some way to participate in the government of the country. I had read my *Hansard* from 1950 and was able to appreciate the value of the contributions made to debates in the house by the nominated members. I had previously talked with friends on the subject. I had conceded that a wholly elected chamber was constitutionally progressive but I also wanted to see the country benefit from the talent and capability of these people who did not seem to have a chance at the polls under adult suffrage, at least during a transitional stage to the ultimate of constitutional progress. So the memorial pleased me.[3]

That "these people" were seriously concerned over their fate in a fully elected legislature is manifested in a number of articles from the newspapers of the period. Canon M. E. Farquhar, for example, whose "Candid Comments" in the *Guardian* usually reflected an Old Guard attitude toward political progress, stated the problem in terms very similar to the way the P.N.M. activist just quoted put it. Reading the speeches delivered in the legislature, the Canon observed, made one realize how barren and poverty-stricken that body would be if it were deprived of the nominated members. If dependent on the popular vote, he was convinced, these able persons would not be allowed to give service to the community:

> As against this point of view it will be argued that Sir Gerald Wight [a leading Trinidad tycoon] once contested a seat with success. With respect to Sir Gerald nearly all the circumstances in his favor were specially unique. He was a popular personality who, without actually committing himself, managed to convey the [false?] impression of possessing generously liberal political and social instincts. It is doubtful now that he would make the same impression.[4]

The handwriting was on the wall for all to see: the days of direct control of the government by the white ruling class were over. While Williams' proposal to provide a place for them in a Senate with limited powers might be interpreted as kicking them upstairs where they could work a minimum of mischief, his specific short term economic policies, as distinguished from the vague, all-encompassing generalities of his philosophy on the state's role in economic affairs, could not have been less controversial. As already suggested, he duly affirmed the Jamaican and Puerto Rican model. From the outset of his lectures on economic development at the University he advocated the establishment of the very Industrial Development Corporation which many businessmen had themselves favored, and which was a logical extension of the 1950 Pioneer Industries Ordinance with its tax holiday and other incentives for the private investor. What the business community was unable to do for itself the P.N.M. would do for it: assure it of a place in the councils of government and promote local investment and prosperity.

If the Trinidad commercial elite had responded to these early P.N.M. proposals for political accommodation and government assistance with a calculating assessment of economic self-interest, then the ensuing history of Trinidad politics would be intelligible in Marxist terms. Instead, they responded less in terms of economic class interest and more as a status group anxious and resentful that its traditional position of social and political supremacy was coming to an end. With the P.N.M. victory of 1956, major sections of the commercial community withdrew into an anxious, stony silence, relinquishing public criticism of the P.N.M. to the condescending editorials of the *Guardian* and the sometimes semi-hysterical jeremiads of the opposition members of the Legislative Council. That the black masses had elevated an essentially gradualist, reform oriented, middle class group to political eminence counted less than the historic shift in status and power which the advent of the P.N.M. signaled. Trinidad politics entered a spiral of political polarization between the P.N.M. and its opponents in the business community and among most of the East Indian members of the legislative opposition. This climate of acrimony and mutual suspicion reached fever pitch during the General Elections of December, 1961, when the opposition Democratic Labour Party ("neither democratic, supported by labour, nor a political party" was a favorite taunt of P.N.M. spokesmen) charged, among other things, that Dr. Williams had made large deposits of gold in a Swiss bank and was preparing to flee the country.

Thus a crisis of political legitimacy had accompanied the P.N.M. into office. The traditional elites of Trinidad were not prepared to accept the overnight transition to party politics which was introduced in 1956; least of all were they prepared to accept the idea that Dr. Eric Williams could for long maintain himself in office by democratic means. It is important to bear in mind that from 1956 to 1961 the P.N.M. was indeed a minority party; 61 per cent of the votes cast in 1956 had gone to non-P.N.M. candidates. The opposition could charge that only an Oxonian conspiracy between Dr. Williams and Governor Beetham had made possible the establishment of the P.N.M. tyranny. This was, in a sense, perfectly true; had Beetham and the Colonial Office not exercised their authority to tilt the scales in favor of pro-Williams nominees to the Legislative Council, the Oxford graduate would not have been able to monopolize the Executive and bring party discipline to bear on all of the government members of the legislature. Formerly influential opposition politicians were almost totally isolated from policy-making positions, their alienation accentuated by the bitterness of the feuds which continued to rage until almost the advent of independence. This was, perhaps, the heaviest social cost of modernizing the Trinidad political system along British lines. There were those who wondered privately if it had been worth it, or even necessary. "I think Dr. Williams made a fetish out of party discipline," an astute, erstwhile member of the P.N.M. inner council said. "He was so eager to avoid the anarchy of the old system that he went to extremes in the other direction."

Extreme or not, the P.N.M. under the expert leadership of Dr. Williams, the specialized parliamentary skills of Dr. Patrick Solomon — the only P.N.M. leader with previous experience in the colony's legislature — and the broader legal and constitutional advice of such close associates as the barristers W. J. Alexander and A. N. R. Robinson, made dramatic strides in modernizing the political life of the islands. From a system of multi-party instability, individual Ministerial autonomy and inadquate safeguards of the public purse, operating under the paternalism of a colonial establishment, the P.N.M. inaugurated an era of coordinated single-party responsibility for all phases of government. A two-party system emerged almost overnight: in 1956 there had been six political parties running nine or more candidates for the Legislative Council; by the time of the elections to the federal parliament in 1958 the P.N.M.'s solidarity had compelled a somewhat odd assortment of old-style political individualists to make common cause with a group of East Indian politicians. Lacking an outstanding leader after Bhadase Maraj withdrew from politics, this coalition called upon Dr. Rudranath Capildeo to forsake his teaching position at the University of London and return to Trinidad to match "knowledgism" with Dr. Eric Williams. Although Dr. Capildeo would give the Democratic Labour Party an aura of academic distinction aimed at rivaling that of the leader of the P.N.M., he inherited a very loosely organized party and occupied a position of leadership quite unlike that of Williams. He too, to be sure, became the recipient of charismatic devotion on the part of many in his ethnic minority, but for reasons that will be seen in the following chapter, he never achieved the degree of personal control over his political associates which Dr. Williams had exercised. Dr. Williams had attracted disciples; Dr. Capildeo had been summoned by men of far greater political experience, and political ambition.

With one "doctor" leading the predominantly Creole political party and another "doctor" rallying East Indian support for the politicians who chiefly represented that ethnic minority, the Trinidad two-party system emerged in a form which strongly tended to parallel the island's ethnic structure. Vertical ethnic and status group consciousness and conflict took precedence over horizontal class conflict of the type which had characterized the ideology of Cipriani, Butler and the earlier socialist radicals. Both parties rested heavily on the charismatic appeal of their respective men of knowledge; neither was initially based directly on strong support from the major trade unions. Despite the formal similarities to the British political system, therefore, political bifurcation in Trinidad tended to take place along ethnic rather than class divisions in the social structure. There was no "labor" versus "conservative" party. Sections of "big business" casting about for a basis of mass support, and viewing the thrifty Indian as a lesser evil, turned for a time to Dr. Capildeo and the D.L.P. but, as he told me with bitterness during the heat of the 1961 campaign, such support had proved to be chimerical.

While politics generated racial tension between Indian and Creole and between the new men of power and the old, the P.N.M. successfully attempted to disarm one traditional source of opposition to state-inspired reforms. No sooner was the ink dry on the Tobago agreement over Chaguaramas than the P.N.M. government announced that it had signed a Concordat with the heads of the islands' denominational boards of education.[5] The circumstances surrounding the decision to come to terms with religious authorities, particularly the Roman Catholic Church, on a basis considerably short of Dr. Williams' original position advocating state control of education, were not elicited with enough clarity and consistency to bear a lengthy attempt at reconstruction. Several key points, however, seem clear. The first was that what one P.N.M. leader described as "the old teachers' bloc" in the party continually pressed for action which would produce drastic reforms in the structure of control over the administration and curriculum of the denominational schools. The old teachers' bloc contained some of Williams' oldest and closest supporters; indeed, he had been projected to public eminence with the assistance and support of many in this group. The T.E.C.A. leaders, in all likelihood, expected that once in power Williams would be prepared to carry the fight for educational reform to the limit. Under the chairmanship of J. Hamilton Maurice, a distinguished teacher and educator who had returned to Trinidad from his post as Director of Education in Dominica just as the P.N.M. was being formed, a commission to enquire into the structure of the educational system and to recommend reforms was established. Given the number of teachers and ex-teachers in the P.N.M. the entire subject of educational reform was one which aroused considerable interest. In 1959 the Maurice Report on education, which included the recommendation that the government should entirely take over the maintenance of the secondary schools and have sole responsibility for hiring, transferring and dismissing teachers, was published. This was considered completely unacceptable by several of the denominational representatives on the commission, and they refused to sign the final document. In 1960 the P.N.M. Cabinet issued its proposals, based on the recommendations of the Maurice Report, but in many instances it rejected the specific suggestions of the report, including the more radical provisions just mentioned. Even these proposals, however, were either ambiguous and unacceptable to some of the denominational boards, and so further negotiations were carried out which finally produced the Concordat, in which several key concessions were made with respect to hiring teachers and in the prerogatives to be exercised by the boards in the placement of pupils at the secondary level. One major criticism leveled against the latter arrangement was that it permitted the boards to select, irrespective of performance on placement examinations, some pupils of their own choosing in the secondary forms.

The maneuvering surrounding the Concordat was perhaps one of the most intricate political problems which Williams had faced. On this issue, convictions in the party tended to run high and in extreme directions. Interview data gathered by the writer indicated that the top leadership of the party was very closely divided on the issue. The Cabinet itself appears to have been split almost in half. The process of decision on this issue differed from that on most crucial party matters in that it was apparently never taken before party organs for discussion and decision. To be sure, the party program had been vague as to what educational reforms would be carried out, but it was probably also true that there was some feeling that it would be unsafe to take this issue to the party. At any rate, the Concordat was a Cabinet level decision. One leading member of the old teachers' bloc who was disappointed in the action taken stated: "The Cabinet took fright on this issue. But it is probably not finally settled." Interview results on this decision showed this interesting pattern: despite the religious affiliation, or degree of religious participation, those P.N.M. leaders who were or had been teachers, strongly favored more drastic changes in the educational system. Dr. Williams' own action in this issue was difficult to ascertain. Many believed that he had himself privately favored greater changes in the system, but that calculation of the political consequences and a willingness to let his colleagues in the government take the major responsibility for decision had prevented him from personally championing the more militant reforms advocated by the teachers.

The political consequences of the Concordat were, it appears, rather along the lines which had been hoped. Many professed to see in

Dr. Solomon's carrying of the ceremonial canopy in the Catholic procession on Corpus Christi day in 1962 an omen of solid state-church relationships; moreover, when the Archbishop postponed a traditional pilgrimage to the Catholic church atop the Laventille Hills in order that the devout might instead turn out to welcome Dr. Williams back from the independence talks in London in May of 1962, most were convinced that church-state differences were indeed at an end. The breach between secular and transcendental authority was being healed in the Creole-Christian community, and the "Communist" bogey in the form of C. L. R. James had been excommunicated, but the East Indians were in a state of high panic.

CHAPTER 9 Fragments from a Life: The East Indian Reaction

As soon as [the ship] touched the quay . . . I began to feel all my old fear of Trinidad.

– Vidia Naipaul, *The Middle Passage*, 1962[1]

On a lovely Sunday afternoon in October, 1961, I sat among a group of D.L.P. dignitaries while, on the platform a few feet away, Dr. Rudranath Capildeo cried out to a gathering of 30,000 East Indians standing on the Savannah to "arm yourselves with weapons and get ready to take over the government of this country." A few weeks before, he had exhorted his followers to smash the voting machines which the P.N.M. government was installing for the December elections. The dominant tone of the D.L.P. campaign was one of fear and hysteria; it was impossible for an outsider – as I was then – to comprehend the self-defeating tactics which Dr. Capildeo employed. It was evident, however, that there was a deep, non-rational bond between this troubled genius and his followers; but, like most non-Indians in Trinidad the nature of that communion was obscure to me. Three years later, however, Dr. Capildeo invited me to his home for a series of wide-ranging interviews. His candor was remarkable and refreshing; he acted like a man who had come to terms with life but who was still receptive to the most unorthodox speculations. While taking notes on our interviews I repeatedly cautioned him to tell me, since I was preparing a book on Trinidad, what should be kept off-the-record, but he waved these caveats aside. As a result, I was privileged to enter that Trinidad East Indian world of which Vidia Naipaul, peerless West Indian writer, has been the brilliant, melancholy chronicler. The following is my understanding of the story Dr. Capildeo told me.

The ancestors of Dr. Rudranath Capildeo can be traced back to 700 A.D., and perhaps even earlier. Their Brahmin roots were in the United Provinces, in the city of Gorakhpur not far from Nepal and the foothills of the Himalayas. They were minor aristocrats – a clan of small princelings who owned several villages around Gorakhpur. In the last quarter of the nineteenth century one of the sons of the family was sent by railway down to Calcutta to further his religious studies. On his way home to his lodgings one night, he was seized by a press-gang from a ship engaged in recruiting indentured laborers for the West Indies. The next time he touched land was in Port of Spain after the long voyage across the Indian Ocean, around the Cape of Good Hope and the Atlantic. His protests to officials in Trinidad were useless; the Coolies were always claiming they had been shanghaied once they reached Trinidad and decided they did not want to remain.[2]

The abducted youth was Rudranath Capildeo's father, Pundit Capildeo, as he came to be called in Trinidad. After working out his term of indenture on the cane fields of Caroni, he acquired the usual compensation of a small piece of land and share-cropped on soil owned by larger landowners. Pundit Capildeo refused to learn English (except to sign his name: the humiliation of "making his mark" could not be tolerated), but nonetheless married well. Around the turn of the century he was wed to Rosalie Soogee Gobin, whose father was in charge of refining procedures in one of the sugar factories. The elder Gobin had at least put on the appearance of converting to Roman Catholicism, but as soon as fifteen-year-old Soogee married Pundit Capildeo she rejected her family's opportunistic conversion. The next year, 1900, the first child was born, the first of nine girls and two boys. Rudranath, born on Carnival Tuesday in 1920, was the penultimate offspring.

The early environment and education of the young Capildeo was divided between the Hindi and Sanskrit taught at home and the religious and secular education provided by the Canadian Mission School in Chaguanas. Most of the teachers in the school were Indians who had converted to Presbyterianism, and the proseletyzing was prominent in the curriculum. Unless the pupil himself was a proselyte he did not enjoy full favor. There was an economic advantage, too; it seemed that it was the converts who always had books and shoes. Books were scarce; Rudranath frequently found himself huddled with three or four other classmates, all reading the same book.

One of the teachers in the school made a strong impression on young Capildeo between the ages six and ten. Samuel Ramoutar was an exceptional, fair-minded, and compassionate teacher who could make academic subjects come to life. During discussions of government he had the boys take the roles of various government officials. On one occasion, while a classmate was made Prime Minister, Rudranath, wearing a hat adorned to represent a crown, played the part of Constitutional

Monarch. When Capildeo was nine, however, his early education in Chaguanas came to a halt. For two years he was bedridden with rheumatic fever. Physical frailty and acute emotional sensitivity would continue to plague him through much of his early adult life.

In 1925 Pundit Capildeo died during a visit to India. By the time of his death, however, the Capildeos had risen to the rank of one of the leading Hindu families. The elder Gobin had provided capital to open a shop in Chaguanas, and Pundit Capildeo, with the assistance of Indian laborers, had built that quaint, imposing edifice known to this day in Chaguanas as Lion House. An oddity of the house was that it covered every square foot of a lot running at an angle back from the main street, and so the rooms took the shape of parallelograms. (Lion House became the prototype of the "Hanuman House" described by Naipaul in *A House For Mr. Biswas.*) The Capildeos operated a general store, and it was during a business-pleasure trip to India, where he would buy Indian merchandise for sale in Trinidad, that Pundit Capildeo died.

When Rudranath was eleven and had recovered from his bout with rheumatic fever, the widow of Pundit Capildeo suddenly decided on an astonishing course of action for an Indian woman of her generation. She traveled into Port of Spain, to Queen's Royal College, marched into the office of the principal, Mr. Cambridge (from Oxford), and requested that the school enroll Rudranath as a student. Impressed by her daring and determination, the principal agreed, and thus in 1931 Rudranath was placed in the preparatory class of the school where he would be briefly exposed to instruction under the celebrated Island Scholar about to leave for Oxford, Eric Williams.

Now began a seven year ordeal, culminating with Capildeo himself winning an Island Scholarship in 1938. The staff of the school itself was magnificent; after many years of educational experience, Dr. Capildeo would regard it as the most powerful secondary education he had heard of. The teachers were chiefly expatriates, Oxford and Cambridge graduates in the main; but the staff also included one Indian, and above all, G. E. Pilgrim, a light-skinned Barbadian instructor who taught mathematics and led the Cadet Corps. Capildeo did poorly at arithmetic, but he excelled in Geometry, Spanish and Latin. English compositions, however, were torture. From his environment in a Hindu home in the heart of Caroni he had learned to speak a pidgin English and viewed the language as a difficult foreign tongue.

Enrollment at Q.R.C. did not lead to escape from Lion House and Chaguanas, an environment which he found increasingly oppressive. Quite the contrary: his mother escorted him from Lion House via the government railway into town every Sunday evening, to a small house in lower Luis Street in Woodbrook, which Pundit Capildeo had casually acquired some years earlier, and she remained with him throughout the week until Friday, when they would both return to Chaguanas. During the weekends Rudranath worked as an unpaid clerk in the family shop, and then on Sunday evening, after loading up provisions of flour, rice and fish for the coming week, mother and son would return to town for another round of scholarship. This rigid, extremely frugal schedule, which meant that he had little time for recreation and camaraderie in the social life of the capital, was adhered to for almost the entire seven years at Q.R.C. In 1937, however, after he had sat for the Island Scholarship for the first time, and had placed seventh, he gave his mother an ultimatum: either she must free him from his duties at Lion House so that he could devote all his time to studies, or she must guarantee him the price of the scholarship, £2,000, if he failed to win on his second try. Mrs. Capildeo chose to release him from his family business chores, and so Rudranath could devote all his energies, fifteen and sixteen hours a day, to "the terrifying ordeal" of studying for the scholarship.

There were few other Indian boys at Q.R.C. during the early Thirties. Out of 366 scholars enrolled during one year, 60 were of European descent, 6 were Indians, while the majority of the remainder were Negroes, largely sons of civil servants and professional families. Although his closest friend was a Negro, young Rudranath's experiences with many of the Creoles were highly traumatic. To them he was the little Coolie boy from Chaguanas. Some Negro classmates, exercising what they implicitly believed was the Creole birthright, taunted and bullied him. He was continually involved in fights. Once, when he was a few years older, he knocked down an antagonistic fellow member of the Cadet Corps, and would have killed him with the butt of a carbine, but was restrained before he could land the blow. His humiliation as a "Coolie boy" was not limited to the sadism of his classmates, however, for even his teachers made occasional sport of his backwardness. Every Friday morning a course in religious knowledge was given by a spokesman for one of the island's many denominations. While waiting for this class to begin one morning, an instructor held up a ruler before the class and asked, "Tell me, Capildeo – what is it you worship? Is this what you worship?" The slur at Hindu "idol worship" was much appreciated by the Christian scholars in the class. In that competitive Public School atmosphere, however, "sneaking" was considered the greatest crime, and Capildeo had to learn boyhood stoicism. The scars of this boyhood oppression, however, would never completely heal. To stand up for the rights of Indians, to strike back, to even the score for past perceived injustices, would become a rallying theme in the angry rhetoric which marked Dr. Capildeo's pre-independence political speeches.

Although he eventually learned to give a good accounting of himself in response to the perpetual bullying that seemed to be inflicted on him, Capildeo's competitive energies were channeled chiefly into his performance in the classroom. The scholarship was the gate to freedom. He dreamed of the scholarship day and night. His home life was unhappy; his mother was haunted by the traditional Indian anxiety and insecurity over land and money. And then, in 1938 – by which time the number of Indians at Q.R.C. had already risen to 60 – he won the scholarship. His decision to include math among his subjects had been made solely on pragmatic grounds: it was possible to obtain a higher score in mathematics than in the humanities, and he scored the highest mark ever obtained in that subject. He prepared to go to the University of London to study medicine. The gate to freedom outside Trinidad swung open, and on August 7th, 1939, after putting in the usual period of the scholarship winner teaching at Q.R.C., Rudranath Capildeo left Trinidad on the German liner *Caribbia*, leaving behind him a family determined that more "Readers and Learners" (as the flock of young scholars are called in *Biswas*) must be produced.

Far more than Eric Williams at Oxford, young Capildeo in Trinidad in the Thirties was almost totally oblivious to contemporary politics. He was sorry for the hungry workers who marched behind Uriah Butler, but he had no firm political opinions. From boyhood, however, he had been fascinated by the stories of great battles and military achievements. From local press accounts of Nazi Germany, he had developed a very high opinion of Hitler and the Third Reich. Hitler was quite a fellow. Aboard the *Caribbia* pictures of Hitler were everywhere; there were members of the German-American Bund on the ship, and at certain hours the passengers would be barred from the lounge while the crew was given Nazi indoctrination. Thus began his first direct exposure to the conflicts in European ideologies and history which would become an absorbing and emotionally-significant adjunct to his formal studies in science.

Arriving in Plymouth, he took the train to Paddington Station. His first glimpse of England produced a reaction of shock. The sameness of the buildings, the stark shabbiness and poverty everywhere were totally unlike his idea of what the Mother Country was like. Met by his cousin in London, he was taken around to 211 Albany Street, near Regent Park, where he obtained lodgings which he would view as his first real home. His landlady was Jewish, a Menshevik exile from Kiev, and with her and her husband he would spend many hours in heated political debate. In Trinidad he had been taught a vague loathing of the Bolsheviks, but in the company of these Russian nationalists, during these first months in London at the outbreak of World War II, he began to acquire a broader world-view.

In October of 1939, the Science faculty of the University of London was evacuated to Bangor, North Wales, and then began a period of acute emotional depression and physical disability. Try as he might, Rudranath could not make friends. His roommate, a Jamaican Negro, was very popular and was continually being invited out; the vista of studies for another five or six years seemed to stretch out as an eternity. Unaccustomed to some of the science subjects in the curriculum, the previous security of his supremacy in the classroom was not there to buoy him up. He desperately wanted to go home to Trinidad. It had all been a mistake. In January of 1941, the strains generated by the war, the new depressing environment, his lack of personal popularity and his slipping academic achievements landed him in the hospital with another bout of rheumatic fever that lasted a full year. It was a bitter time of self-recrimination and loneliness. He realized that he had never acquired any opinions of his own; that, despite his exemplary and virtuous life as a Brahamin son and scholar, he would now die in the gloomy atmosphere of the poor ward of a North Wales hospital.

But despite the pain and depression his body stubbornly refused to die. As an extremely religious youth he prayed intensely. He could not understand why this had happened to him. He had believed that by observing religious forms and ceremonies and by following God's commandments blessings would be showered upon him. Looking back on his life he realized how shallow and untrue this simple faith had been; if God existed he was not concerned with the suffering of ordinary people. Rudranath now determined that he would break through the crust of conventional piety and that he would do and say what he pleased. To pass the endless hours and to escape from the constant pain he began to learn Welsh and make friends with other patients in the ward.

It was the beginning of a period of great success. He declared himself to be an absolutist agnostic, convinced that what other people thought they knew they did not really know. He began reading in comparative religions, trying to build a new, more mature world-view for himself. When he was discharged from the hospital he found that his legs were too weak for him to perform the laboratory work required for the medical course, and he was forced to switch to mathematics. But now he discovered an entirely unexpected consequence of this period of physical and spiritual turmoil: his mind seemed to be opening up, his comprehension increasing daily. He had previously regarded science and mathematics as formal structures consisting of fixed axioms, laws and logical procedures; he had not even understood that the Newtonian mechanics he had studied at Q.R.C. had a real-world referrent. In a rush of insight he now understood for the first time the manipulative, creative procedures of mathmatical and scientific thought. He began producing solutions to math problems which astounded his instructor. He became fascinated with the meaning and origins of numbers; he was made Treasurer of the student Mathematics Society; and in 1943 he was awarded a B.Sc. with first class honors in mathematics and physics.

Proceeding on to graduate work at Bangor, Capildeo now entered fully into student life. The shy Coolie boy, "the little frog spawned in the water who had almost died on land," was no more; instead, there emerged a rather conceited young man who seems to have been highly conscious of his superior gifts. When he was approached to stand for a post on the committee of the students' Union he replied that he did not wish to do so, but if they really wanted him they would see to it that there was no opposing candidate. It was so arranged.

He revelled in controversy, deliberately choosing the most unpopular side in the debates he now joined. He supported euthanasia and Communism. He led the Communist party in the elections for the student mock parliament and won a huge majority of seats, defeating both the Welsh Nationalists and the Conservatives. He became an avid reader of newspapers and periodicals, especially the *New Statesman* and *News Chronicle*. The war reawakened his childhood passion for great battles and warriors. He was enthralled by the Russian resistance led by Stalin, a fellow Oriental after all. Ideological consciousness among the students was acute. The socialist societies and the Communist society were at dagger points; the Conservatives and Communists got along rather well, however. During this hectic period of deep involvement in political affairs Capildeo was even invited to deliver a sermon in a local church, and on the appointed date it was packed with students who would not miss this spectacle of a pagan in the pulpit. When he had concluded his strong plea for social awareness and reform, the students shocked the congregation by breaking into applause. It was a wild and stirring night. By 1944 he had been elected President of the Men's Union and, with the war drawing to a close, participated in the re-establishment of the University in London. In 1945 he was awarded the M.Sc. in mathematics with a mark of distinction. He had achieved everything he had set out to do – and more.

Capildeo was now twenty-five years old. Fifteen years would pass before he was chosen to rally the opposition to the P.N.M. in Trinidad.

These were years of achievement and drift. He had developed a deep affection for England and would have remained there after receiving his Master's degree but for the fact that, rightly or not, he felt that as an Indian his chances for a permanent University post were slight. In September of 1945 he returned to Trinidad and accepted a teaching position at Q.R.C. Once again he lived with his mother on Luis Street, cycling to and from the College.

The year he spent back at Q.R.C. would end in disaster, but in the meantime, he found distraction in the political events which were sweeping the colony. His elder brother Simbhoonath entered politics in 1946 as a candidate to the Legislative Council for the United Front. Although Simbhoonath had not gone abroad to study he had nonetheless achieved the rank of solicitor, and through such activities as participation in the East Indian Debating Association he had attained some stature in the Indian community. Rudranath's first brush with real politics came during this campaign in which he assisted his brother in mustering the vote for the United Front candidate in Caroni.

The 1946 election in Trinidad, the first held there under universal suffrage, coincided with two other events of great importance. The first, of purely local significance, was the centennial celebration of the beginning of Indian immigration to Trinidad; the second, of world-wide significance, was the imminent advent of independence for India. From 1945 can be dated the renaissance of Indian consciousness and culture in the colony. Ranjit Kumar, who had come to Trinidad from India in 1935 in connection with the distribution of the first Indian film, *Bala Joban*, and who had remained to become an assistant city engineer in Port of Spain, donned the largely discarded Indian *dhoti* and entered the 1946 election campaign. The year before, orators at the Indian centenary observances had stressed their loyalty to Mother India and their determination to keep the Indian community intact and to disseminate Indian culture more vigorously.[3]

Rudranath Capildeo, the sophisticated university scholar, took no part in this resurgence of Indian feeling. Instead, he suddenly found himself threatened with dismissal from his job. He had written an article for the *Guardian* which argued that the output of science students at Q.R.C. could be radically expanded and that the College should become the nucleus of a University College. Independent public declarations of educational policy did not sit well with the Director of Education, who threatened to call a commission of inquiry to investigate this insubordinate behavior by a staff member. Under the circumstances, Capildeo probably did the wisest thing: against the protestations of his mother he sold his books and fled back to Mother England.

Capildeo now begins the struggle up through the ranks of an academic career at the University of London. Starting in 1946 as Junior Demonstrator, he rises to Senior Demonstrator, Temporary Assistant Lecturer, Assistant Lecturer and, finally, in 1950, is made a full Lecturer. In the meantime, he has done his Ph.D. with a thesis on "The Flexure Problem in Elasticity," a problem with very practical implications in the field of aerodynamics. He is beginning to feel secure in his academic competence and prospects; he finds that in a seminar with some of Britain's leading scientists he can easily hold his own. The lingering fear that the European always, somehow, had something up his sleeve to make him one-up is finally dispelled. He makes a noble resolve: as a scientist he will not succumb to the pressures of publish-or-perish, he will not waste his time in pot-boiler research. He will tackle the big problems such as the Theory of Relativity. He is troubled by it. Why? He begins to keep to himself; gives up all political concerns; acquires the reputation of being something of a crank. In 1954 he is again stricken ill and takes a leave of absence from the University. For a change of scene he accepts a job in the Sudan for a year. After a promising beginning it ends in a fiasco of intrigue and misunderstanding.

Back in England Capildeo begins to read for the law. Following his mother's death in 1952 he has become a man of independent means. There was a brief trip back to Trinidad in 1953 to settle the estate. With Bhadase Maraj, who now is a dominant figure among Trinidad's Hindus, and Simbhoonath, an officer of the Hindu cultural organization which Bhadase heads, he discusses the possibility of establishing a Hindu school with himself as its principal. Nothing comes of the proposal. He acquires a home in Brighton and during the following years his life runs in a cycle between the months of involvement and discontent in Trinidad and the periods of rest, resuscitation and scholarly output in England.[4]

The great events which marked the beginning of P.N.M. rule in Trinidad find Rudranath living in the colony as a practicing barrister. He enjoys his law practice but is appalled by the facility with which some of his colleagues can convert their offices into bedrooms in order to obtain payment from impecunious lady clients. He is horrified when a young lady client of his own inquires if perhaps her favors might substitute for cash payment. He is rescued from this diversion from his scientific training by an offer from the P.N.M.

government to become principal of the Trinidad Polytechnic. In the midst of speculation that the offer is an attempt to side-track a possible adversary from a career in politics, Capildeo accepts the job and during the following year acquires a reputation as a superb educational organizer and administrator. Once again he has reached a pinnacle of fame and success. At the insistence of friends and the then-publisher of the *Guardian*, however, he soon leaves the Polytechnic to become Political Leader of the Democratic Labour Party in order to lead the struggle against the new black tyranny in Trinidad.

It is a decision he will soon regret. And yet, at the outset, the decision to enter politics in Trinidad seems a highly reasonable course of action for him to follow. He is the son of a late Pundit from Chaguanas, independently well-to-do, an intellectual with dual qualifications in science and law, personally attractive, and has a wide circle of admirers. At forty Dr. Capildeo can rightly be called "Trinidad's Most Educated Man" and can readily be cast in the role of savior of a minority still sensitive to the epithet, "ignorant Coolie." But he encounters two great obstacles to success in his newly-found political career: the nature of the Democratic Labour Party – and himself.

The D.L.P. had come into existence in 1958 for the purpose of contesting the federal elections in March of that year. It was organized as the Trinidad wing of a loose confederation of parties led by Bustamante of Jamaica and was fashioned to oppose the Manley-Adams-Williams coalition. In Trinidad as elsewhere it was essentially a collection of politicians currently in opposition in the local legislatures. Only in Jamaica, in the form of Bustamante's Jamaica Labour Party, was it an organized party in the proper sense. In Trinidad it represented a wide assortment of opponents to the P.N.M., predominantly East Indians and businessmen. Although Manley and Adams succeeded in winning majorities for the federal legislature in their islands and would be able to form the federal government, the D.L.P. in Trinidad won a surprising victory over the P.N.M. This had two important consequences: it added new fuel to the charge that the P.N.M. represented a tyrannical minority in Trinidad, and, as the feud between Adams and Williams developed over Chaguaramas and other issues, it had the ironical effect of now leading the traditionally anti-federalist East Indians to embrace the federal government as their new guardian. From the floor of the federal house on St. Vincent Street in Port of Spain, anti-P.N.M. politicians like Albert Gomes and Ashford Sinanan found higher ground from which to launch a verbal barrage against Dr. Williams and the P.N.M.

But, as against this history of recent political success, the Trinidad

D.L.P. can offer Dr. Capildeo little in the way of a coherent political orientation or organization. It is a collection of politicians, as he views it, united only by diverse personal interests and a common opposition to the P.N.M. Privately, he expresses the view that it is based solely on a conspiracy of fear. If the P.N.M. can be accused of organizational defects and inconsistency in some aspects of policy, the D.L.P. solves these problems by remaining almost totally unorganized and bereft of any clear policies whatsoever.

Thus, when Dr. Capildeo enters politics his personal political views, which are broadly socialist, are almost totally irrelevant. His task is simply to enter the ring and match knowledgism with Dr. Williams. But he is temperamentally ill-suited for the role of belligerent challenger in a tense political climate. Once again, in a situation of stress, he suffers a severe breakdown. His nervous system is shattered; he experiences uncontrollable hysterical episodes in which he becomes as "weepy as a child." He makes the astonishing public proposal that Trinidad's tourist trade can be enhanced if a tunnel is blasted through the Northern Range to Maracas Bay. Gleefully, Creole Trinidad seizes on these incidents: he becomes nicknamed The Mad Scientist and is so immortalized in a popular calypso.

In the midst of this public vilification and nervous exhaustion Capildeo begins another intensive period of self discovery. This time it leads him . . . to God. The route, however, is a circuitous one. He has known for some time that he has been running from something. He has been living in grand style and can afford almost any material indulgence he pleases, but he has begun to feel shabby. In desperation he has turned to holy scripture, frantically searching the Bible and the Gita for clues to his condition. After a thorough hospital check-up reveals no physical malfunction, he is prepared to accept a very difficult truth about himself suggested by Jesus's apparently ridiculous question to the man who had waited 38 years for a miraculous cure at the side of the pool in Jerusalem: "Wilt thou be made whole?" (John 5: 1-10). Was it possible that he himself was ill because, in some remote region of his soul, he did not desire, or felt he did not deserve, to be well?

Deeply troubled and confused Capildeo leaves Trinidad and returns to Brighton, his life in shambles. By chance he comes across a copy of a book by C. E. Barker, *Nerves and Their Cure.* The author is living nearby and Capildeo makes an appointment to see him. Barker immediately makes a deep impression on him; he is told that healing is a matter of restoring the harmony of the mind and body. Jesus is one agent by which this internal force could be channeled. He assures Capildeo that he will get well. Leaving Barker's house

Capildeo receives an intimation of the mystical experiences which will become possible for him: incredibly, he seems to fly down the road for three miles.

Still in a state of emotional and spiritual chaos, Capildeo is nonetheless compelled to cut short his visits with Barker to return to Trinidad for the election campaign of 1961, now only a few months away.

From the D.L.P. *Statesman*, May 13, 1961:

> MAN WITH A MISSION
>
> The sun blazed down. Heat waves shimmered up from the roadway. Shoes were covered with dust. But the steady procession of cars, trucks, buses and jitneys kept rolling into Piarco on May 1 – Labour Day.
>
> Hundreds of Party ties – with a blazing torch were being sold. Thousands of Party buttons were pinned down on shirts, coat and dresses. The children and women gulped down 'soft' drinks while here and there some young men guzzled down cold beer. The air was charged with excitement and expectation . . .
>
> The speck in the distance grew bigger and bigger and in a short while the B.W.I.A. plane thundered down the runway, turned and taxied in. The door opened and the passengers began to alight as a strange hush fell upon the waiting crowd.
>
> Finally Dr. Rudranath Capildeo appeared and waved. The crowd surged forward like a river bursting its banks. A deafening roar went up as the Doctor came down the ramp to embrace his sisters . . .
>
> Members of the Executive, led by Mr. Ashford Sinanan and Dr. Forrester, managed to clear a path and lead Dr. Capildeo to the platform. After months of hoping that Capildeo's health would improve rapidly enough to permit him to return to lead the D.L.P. in time for the General Elections, after the tension and excitement of the last moments, many wept openly in that emotion-packed moment . . .
>
> And then came Dr. Rudranath Capildeo – A Man with a Mission. His straight-from-the-shoulder speech was punctuated by deafening cheers. In language which showed the poetry in the man's soul, in words that revealed a fearless and inexorable desire to follow the path of truth, in a manner which showed that principle would not be sacrificed for expediency . . .

Dr. Capildeo told them that, despite the atmosphere of disloyalty and intrigue within the D.L.P., the crisis created by the P.N.M.'s destruction of the Civil Service, the judiciary, and practically every other phase of life had made his presence necessary. He told them that the damage would take years to repair, but they need not be dismayed because "*he knew something about relativity and would contract the time.*" The throng then disbanded to form a mammoth motorcade to Port of Spain.

It was a brave front, but he was still melancholic and deeply disturbed. His closest friends and associates realized he was very sick and a search was made in England for a healer and medium who would come to Trinidad to help him. Contact was made with one of the top practitioners in this art – a Mrs. Collins. She, however, was much in demand and at first refused to come. Then she came. She had received insistent spiritualist messages that she must come. Capildeo was not surprised; Barker had already discussed spiritualism with him and, as a physicist not unresponsive to unconventional speculations, Capildeo was prepared to accept the validity of such phenomena.

Mrs. Collins turned out to be a very jolly middle-aged woman, not at all the austere mystic he had imagined. His friends were harassing her for information about the elections. She was no sooner off the plane than she had announced the as-yet-secret date of the elections. Capildeo himself was intrigued with her gift of prophecy. He handed her a newspaper advertisement which contained the photographs of the D.L.P. executive. She scrutinized the faces and pointed to one of them: this man could not be counted on. Capildeo was astounded. She had pointed to the one man in the executive in whom he had complete confidence: Ajodhasingh, the renowned and gentle masseur from south Trinidad. Bewildered, he asked who on the D.L.P. team he could trust. You can trust no one on this team, Mrs. Collins told him. A few months later Ajodhasingh died, and all Trinidad mourned for him.

Mrs. Collins' treatments consisted of the laying on of hands. She always insisted that Capildeo request the healing before she administered it. Her hands would become icy cold or hot; he was in no doubt that there was a flow of energy taking place. Still, improvement did not come immediately. A group was formed for a holiday in Tobago and the treatments continued there. One night he startled his sister at dinner when he began to laugh and joke, the first time she had seen him behave in this manner for years. He began to get better . . . he had a vision of the sea, blue and peaceful . . . he was getting a glimpse of the world beyond appearances, the world which the Gita described in the cryptic verse that asserts that the unreal never is, and the real never is not. After ten days Mrs. Collins returned to England. But Capildeo now was on the road to inner discoveries and revelations which he had never before imagined to exist.

Before he could be released to return to England to practice these new arts of healing, however, he had a bitter political campaign to wage. In Port of Spain he was brutally heckled. One evening, during a speech from the verandah of a house at a corner of Victoria Square, he attempted to explain the implications of science for the economic development of the country. As I looked on incredulously, his Negro antagonists howled and raged like crazed animals against the cast iron fence which fortunately separated the house from the street. It was a hideous ordeal, but he bore it with fortitude. Somehow sensing his vulnerability the mob, under the eyes of the alert but inactive police, redoubled their taunts: Mad Scientist, Mad Scientist. The D.L.P. campaign soon withdrew from the streets altogether and was conducted indoors, chiefly in private homes.

Capildeo had already reached the end of his tether. He had already decided to meet steel with steel. The alleged bullying and victimization of Indians by the Negroes would be met blow for blow. Was the government introducing voting machines to confuse the Indian country voters? "Smash the voting machines!" Was the government of black fascism going to refuse to yield power to the democratic majority? "Arm yourselves with weapons and prepare to take over the government of this country!" Like the Hindu astrologers in India who had predicted the end of the world would come at the end of 1961, Dr. Capildeo and his colleagues seemed to insist that prediction would be fulfilled in Trinidad unless the D.L.P. won.[5]

Repeatedly in the months preceding the General Elections in early December of 1961 Dr. Capildeo cried out to his followers to take violent action. He was listened to solemnly, sometimes with great devotion. But, aside from some reprisals against P.N.M. candidates in the country districts and one night of terror in an eastern suburb of Port of Spain, no mass action against the government materialized. His call to violence, designed to end forever the ancient stereotype of the weak and fearful Coolie which had made Indians the prey of Negro bullying and arrogance, went unanswered. Rather than gaining support, the D.L.P. now lost support. Intended by some business interests to serve as the party of order, it became the party of disorder. It was decisively beaten at the polls, winning but one-third of the seats to the legislature, and those primarily on the basis of heavily East Indian country districts. Throughout the campaign the P.N.M., with considerable sagacity, refrained from lodging official charges against Dr. Capildeo.

During the months between the elections and the final independence negotiations in London the following May, Dr. Capildeo continued to lead the struggle against the P.N.M. from his new position in the legislative opposition. But misery piled upon misery as he sustained highly painful and temporarily crippling injuries in an automobile accident. The final blow came when Reginald Maudling, the Secretary of State for the Colonies, called him for a private audience at the beginning of the independence talks at Marlborough House. No matter what protests he and his delegation made, Maudling told him, Trinidad & Tobago was going to become an independent nation, and that was that. Later, during a recess in the conference, Dr. Williams approached him on a balcony at Marlborough House and an informal truce was declared.

Perhaps it was just as well. He has fought the good fight as he saw it to the bitter end. He can now, in good conscience, begin a partial disengagement from politics and devote himself fully to the discovery of the inner self and the ultimate nature of being. In his attitude toward the methodology of revelation he is eclectic. But he finds in the method of the Zen Bhuddists a highly successful technique: he must renounce the haughty, arrogant self which had arisen out of the ashes of his early torment as a student in Wales in order to practice the art of loving his fellow man and communing with the absolute. Empty the mind of all thoughts; fasten on a phrase or series of words and repeat them over and over; look at people and regard them with compassion. Riding in the London underground he looks at those about him and, inwardly repeating his private litany, he attempts to will loving. From willing these states of compassion they begin to achieve a force of their own; a process of spiritual transfiguration slowly gains momentum.

One day, while he is seated in his study, the ultimate revelation comes. He feels a tingling sensation throughout his body, a profound sense of withdrawal into the self. Then the illumination begins . . . the edges of the carpet begin to glow . . . the room is suffused with soft, brilliant colors . . . he is filled with an ineffable sense of peace.

Two years later, in 1964, after a spiritual voyage of unknown itinerary, Dr. Capildeo, forceful and self-possessed, announced to a D.L.P. convention in San Fernando that the party's ideology would be that of "democratic socialism." He cited the ultimate values of Islam, Christianity and Hinduism in support of the party's new political direction. It seemed like a good beginning, a fresh start. But from where I sat on the convention platform it was evident that at least nine out of ten of the delegates were East Indians.

CHAPTER 10 Aftermath of Independence

A nation, like an individual, can only have one Mother. The only Mother we recognize is Mother Trinidad & Tobago, and Mother cannot discriminate between her children. All must be equal in her eyes.

— Eric Williams, 1962[1]

During the formal opening of the Trinidad & Tobago parliament on August 31, 1962, four local private airplanes buzzed a feeble salute to mark the historic occasion. The following day, while U.S. military bands played for appreciative audiences from the Woodford Square bandstand and elsewhere in the island, a squadron of some twenty carrier-based U.S. Navy helicopters repeatedly swooped over Port of Spain in precision formation. The same evening the U.S. Consul General held a mammoth cocktail party at Chaguaramas in honor of the large independence delegation from the United States. The delegation contained so many distinguished American Negroes that one of them was overheard to refer humorously to the group as "the Minstrel show." The party at Chaguaramas was charged with an atmosphere of good will despite, or because of, Dr. Williams' absence. Local businessmen, East Indian and Negro politicians milled about chatting with foreign visitors, joking with each other, all enjoying a mood of mild elation and relief that the independence issue had finally been settled.

This mood had been in the air for a number of weeks following the final trip to London in May when the date for independence had been set. An era of good feeling had set in. East Indian politicians had ceased prophecying disaster and had instead issued assurances that all would be well. Dr. Williams' conciliatory approach to Dr. Capildeo on the balcony at Marlborough House had resulted in a partisan detente. An almost miraculous easing of tensions followed. The casual lounger on Frederick Street during the weeks before independence could notice a marked increase in the number of East Indians shopping in town on Saturday morning. Bhadase Maraj had telephoned Dr. Williams in London after the independence talks and had told him,

"Bill, I have always maintained that you had more brains than the rest of those fellows put together." The wife of a leading East Indian politician wrote a letter to the *Guardian* in which she praised Dr. Williams' great qualities as a leader. Miss Nigeria attended the independence festivities and was all the rage at a Woodbrook dance during which she performed the high-life. Following this performance the winner of the independence calypso contest, Lord Brynner, gave a satirical rendition of his own inspirational composition which featured an impious and acclaimed alteration of the lyrics containing the national motto, "Together We Aspire, Together We Achieve," to "Together We Perspire, Together We Conceive."

The Mighty Sparrow, many felt, had not been "up to standard" in his independence calypso, when he told foreign visitors to "spread the word anywhere you pass – tell the world here's a model nation at last." This view, it is fair to say, not even such a devoted Sparrow fan as C. L. R. James, who regarded the Grenadian immigrant as the greatest popular political analyst the West Indies had produced, would endorse. James had temporarily left the model nation a few weeks before to return to his writing desk in London; Albert Gomes and his numerous family had also left the island for the U.K. Sir Learie Constantine "went home" to London as Trinidad's High Commissioner, after receiving a silver salver at a memorial cricket match played in his honor. A professor from Puerto Rico, longtime perceptive analyst and supporter of the P.N.M., left the island after the independence celebrations, but not before he had issued a press release at the airport in which he maintained that, now that the P.N.M. "oligarchy" had taken Trinidad to nationhood, the time for the socialist reconstruction was at hand.

If it was, few in Trinidad showed much sign of being aware of the fact. Carnival in 1963 was, as always, "the biggest and best" ever. A few months before Dr. Williams had negotiated a difficult settlement between a major trade union and the employers, and a few months later he embarked on an almost village-by-village tour of the island in an unprecedented "Meet The People" tour which prompted Bhadase Maraj to purchase a two page advertisement in the P.N.M. *Nation* which stated, *inter alia,* ". . . speaking strictly from an entrepreneur's point of view, such visits, with emphasis laid as it is on agriculture and production generally, could only lead to prosperity for those persons who, by and large, have been denied this right because of the historical pattern by which this society was developed. This has led me to the conclusion that better days are ahead for businessmen . . ."

Early in 1962, a few months before independence, a Special Convention of the P.N.M. had voted unanimously in favor of a resolution proposing that Trinidad & Tobago should go on to independence alone. The Jamaican referendum on federation had taken that island out of the provisional union the preceding September; politicians from the smaller islands were still advocating an Eastern Caribbean rump federation with Trinidad to continue as the capital, but Trinidadians were not disposed to relieve the Colonial Office of its financial burdens in the poorer small islands. Dr. Williams broke this news to the Secretary of State for the Colonies, Reginald Maudling, and the British, having agreed to the Jamaican secession, had little choice but to allow Trinidad to do likewise. The P.N.M. convention left the door to future political association slightly ajar: the smaller islands might eventually be joined to Trinidad & Tobago as integrated constituencies within a unitary state. Thus, what had begun as a pan-island experiment to liquidate British imperialism in the Caribbean had by 1962 resulted in the formation of two new island nations, Jamaica and Trinidad & Tobago, while the remaining islands continued under colonial rule, their future status and prospects uncertain. By 1966 Barbados and Guyana would also attain a separate independence. The ultimate consequence of the historical development of multi-nucleated political administration under colonialism with its structure of parallel, but separate, island administrations was to make it possible for local loyalties and exigencies to take precedence over the cultural homogeneity of the area in the formation of the new national boundaries. Out of one people the Colonial Office had succeeded in making four new nations.

The position of the P.N.M., as enunciated by Dr. Williams and implemented in governmental action, on decisions affecting the final boundaries of the new nation of Trinidad & Tobago, the degree of national sovereignty it would expect to exercise in economic matters, and its global alignments, finally come down to one paramount consideration: local economic self-interest. In the agitation over Chaguaramas Williams embarked on a course which, while it may have demonstrated the P.N.M.'s determination to teach the bearers of the "colonial mentality" a lesson, also clouded his attitude towards the Monroe Doctrine and could not be easily reconciled with his *Realpolitik* embrace of American economic penetration of Trinidad. Williams would continue to express ambivalent attitudes over the continued dependency and metropolitan control of the Trinidad economy, but like most West Indians, acutely conscious of limitations for economic growth, he would continue to look abroad to the industrialized nations for the major impetus to economic development. At the special P.N.M. convention dealing with the issue, the severence of Trinidad from the remaining islands of the post-referendum federation was argued almost exclusively on economic grounds: Trinidad did not feel itself prepared to take on the economic burden posed by continued union with the small islands.

There was certainly nothing ignoble in the efforts of West Indian nationalists to tailor decisions affecting external relations to the maximum economic welfare of the islands to which they felt a primary loyalty. This did, however, give a certain sense of unreality to the political and ideological stances taken by some of the militant nationalists. If nationalism could not promise a better life for the people, what was it good for? But while insisting on political independence and its corollary of local autonomy and solidarity, the nationalists who had emerged in the West Indies were at the same time convinced of the need for continued, and hopefully, even accelerated rates of foreign investment in the local economies. We have already seen that Dr. Williams would attempt to present a basic political and economic world view which could place Eisenhower and Nehru in the same camp, thus debunking the traditional west Indian ideological divisions between socialists and capitalists. This pragmatic (or, as some would charge, "opportunistic") approach to economic affairs was not the only instance in which accommodation and compromise on key issues would mark the statesmanship of the P.N.M. political leader. Despite the aggressive language which often marked his public utterances the record of Williams' stated policies and performance in office shows him to have been generally accommodative in design and compromising in execution.

Trinidad had travelled a long, sometimes exciting, but on the whole smooth road to political independence. The major reasons for this smooth transition were suggested at the outset. The long colonial tutelage exercised by Great Britain in the Caribbean inculcated in the majority of the population knowledge of, and a desire for, the standards of life and the political institutions of the Mother Country. The ideology of the advanced community was, however, best understood by those local persons who were drawn into the international society and institutions of higher learning by which the metropolitan power willy-nilly built in the provincial administrative region a middle class stratum arising out of educational achievement. In Trinidad, the ladder of opportunity in the Negro section of the society was, given the social values of the ex-slave and the tendency of the commercial community to close ranks against Negro mobility in business establishments, very largely limited to academic achievement. The educated, worldly man of color was a West Indian phenomenon about which a number of nineteenth century visitors remarked. After the abolition of slavery the West Indies were never to undergo the social turmoil of a Reconstruction. In Trinidad the transition from slavery was eased by the presence of an already substantial stratum of free coloreds, many acculturated to the values of the white French Creole elite; and thus race and the possession of the upper class style of life tended to be viewed as a matter of degree rather than an all-or-nothing attribute. There were degrees of "Negroness," and a "respectable" style of life and social status were associated with skin color as indices of social worth. Some of those, particularly in the urban areas, who had neither the requisite color nor the opportunity to rise through the narrow sieve of social mobility responded by developing a rebellious lower class culture centered around the *jamettes* of the urban underworld. The Negro section of the society tended, therefore, to be divided into two classes: those who had achieved some position of respectability in the colonial society and those who had not.

From this process the East Indian laborers who came to "save" the agricultural economy after the end of slavery were largely excluded for several generations. Their passion for thrift arose in connection with plans to return to the home country and was later put to use in the acquisition of land in the colony. But a colony is not a "nation"; Trinidad was a province in a great global system of administration, and though the ex-slave was permitted to retain few memories of Mother Africa and had acquired an indigenous "Creole" identity, the East Indian, like the educated colored middle class and European elite, tended to view himself as belonging to a center of culture remote from the little island in the Caribbean.

There thus began developing in nineteenth century Trinidad a system of horizontal and vertical social differentiation within which existed both common and differential criteria of prestige. Within the Negro section of the community color and education tended to be highly correlated with social position, but color tended to diminish in actual importance in determining mobility as educational opportunity and achievement increased over the years. Color preference was most strongly reinforced by the tendency, particularly in private commercial establishments, to discriminate among employees on the basis of color. But a few men of humble antecedents and dark complexion, with intelligence and energy, could move ahead through the limited system of mobility afforded by the educational system into positions of limited responsibility in the civil service, or possibly, to a professional career.

Within the East Indian community the situation was somewhat

different. The East Indian realized what few Negroes would be willing to concede – that as a group the East Indians far more closely resembled the Europeans in racial characteristics than did the Negroes. Moreover, Hinduism was an exclusive, hereditary tradition. This fact was given additional social reinforcement as the nation of India emerged on the stage of modern nations. The East Indians in Trinidad, therefore, tended to be united not only on the basis of a sense of separate national-religious and racial identity, but even as some of their members achieved prominence in the professions and in business, the stereotype "Coolie" was retained in the Creole mind and worked to retard the assimilation of East Indians to the values of the majority ethnic group.

The consequence of this pluralism in Trinidad was that, in a small society in which at least a *de facto* extended kinship system prevailed in the Negro lower class, and the *de jure* forms were observed in the middle class, Negroes were seldom related by kinship to East Indians, East Indians were seldom related to local whites, and the latter at least claimed to be unrelated to either. In the middle minorities, on the high colored fringes of the Negro community and in the upper middle stratum of the East Indians, there developed a kind of fair-skinned "society," small in number, but tending to maintain the image that success and beauty were a consequence of approaching upper class European styles of life and Caucasian physical appearance.

The political consequences of these structural features of the society have been shown: it was not before the successful middle class Negro community managed to unite in sufficient numbers behind a leader capable of attracting a wide charismatic following in the Negro lower class that a majority political party could be formed. Once that had happened, the rest was fairly automatic. The East Indians, who had already been culturally united, particularly in the majority Hindu section, formed a rather feeble association with a local white commercial elite which was looking for a basis of mass support by which its political power could be continued. That alliance proved largely unworkable for two reasons: there was not such a high degree of attraction by the white elite to the East Indian leaders as perhaps some of the latter imagined, and under Dr. Capildeo's leadership the East Indian movement began to develop overtones of social chaos which made the P.N.M. government look like a rock of stability in contrast. Thus, in the elections of 1961 the white commercial elite seems to have split in its support. There were strong feelings against Dr. Williams and his "People's Nigger Movement," but these were tempered by the realization that the party had maintained order and that after the elections it was clearly the political force that would have to be contended with for the foreseeable future. This conclusion the East Indian politicians resisted for as long as possible, charging in the first instance that since 1956 the P.N.M. had ruled fraudulently as a majority party when in fact it had obtained only 39% of the vote, and in the second instance that it had defrauded the electorate in the 1961 elections by the introduction of the nefarious Voting Machine.

This posture, however, could not be maintained indefinitely; as independence came, the realization that Dr. Patrick Solomon, the Minister of Internal Affairs, now commanded the only police and military force in the island must have had a sobering impact on future political calculations. Politics suddenly became a rather more serious undertaking because power finally had become local. The beginning of an attempt to increase mutual trust was mandatory; the alternative was continued serious hostility between Negroes and East Indians, possibly erupting into bloodshed on a mass scale. From point of view of purely naked power the P.N.M. and the Negro community easily held the winning hand. Dr. Capildeo could neither starve the country (as he had sometimes boasted in private that he might), nor could his minions from County Caroni, should he mount the offensive which he had publicly threatened, expect to arrive in downtown Port of Spain without having their ranks decimated by the seasoned combat troops from "behind the bridge." In retrospect, it may seem ludicrous to speculate on these possibilities, but one had the impression that, while Capildeo's call to action was largely a hostile outburst calculated to instill in the East Indian masses the same fanatical pride that Dr. Williams had produced among the Negroes, it nonetheless might inadvertently have led to serious disturbances of the kind suffered in Guyana during 1963 and 1964 when massive outbreaks of violence took place between Negroes loyal to Mr. Burnham and the East Indian followers of Dr. Jagan.

The rise of East Indian militancy after World War II, and the emergence of the Hindu community as a fairly solid bloc in the era of universal suffrage, created a new political situation from that which had been envisaged by the earlier middle class radicals like Cipriani. In place of class struggle against the white employers and political directorate, a movement which Uriah Butler brought to a climax in the late Thirties, there developed an increasing tendency to vote on the basis of ethnicity. As long as inter-ethnic conflict was at a low pitch, a group identity based on common lower class status gave support to the radical labor ideologies of Cipriani, Butler, and the postwar socialists. But by 1950 East Indians were on the Legislative Council Executive, they had succeeded in business, they were coming up in the professions. "We going up!" became the cry in the sugar belt by which East Indian politicians rallied ethnic group support. The process of greater ethnic polarization between East Indian and Negro was thus aggravated as the latter became aware of the political strength of the former arising from the Indians' sense of ethnic solidarity. Thus class resentments among the Creoles were augmented by resentment against a traditionally inferior group which suddenly emerged as a rival to claim its place in the sun.

The period from 1950 to 1955 was the critical transitional era in Trinidad politics: corruption in public life, a feeling of political frustration on the part of the divided trade union movement, a growing sense of dismay in the Negro middle class towards what they viewed as the power of unscrupulous politicians from the East Indian sector and the petty bourgeois of the middle minorities, combined with a desire to keep abreast of the respectable political movements of Negro politicians elsewhere in the area, gave rise to strong feelings favoring political reform. Besides, the time was clearly far past when politics would be an avenue of protest only. Political independence was definitely in the offing, although no one knew when or in what form.

It is in that context that the rise of Dr. Eric Williams and the P.N.M. must be seen: as a middle class reform movement out to clean the augean stables of Trinidad politics and to bring the government up to par with political developments in Jamaica. Such a movement might have had a more radical political ideology; there was a considerable residue of radical opinion among trade unionists, and the deprived Negro lower class would then, as today, be ready for anything. During the agitation over Chaguaramas Dr. Williams found it possible to issue quite radical pronouncements, to work closely with C. L. R. James, to take on the giant to the north, and he could quite easily have led a march of thousands to the gates of Chaguaramas.

Such a radical movement might have developed, but the odds were heavily against it. The middle class Negro community contained a few radicals, but the general level of a radical ideological consciousness or commitment was quite low. The middle class center of political gravity was well to the right of the radical firebrands who made a brief union in the United Front after World War II. In this the Trinidad middle classes did not differ from the general political consciousness to be found in the predominantly civil service, professional wing of nationalist parties elsewhere in the West Indies. The view prevailing in this stratum was that the local economy and society were basically a going concern that required more competent management and a greater attention to the problems of raising the level of amenities and opportunities for the entire population. Among the intellectuals of the middle class there had been, to be sure, a much stronger exposure to the labor-socialist milieux of the metropolitan country: colonial university students had naturally gravitated toward those groups and ideologies which accepted them socially and viewed them as the vanguard of the diffusion of enlightenment to the colonies. This was true not only of Negro professionals, but of East Indian professionals like Dr. Capildeo as well; was not Nehru among the great men of the century?[2]

But the ideological sympathies acquired in the metropolitan countries tended to become sharply attenuated under conditions of life in the West Indies. West Indian intellectual life was not merely a "kindergarten," as C. L. R. James had pointed out; it was practically nonexistent. The sophisticated tastes in art, literature, cinema, and social thought acquired in London, New York, or Montreal were given little scope for expression or appreciation once the student had returned home to Trinidad. The educated man was seen primarily as a successful competitor in a scramble for status afforded by the educational system: what he knew counted for far less than what he symbolized as a harbinger of hope and aspiration for the ordinary citizen. In the everyday round of basically undemanding work in which the West Indian graduate soon found himself enmeshed, and in the relatively affluent and entertaining life which was his for the asking, there was little stimulus to serious political activity.

Thus, when C. L. R. James returned to Trinidad in 1965 he was unable to attract any substantial number of middle class intellectuals to the formation of a new party. James had gone to Trinidad to cover a cricket match for the British press, only to find himself placed under virtual house arrest during an outbreak of periodic unrest in the sugar belt. This apparently galvanized him into action against the P.N.M., but the elections of November, 1966, proved to be almost an exact duplicate of the 1961 elections. Once again, the "Negro" party won two-thirds of the seats, the "Indian" party under Dr. Capildeo's leadership obtained the remaining one-third. James, and all of the candidates of his Worker's and Farmer's Party, lost their deposits. There were no niceties in the P.N.M.'s attack against the W.F.P.: it was variously alleged that the party contained "pederasts," "Communists," and, in one memorable headline in the P.N.M. *Nation,* it was alleged that Trinidad was suffering from *Too Damn Much Democracy.*

The tone of public life in Trinidad had deteriorated to a level which could hardly have been anticipated a decade before when the University of Woodford Square was founded. The reasons for that deterioration were not to be found simply in the fact that the P.N.M. had remained in power for so long, but in the ultimately precarious ideological position in which the leadership had placed themselves. The decision to bend over backwards to attract foreign investment meant that an atmosphere of security and well-being had to be generated within the local and expatriate upper middle class business community. These were the classes whose views and contacts would be crucial in creating investor confidence. Consistent with this policy was the posture adopted — the lessons of the Chaguaramas debacle had been learned only too well — that the P.N.M. was a bastion against the "Communist threat." Moreover, the "nationalist" synthesis which the P.N.M. claimed to have achieved was not only mythical, but was highly functional in preventing the emergence of class-based politics which might upset the neo-colonial commitments already entered into. That is, while the P.N.M. leadership had not wanted, and had indeed deplored, the ethnic basis of the two party system, they must also have realized that a vertical, ethnic opposition had forestalled the emergence of a working class party which might disrupt Trinidad's cultural and economic integration within the Anglo-American orbit. The East Indian opposition pseudo-party, although Dr. Williams and others would grumble about "the problem of a weak opposition," in fact represented a gift from the gods: the opposition benches, the commitment to a Westminster model insisted, had to be filled by vocal, angry men. The Westminster model fortunately did not specify that the opposition should represent a radically different social and political outlook. Trinidad had, in short, become an advanced Western democracy.

So much, and more, is the past history of Trinidad & Tobago. It is a record of social progress which, if it is disappointing in some respects, presents certain universal themes and problems with which the world itself must contend: the uprooting, shifting and dissolution of traditional cultures; the social and personal dislocation resulting from the implosive effect of technology; the greater social universalism and the ambiguities of human equality arising from the transition from the agrarian to the urban-industrial society; the brute limitations on development imposed by the division of the world into the strong and the weak, the rich and the poor; and the gropings of intellectuals to define and channel these forces. If the adjustment most Trinidadians have made to these global dilemmas is any indicator, however, mankind can look forward to a future in which life is more joyous as well as more absurd.

Perhaps we in the industrial nations will someday adopt Sparrow's slogan and help to create in Trinidad "a model nation at last" — just to see how it might all turn out. Instead of military bases, supply depots, bullets and death in a strange jungle — a planned city — Iēre — on the beach and under the tropical rain forest near the Trinity Hills, with publicly-owned light industries, electric pirate taxis and a high-rise civic center near Williams Square, communicating by high-speed monorail to Port of Spain and beyond to the West Indian capital at Chaguaramas. Surrounding Williams Square would be the Interfaith Cathedral, the Capildeo Experimental High School, the James-Padmore Institute for Advanced Social Studies and the Mighty Sparrow Center for the Performing Arts. In the center of the square itself, of course, would stand a (small) statue of Eric Williams with an inscription directed at all future West Indian intellectuals: HE CAME HOME, AND HE STAYED HOME.

Footnotes to Chapters

NOTES TO CHAPTER 1

Trinidad and the West Indian Setting

1. *Party Politics in the West Indies*, San Juan, Trinidad: Vedic Enterprises, p. 89.
2. "Special Convention Data," Port of Spain: People's National Movement, 1962, p. 12.
3. R. B. Davison, *West Indian Migrants*, London: Institute of Race Relations, Oxford University Press, 1962.

NOTES TO CHAPTER 2

A Sociologist's Baedeker to Trinidad & Tobago

1. J. Melville and Frances Herskovits, *Trinidad Village*, New York: Alfred Knopf, 1947, p. 6.
2. *Ibid.* A later writer, however, has plausibly argued that the African heritage had little to do with the origins of the pervasive non-legal union in Trinidad. See Dom Basil Matthews, *Crisis of the West Indian Family*, Trinidad: Government Printing Works, 1953. Recent studies on African retentions in Trinidad include: Andrew Carr, "A Rada Community in Trinidad," *Caribbean Quarterly*, III, 1953, pp. 35–54; George E. Simpson, "Folk Medicine in Trinidad," *Journal of American Folklore*, October–December, 1962, Vol. 75, No. 298, pp. 326–340.
3. Daniel Crowley, "Plural and Differential Acculturation in Trinidad," *American Anthropologist*, 1957, Vol. 59, pp. 817–824. For a comparison with predominantly Negro Jamaica see Leonard Broom, "The Social Differentiation of Jamaica," *American Sociological Review*, Vol. 19, pp. 115–125.
4. Morton Klass, *East Indians in Trinidad, A Study in Cultural Persistence*, New York: Columbia University Press, 1961, p. 239.
5. Eric Williams, *History of the People of Trinidad and Tobago*, Port of Spain: P.N.M. Publishing Co., 1962, p. 280.
6. Klass, *op. cit.*, p. 243.
7. Vera Rubin (Consulting Editor), "Social and Cultural Pluralism in the Caribbean," papers from a conference jointly supported by The New York Academy of Sciences and The Research Institute for the Study of Man, New York, May 27 and 28, 1959; *Annals of the New York Academy of Sciences*, Vol. 83, Art. 5, pp. 761–916. Among the contributors, Daniel J. Crowley, "Cultural Assimiliation in a Multiracial Society," pp. 850–854, and Morton Klass, "East and West Indian: Cultural Complexity in Trinidad," pp. 851–861, provide the most acute discussion of the situation of the East Indians in Trinidad. From an over-all societal standpoint, in the opinion of the present writer, Crowley's account, which carefully distinguishes between different areas and the degree of retention of various Indian cultural traits, is the best brief summary currently available.
8. Williams, *op. cit.*, p. 280.
9. Arthur and Juanita Niehoff, *East Indians in the West Indies*, Milwaukee: Milwaukee Public Museum Publications in Anthropology, 1960, *passim*.
10. *Ibid.*, pp. 43–45.
11. Since this was written Jack Harewood, Director of Statistical Services for Trinidad & Tobago, has published *Employment in Trinidad and Tobago, 1960*, Institute of Social and Economic Research, University of the West Indies, Jamaica. Based on the 1960 census data, Harewood arrives at a total of 29,600 unemployed out of a total labor force of 278,100, or, 10.6 per cent of the labor force are

identified as subject to long or short-term unemployment. When the substantial figures on under-employment are included in a reckoning of total labor force time lost due to both unemployment and underemployment, the figure becomes 45,000 man-years, 16.2 per cent, lost from the theoretical maximum available in the labor force. Harewood's analysis discloses that while percentagewise relatively fewer Trinidadians were in the working population in 1960 than at the time of the 1946 census, this decline can be accounted for largely by age shifts in the total population, the decline in employment of the elderly in agriculture, and the larger percentage of adolescents in school. Although he finds a general up-grading in the skill-level and income of those who worked, he warns that ". . . should population growth continue in the future as rapidly as it has in the recent past, the economy will undoubtedly be hard-pressed to provide a sufficient number of productive, well paid jobs, to ensure a continuation of this increase in real output per head, or even to prevent a reversal." *Ibid.*, p. 81.

NOTES TO CHAPTER 3

Origins of a Sense of Nationhood

1. Quoted in J. H. Collens, *Guide to Trinidad,* London: Elliott Stock, 1888, p. 9.
2. Andrew Pearse, "Carnival in Nineteenth Century Trinidad," *Caribbean Quarterly* (Trinidad Carnival Issue), Vol. 4, Nos. 3 and 4, March-June, 1956, pp. 175–176.
3. Adapted from Pearse, *idem.*
4. Quoted by Pearse, *idem.*
5. Quoted by Pearse, *idem.*
6. *Idem.*
7. *Idem.*
8. Gertrude Carmichael, *The History of the West Indian Islands of Trinidad and Tobago, 1498–1900,* London: Alvin Redman, 1961, p. 223.
9. Klass, *East Indians in Trinidad, op. cit.*, p. 22.
10. Eric Williams, *History of the People of Trinidad and Tobago, op. cit.*, p. 121.
11. Collens, *op. cit.*, pp. 7–8.
12. *Ibid.*, pp. 37–39.
13. *Ibid.*, p. 257.
14. *Ibid.*, p. 270.
15. *Ibid.*, p. 260.
16. *Ibid.*, p. 78.
17. *Ibid.*, p. 277. For a comprehensive, global perspective on British colonial policies and expansion in the nineteenth century, see C. E. Carrington, *The British Overseas,* Cambridge, England: Cambridge University Press, 1950.
18. Carmichael, *op. cit.*, p. 369.
19. James Anthony Froude, *The English in the West Indies*, London: Longmans, Green, and Co., 1888, p. 76.
20. Charles Kingsley, *At Last: A Christmas in the West Indies*, London, Macmillan and Co., 1874, p. 90.
21. Froude, *op. cit.*, p. 87.
22. Collens, *op. cit.*, pp. 38–39.
23. *Loc. cit.*
24. *Ibid.*, p. 9.
25. Pearse, *op. cit.*, p. 191.
26. Williams, *op. cit.*, p. 213.
27. Quoted in Williams, *loc. cit.*
28. *Ibid.*, p. 214.
29. *Ibid.*, p. 215.

30. Pearse, *op. cit.*, p. 188.
31. *Ibid.*, p. 193. Barbara Powrie in "The Changing Attitude of the Coloured Middle Class Towards Carnival," *Caribbean Quarterly* (Trinidad Carnival Issue), *op. cit.*, p. 226, suggests that the highly competitive ethos of the colored middle class necessitated some kind of periodic "safety valve" such as Carnival.
32. *Ibid.*, pp. 185–186.
33. Daniel J. Crowley, "The Traditional Masques of Carnival," *Caribbean Quarterly* (Trinidad Carnival Issue), *op. cit.*, p. 220. See also his "Toward a Definition of Calypso," *Ethnomusicology*, 1959, Vol. 3, No. 2, pp. 117–125. As frequently happens in investigations of the nineteenth century origins of Trinidad culture, Crowley can give eight different theories to account for the origin of the term "calypso."
34. *Ibid.*, p. 217.
35. Pearse, *op. cit.*, p. 192.
36. Quoted in Lloyd Braithwaite, "The Problem of Cultural Integration in Trinidad," *Social and Economic Studies*, March, 1954, Vol. 3., No. 2, p. 87.
37. Hewan Craig, *The Legislative Council of Trinidad and Tobago*, London: Faber and Faber, 1952, p. 28.
38. Quoted in Craig, *ibid.*, p. 31.
39. *Ibid.*, p. 32.
40. *Ibid.*, p. 29.
41. Williams, *op. cit.*, p. 225.
42. Braithwaite, *op. cit.*, p. 85.
43. Quoted in Craig, *op. cit.*, p. 29.

NOTES TO CHAPTER 4

The Education of Young Colonials at Home and Abroad

1. H. Coleridge, *Six Months in the West Indies in 1825*, London: John Murray, 1826, p. 321.
2. This chapter was written before the appearance of Shirley C. Gordon's invaluable compendium of colonial documents, *A Century of West Indian Education*, London: Longmans, Green and Co., Ltd., 1963. More complete documentation of the process described here for Trinidad is available for the entire West Indies through these documents. In a circular dispatch from the Colonial Office dated January 26, 1847, for example, the following points are stressed: "a) Religious Education — to inculcate the principles and promote the influence of Christianity; b) The English Language — to diffuse a grammatical knowledge of the English language as the most important agent of civilization for the colored population of the colonies; c) Requirements of Small Farmers — to communicate such a knowledge of writing and arithmetic . . . as many enable the peasant to economise his means, and give the small farmer the power to enter into calculations and agreements . . . ; d) Relationships With Authority — The lesson books of the colonial schools should also teach the mutual interests of the mother-country and her dependencies [sic]; the rational basis of their connection, and the domestic and social duties of the colored races." *Ibid.*, p. 58.
3. Carmichael, *op. cit.*, p. 33.
4. *Ibid.*, p. 224.
5. *Ibid.*, pp. 252–253.
6. *Education Report, 1959, of Committee on General Education,* (The Maurice Report), Port of Spain: Government Printing Office, 1959, p. 9.
7. *Ibid.*, p. 12.
8. Quoted in Carmichael, *op. cit.*, p. 265.
9. Collens, *op. cit.*, p. 246.
10. *Ibid.*, p. 245.
11. C. L. R. James, "Nationalist Strain," *New Statesman*, January 18, 1958, pp. 67–68.

12. C. L. R. James, "Notes on the Life of George Padmore," *The Nation*, October 2, 1959.
13. *Idem.*
14. Eric Williams, "Education of a Young Colonial," *The P.N.M. Weekly*, August 30, 1956.
15. *Idem.*
16. *Idem.*
17. *Idem.*
18. C. L. R. James, *Beyond a Boundary*, London: Hutchinson and Co., 1963, p. 157 and *passim.*
19. Matthews, *op. cit.*, p. 95.
20. C. L. R. James, "Andrew Arthur Cipriani," *Guardian* (Independence Supplement), August 26, 1962.
21. C. L. R. James, "Dr. Eric Williams, P.N.M. Political Leader – A Convention Appraisal," *The Nation*, March 18, 1960.
22. Edward Shils, "The Intellectual in the Political Development of New States," Committee on Social Thought, University of Chicago (mimeographed), n.d., pp. 19–20.
23. *Idem.*
24. C. L. R. James, "Notes on the Life of George Padmore," *op. cit.*
25. *Idem.*
26. *Idem.* See also "From Tacarigua to Moscow: Padmore's Early Life," J. R. Hooker, *Trinidad & Tobago Index*, Winter, 1966. Dr. Hooker's *Life of George Padmore* is in press.
27. *Idem.*
28. Personal interview with Mr. James, 1962.
29. Kwame Nkrumah, *The Autobiography of Kwame Nkrumah*, Edinburgh: Thomas Nelson and Sons, Ltd., 1957, p. 44. Padmore's account of the education of future nationalists, his own career, and related topics, will be found interspersed through his *Pan-Africanism or Communism?*, London: Dennis Dobson, 1956.
30. *New Statesman* (Jubilee Number), April 19, 1963, p. 543.
31. Learie Constantine, *Colour Bar*, London: Stanley Paul and Co., 1954, p. 68.
32. Fenner Brockway, *Inside the Left*, London: George Allen and Unwin, 1942, p. 326.
33. Frederic Warburg, *An Occupation for Gentlemen*, London: Hutchinson and Co., 1959, p. 206.
34. *Ibid.*, pp. 217–218.
35. *Ibid.*, p. 211.
36. *Ibid.*, pp. 214–215.
37. Eric Williams, "A Colonial at Oxford," *The Nation Christmas Annual*, 1959, p. 89.
38. James, "Dr. Eric Williams, P.N.M. Political Leader — A Convention Appraisal," *op. cit.*
39. James, *Party Politics in the West Indies*, *op. cit.*, p. 158.
40. Eric Williams, *My Relations with the Caribbean Commission, 1943–1955*, pamphlet published by Dr. Eric Williams, July 5, 1955, pp. 33–34.
41. Williams, "A Colonial at Oxford," *op. cit.*, p. 91.
42. *Ibid.*, p. 92.
43. Eric Williams, *Capitalism and Slavery*, New York: Russel and Russel, 1961, p. 268.
44. C. L. R. James, *The Black Jacobins: Toussaint Louverture and the San Domingo Revolution*, London: Martin Secker and Warburg, 1938, pp. 311–312.
45. *Idem.*
46. Karl R. Popper, *The Poverty of Historicism*, London: Routledge and Kegan Paul, 1961. Popper's formulation of "historicism" contains many elements with which I disagree; nonetheless, his discussion of certain determinist tendencies are telling and relevant to this discussion *e.g.:* "Those who desire an increase in

the influence of reason in social life can only be advised by historicism to study and interpret history, in order to discover the laws of its development. If such interpretation reveals that changes answering to the desire are impending, then the desire is a reasonable one, for it agrees with scientific prediction. If the impending development happens to tend in another direction, then the wish to make the world more reasonable turns out to be entirely unreasonable; to historicists it is then just a Utopian dream. Activism can be justified only so long as it acquiesces in impending changes and helps them along." *Ibid.* According to James, ("A Convention Appraisal," *op. cit.*), he and Williams had extensively discussed the latter's thesis for *Capitalism and Slavery* and he noted that Williams had concluded that if emancipation had not taken place from above, it would have taken place from below by a slave revolt. This was true, but the point remains that for James it *did* take place primarily from below; for Williams, primarily from above. I would not split hairs on this issue except for the fact that it was the practical implications of precisely this kind of question which split James and Williams in Trinidad politics 25 years later.

47. Walter Goldwater, *Radical Periodicals in America, 1890–1950,* New Haven: Yale University Library, 1964, p. xii.

48. Dwight MacDonald, *Memoirs of a Revolutionist,* New York: Farrar, Straus and Cudahy, 1957.

49. *State Capitalism and World Revolution,* p. 4, the chief theoretical statement of the Johnson-Forest Tendency, originally published in 1950 and re-published in 1956. During an interview with the writer in 1962 Mr. James referred to this work as "my masterpiece." Probably available today through New World, 20 Staverton Rd., London NW 1.

50. C. L. R. James, *Mariners, Renegades and Castaways: The Story of Herman Melville and the World We Live In,* New York: C.L.R. James, 1953, "Introduction," n.p. An exciting book, in the writer's opinion, as a sociological interpretation of literature. Probably available through same address given in preceding footnote.

51. Lloyd Braithwaite, "Social Stratification in Trinidad," *Social and Economic Studies,* October, 1953, Vol. 2, Nos. 2 and 3, p. 119.

NOTES TO CHAPTER 5

Trinidad in Transition — 1935–1955

1. Much of the information contained in this section was obtained through interviews with participants and close observers of the events described, as well as from contemporary press accounts. Secondary sources dealing with general historical trends in Trinidad since 1930 are, at best, sketchy and incomplete. There exists no study of the Butler movement, and the confused events of the post-war period still await comprehensive research. Dr. Williams' independence *History* treats the period from 1921 to 1956 in only 27 pages.

2. Lloyd Braithwaite, "Social Stratification in Trinidad," *op. cit.*, p. 133.

3. Morley Ayearst, *The British West Indies,* New York: New York University Press, 1960, pp. 82–83.

4. In the West Indian ideological lexicon a "Marxist" is one who is believed to harbor pro-Communist sympathies. The suppression of the Marxist left in the West Indies in the early 1950's was fully supported by such moderate socialists as Grantley Adams of Barbados, who would become the first and last Prime Minister of the West Indies Federation in 1958. According to Adams; Richard Hart of Jamaica, Quintin O'Connor of Trinidad, Dr. Jagan and others had attempted to persuade him to line up West Indian trade unions with the Communist sponsored World Federation of Trade Unions in a revised Caribbean Labour Congress which Adams, as a labor militant a decade earlier, had helped to establish. When Governor Savage suspended the B.G. constitution in 1953, thus setting in train

the events which would split Dr. Jagan and Forbes Burnham and result in the polarization of politics along racial lines of East Indian versus Negro, Adams said that the methods of the deposed Guianese nationalists were ". . . a mere repetition of communist methods throughout the world and for that reason I welcome the ending of the opportunities of mischief which have been imposed on them." Quoted in F. A. Hoyos, *The Rise of West Indian Democracy*, Barbados: Advocate Press, 1963, p. 195.

5. Paul Blanshard, *Democracy and Empire in the Caribbean*, New York: The MacMillan Company, 1947, p. 115.

6. The ethnic distinctions given here are quoted from Daniel Crowley's "Plural and Differential Acculturation in Trinidad," *op. cit.* Crowley, however, ranks these groups according to a hypothetical, subjective, Creole evaluation. The vertical dimension in our scheme is based not on subjective criteria of social rank but on an approximation of social class as determined by objective indicators such as income and occupation. For a much more detailed discussion see Lloyd Braithwaite's "Social Stratification in Trinidad," *op. cit.*, which is still the classic study.

7. Walter Mischel, "Preference for Delayed Reinforcement: An Experimental Study of a Cultural Observation," *The Journal of Abnormal and Social Psychology*, 1958, Vol. 56, pp. 57–61.

8. *Trinidad and Tobago Yearbook, 1953*, Port of Spain: Yuille's Printerie, Ltd., pp. 184–185, 314–317. The precise numbers given here may, for a number of reasons including the accuracy of the compilation, be open to question. The general trend, however, seems unmistakable and should be kept in mind as a part of the local background to the emergence of Dr. Rudranath Capildeo as a political leader, a process detailed in Chapter 9.

9. Under a heading entitled "The Menace of Communism," Dalley wrote as follows: "In the terms of reference under which I was appointed, there was no mention of Communism, but it was an open secret that for some time the Government had been concerned at the spread of communist ideas and methods. The Trade Union Council (which included two of the principal trade unions) still remained affiliated to the communist-run World Federation of Trade Unions; the President-General of the Oil Workers' Trade Union had returned from behind the 'Iron Curtain' and was publicly expressing the greatest admiration for the Soviet system, and added to this, the events in British Guiana had greatly intensified the apprehension that, if not checked, communist propaganda, overt and covert, would result in a very dangerous situation." F. W. Dalley, *General Industrial Conditions and Labour Relations in Trinidad*, Trinidad: Government Printing Office, 1954, p. 33. Soon after, the offending trade unions were brought into line and became affiliated with the international anti-Communist trade union movement.

10. Naipaul, *The Mystic Masseur*, London: Andre Deutsch, 1957, pp. 201–204. Vidia Naipaul is without question the greatest writer of fiction which the West Indies have produced to date. Self-exiled in London for many years this brilliant ironist's works include an account of the 1950 General Elections in Trinidad, *The Suffrage of Elvira* (Andre Deutsch, 1958), and a West Indian travelogue, *The Middle Passage* (Andre Deutsch, 1962). While his relationship to Creole Trinidad — and perhaps to life in general — may be described as "alienated," his penetration into the *genius loci* is unequaled. (For further bibliographical information on Naipaul see footnote 2, Chapter 9, below.)

NOTES TO CHAPTER 6

Founding the University of Woodford Square

1. Conrad B. Valentine, "Sonnet to Dr. Eric Williams," *The Nation*, November 8, 1963.

2. Lloyd Braithwaite, "Social Stratification in Trinidad," *op. cit.*, pp. 152–153.

3. Eric Williams, *Education in the British West Indies*, Port of Spain: Guardian Commercial Printery, 1950, p. 5. D. W. Rogers was himself author of a highly amusing, fictionalized critique of local education entitled *Chalk Dust*, Port of Spain: Cosmopolitan Printery, 1943.
4. *Ibid.*, p. 7.
5. *Guardian*, November 20, 1954.
6. *Guardian*, November 19, 1954.
7. *Guardian*, November 18, 1954.
8. *Guardian*, June 8, 1955.
9. *Guardian*, May 18, 1955.
10. *Guardian*, November 16, 1954.
11. *Guardian*, November 19, 1954.
12. *Guardian*, December 1, 1954.
13. *Guardian*, December 7, 1954 (emphasis added).
14. Eric Williams, *My Relations with the Caribbean Commission, 1943–1955*, *op. cit.*, p. 47.
15. *Ibid.*, p. 33.
16. *Ibid.*, p. 37.
17. *Ibid.*, p. 11.
18. *Idem.*
19. Eric Williams, *Constitution Reform in Trinidad and Tobago*, pamphlet published by The People's Education Movement of The T.E.C.A., Ltd., Port of Spain, August 6, 1955.
20. Andrew Carr, "P.N.M. Reminiscences," *The Nation*, April 22, 1960.
21. *Idem.*
22. People's National Movement, *Constitution*, Port of Spain, 1956.
23. *Report of the Legislative Council General Elections, 1956*, Port of Spain: Government Printing Office, 1956.

NOTES TO CHAPTER 7

A Red Star Over Trinidad

1. James, *Party Politics*, *op. cit.*, p. 110.
2. For a statement of the implicit theoretical orientation of this and the following chapter see Wendell Bell and Ivar Oxaal, *Decisions of Nationhood: Political and Social Development in the British Caribbean*, Denver: University of Denver, (Monograph Series in World Affairs, Nos. 3 and 4), 1964. Also see Wendell Bell, *Jamaican Leaders: Political Attitudes in a New Nation*, Berkeley and Los Angeles: University of California Press, 1964.
3. There is an extensive literature on the pros and cons of federation in the West Indies as well as numerous official publications. For a highly astute and fair-minded post-mortem on its dissolution see Hugh W. Springer, *Reflections on the Failure of the First West Indian Federation*, (Occasional Papers in International Affairs, No. 4), Cambridge, Mass.: Center for International Affairs, Harvard University. A special federation number of *Social and Economic Studies*, June, 1957, Vol. 6, contains a number of important papers and useful bibliographies. The most exhaustive analysis of the various motives of the Colonial Office in sponsoring federation will be found in Jesse Harris Proctor, Jr., "Britain's Pro-Federation Policy in the Caribbean: An Inquiry into Motivation," *Canadian Journal of Economics and Political Science*, August 1956, Vol. 22, pp. 319–331. For an account of the tragi-comical efforts to salvage the federation after the Colonial Office had allowed both Jamaica and Trinidad to withdraw see F. A. Hoyos, *The Rise of West Indian Democracy*, *op. cit.*, pp. 202–228. The high degree of opposition to federation among the Jamaican elites has been empirically documented by Wendell Bell, "Attitudes of Jamaican Elites Toward the West Indies Federation," *Annals of the New York Academy of Sciences*, Vol. 83, Article 5, pp. 862–879.

4. Morley Ayearst, "Characteristics of West Indian Political Parties," *Social and Economic Studies*, September, 1954, Vol. 3.

5. Eric Williams, "The Trinidad Oil Deal," *P.N.M. Weekly*, June 25, 1956.

6. Eric Williams, "Aspects of Caribbean Economy," *P.N.M. Weekly*, July 23, 1956. All dollar values cited here are B.W.I. dollars ($1 U.S. equals approx. $1.70 B.W.I.).

7. *Idem.*

8. *Idem.*

9. *Idem.*

10. *Idem.*

11. *Ibid.*, July 30, 1956.

12. *Idem* (emphasis added).

13. *Idem.*

14. *The Nation*, December 30, 1960.

15. Eric Williams, "The Principal Issues at Stake in the Federal Elections," *P.N.M. Weekly*, February 3, 1958. Full text of a speech delivered at the University of Woodford Square on January 24, 1958. All quotations below were abstracted from this source.

16. Readers familiar with the neo-revisionism of European Social Democracy over the past decade will find the argument presented here very familiar. Among American sociologists this trend became known as The End of Ideology, and various positions were taken toward it, *e.g.*: ". . . the fundamental problems of the industrial revolution have been solved: the workers have achieved industrial and political citizenship; the conservatives have accepted the welfare state; and the democratic left has recognized that an increase in over-all state power carries with it more dangers to freedom than solutions for economic problems. This very triumph of the democratic social revolution in the West ends domestic politics for those intellectuals who must have ideologies or utopias to motivate them to political action." Seymour Martin Lipset, *Political Man*, Garden City, New York: Doubleday and Co., 1960, p. 406.

17. Eric Williams, "The Approach of Independence," address to the Fourth Annual Convention of the P.N.M., 1960.

18. See "Postscript" to David Lowenthal, "The West Indies Chooses a Capital," *The Geographical Review*, March, 1958, Vol. 48, p. 364.

19. *Trinidad and Tobago Legislative Council Debates*, August 7, 1957, Port of Spain: Government Printing Office.

20. *P.N.M. Weekly*, July 22, 1957.

21. Colonial No. 338, *Report of the Chaguaramas Joint Commission*, 1958, p. 16. It was rightly pointed out by P.N.M. spokesmen that the Commission was authorized purely as a fact-finding body and that its report did not contain formal recommendations for the solution of the issue. Nonetheless, the weight of implication in the passage just summarized was certainly discouraging for those who sought to have the naval base moved to another area.

22. *Guardian*, May 15, 1958.

23. *Guardian*, May 24, 1958.

24. *Guardian*, June 17, 1958.

25. *Guardian*, June 11, 1958.

26. *P.N.M. Weekly*, June 23, 1958.

27. *Guardian*, September 22, 1958.

28. C. L. R. James, *Party Politics*, *op. cit.*, p. 50. The major portions of this highly personal study of the workings of the P.N.M. were first circulated by James in mimeographed form among party members in 1960. The published version of his differences with Dr. Williams and the P.N.M. leadership is, with the exception of the addition of a few footnotes, identical to the mimeographed document.

29. *Guardian*, March 8, 1960.

30. *Guardian*, June 19, 1960.

31. *The Nation*, June 3, 1960. Williams was quoted as stating, *inter alia:* ". . . it is axiomatic that we are West of the Curtain and not part of it. There can be no argument about that. This is the anchor of our foreign policy as we emerge into independence . . ."
32. C. L. R. James, "No Alternative But Resignation," *Party Politics, op. cit.*, pp. 76–112.
33. *The Nation*, November 25, 1960.
34. *Idem.*
35. *Guardian*, December 17, 1960.

NOTES TO CHAPTER 8

The Structure and Problems of Power

1. Note on Method: The P.N.M. was not an easy organization to study because of the prevailing aura of secrecy. Although I obtained Dr. Williams' permission to "do what you like" this proved difficult in practice. However, I was able to make a number of friends in the party and I was invited — a rare privilege — to attend one party convention. Aside from extensive formal interviewing I relied mainly on "making the P.N.M. scene" as much as possible, for over a year, and this bore fruit. In addition, at one stage I conducted a positional-reputational study of the top 30 influentials in the party, gathering social background data etc. on them. This was done through exhaustive interviews with three persons highly knowledgable about the inner workings of the party. During these interviews my informants were repeatedly asked to arrange and re-arrange calling cards with the names of the top 30 party members on them in order to reconstruct the various personal groupings and how they had shifted over time. Some months later — never were sociological informants more heavily imposed upon! — the same knowledgables were asked to describe the positions taken by the top 30 on each of a number of major government policies, *e.g.*, Chaguaramas, Pioneer Industries legislation, the Senate, the Corcordat, etc. There was very high agreement between the informants about the positions adopted, but with the exception of the Concordat I was generally unable to isolate any differences in social backgrounds which might account for individual differences in positions taken on issues. The main reason for this was that, by and large, with the exceptions discussed in this chapter, the party took its cue from the Political Leader; the deviant cases were not numerous enough to reveal what causal inputs might have been important had Williams' charisma been less. Nonetheless, I have also tried to emphasize that Williams' charisma, even within the party, was operative only within certain limiting assumptions represented by the socially progressive, but by no means radical, outlook of the Creole middle class.
2. The minutes of the People's Education Group cited throughout this chapter were loaned to the writer by Senator W. J. Alexander, Minister Without Portfolio and Special Advisor to the Prime Minister. I am, however, solely responsible for the inferences drawn from those documents. Other confidential party records were not made available to me.
3. Carr, "P.N.M. Reminiscences," *The Nation*, April 15, 1960.
4. *Guardian*, May 15, 1955.
5. *The Nation*, December 30, 1960.

NOTES TO CHAPTER 9

Fragments from a Life: The East Indian Reaction

1. Naipaul, *The Middle Passage*, London: Andre Deutsch, Ltd., 1962, p. 40.
2. It so happens that Dr. Capildeo is an uncle of Vidia Naipaul. According to several local informants, a number of characters and incidents which have appeared in Naipaul's novels have had real-life counterparts. His major work,

A House for Mr. Biswas (New York and London: McGraw-Hill Book Co., 1961), contains characters and incidents which appear in some degree to parallel the Capildeo family history. "The younger god," of the extensive Indian household at "Hanuman House" is regarded by Dr. Capildeo as based on his own life at "Lion House" in Chaguanas. Despite the possibly factual basis of some of Naipaul's characters, his status as an outstanding West Indian novelist is of course not affected thereby, and the interest of his writings for the sociologist and social historian is greatly enhanced.

A somewhat different account of the life of Dr. Capildeo's father, and a first-hand impression of the ancestral village in India today, is given by Naipaul in "The Village of the Debes," *An Area of Darkness*, London: Andre Deutsch, 1964, pp. 266–267.

3. See *Indian Centenary Review: One Hundred Years of Progress, 1845–1945*, edited by M. J. Kirpalani, M. C. Sinanan, S. M. Rameshwar, and L. F. Seukeran, Port of Spain: Guardian Commercial Printery, n.d.

4. Among his major scientific publications would be: "Flexure With Shear Centres: A General Treatment With Complex Variable," *Proceedings of the Cambridge Philosophical Society*, 1953, Vol. 49, Part 2, pp. 308–318; "The Mathematics of Bird Population Growth and Decline," with J. B. S. Haldane, *The Journal of Animal Ecology*, 1954, Vol. 3, No. 2, pp. 215–223; "The Kinematics of Inertial Frames," *Proceedings of the Cambridge Philosophical Society*, 1961, Vol. 57, Part 2, pp. 321–329. The purpose of the latter paper, the author stated, was not ". . . to contradict special relativity, but rather to fortify, complete and remove from its system irrelevancies and curiosities which cause only mystery and confusion." A brief statement of his later concern with developing a new theory of gravitation will be found in a communication, "Gravity and Rotation," contained in *Nature*, July 11, 1964, Vol. 203, No. 4941, p. 175.

5. For an excellent, detailed, essentially pro-P.N.M. account of the 1961 elections see Gordon K. Lewis, "The Trinidad and Tobago General Election of 1961," *Caribbean Studies*, July, 1962, Vol. 2, No. 2. See also Vera Rubin, "Culture, Politics and Race Relations," *Social and Economic Studies*, December, 1962, Vol 11, No. 4.

NOTES TO CHAPTER 10

Aftermath of Independence

1. *History of the People of Trinidad & Tobago, op. cit.*, p. 281.

2. Wendell Bell found a high degree of correlation between elite perceptions that Jamaica had more to gain than lose from independence and their feelings that self-government within Jamaica had beneficially affected their personal careers. See *Jamaican Leaders, op. cit.*, p. 149. The "self-interest hypothesis" does not, of course, exhaust the range of variables accounting for strong nationalist sentiments. Although the present study focuses on behavioral events rather than attitudes obtained through structured interviews or questionnaires, the findings by both Bell in *Jamaican Leaders* and Charles Moskos, a contributor to this series, regarding the connection between Enlightenment ideals and nationalism is of course generally supported in the Trinidad case. The P.N.M. was quite literally founded as a party of enlightenment. The more critical tone of the present discussion is a result of the fact that we are dealing with the inevitably imperfect attempt to reconcile general democratic and egalitarian ideals with practical difficulties and with other, possibly conflicting, goals and interests.